STREISAND

JAMES SPADA

With Christopher Nickens

DOUBLEDAY & COMPANY, INC.

GARDEN CITY, NEW YORK

1981

STREISAND

THE WOMAN AND THE LEGEND

ACKNOWLEDGMENTS

Special thanks to Karen Swenson, for her assistance, invaluable research help, and suggestions.

Thanks to Bob Scott, Bob Schulenberg, Monroe Friedman, Lester Glassner, Steve Miney, Michel Parenteau, Bruce Mandes, and George Zeno for their generous help.

For their enthusiasm, friendship and advice, nods to Bart Andrews, Randy Porter, Barbara Petty and Steve Mitchell, Rick Parker, Larry Verdugo, Earl Miller, Larry Alexander, Kathy Robbins, Jane Rotrosen, Steve and Fran Gurey, Mike Ruvo, Steve Lachs, Preston Reese, Chris van Scoyk, George Schulman, and Vito Russo.

Gratitude to all those associates of Barbra's who gave of their time and memories.

To our editor, Laura Van Wormer, a thank you for her enthusiasm, her faith, her patience, and the *esprit* that never failed us.

To Jerry and Dan—special hellos.

To Barbra—thanks for being such a fascinating woman.

DESIGNED BY LAURENCE ALEXANDER

Library of Congress Catalog Card Number 80-2983
ISBN: 0-385-17566-3
Copyright © 1981 by James Spada

CONTENTS

Dedicated to our mothers,
MITZI SPADA
(1921–65)
and
TONI NICKENS

INTRODUCTION

THE
STREISAND
MYSTIQUE

It is a very fortunate thing to live at the same time as a performer of legendary status who is functioning at the height of creative power. Most theatrical legends develop after the fact, when the inevitable embellishing moss gathers to enlarge reputations. How thrilling it would be to attend—knowing what we know today about their place in history—performances by Sarah Bernhardt, Edwin Booth, John Barrymore, or Eleonora Duse.

There have been so few living legends that the ones we have are worthy of our fiercest protection. How lucky we are then to be able to experience fully a woman who is already one of the most legendary performers of all time—Barbra Streisand. Even her most vociferous detractors—and like Bernhardt, Duse, Garbo, and almost everyone else worth their legendary salt, she has many—would be deluding themselves to deny that she has for twenty years been choreographing the most successfully multifaceted career in show business history. No one—not Presley, not Sinatra, not Garland, not Crosby—has enjoyed the same level of concurrent popularity on record and in films for as long as Streisand has. She has been at the peak of her recording career and the peak of her movie stardom for the past ten years, and there is no reason to expect a dip in the popularity graph. She has been able to adapt—again with unprecedented success—to changing musical tastes and to reflect in her films many of the permutations of our social values.

Popularity itself, of course, is no guarantee of legend. There have been hundreds of performers who have created a sensation for a short period of time, then faded into oblivion. They did not possess enough substance to prevail: their popularity was unfettered by controversy, they did not polarize public opinion, they were talented but not unusually interesting. None of this can be said of Barbra Streisand.

Streisand has been the subject of raging controversy since her career began. Like sunspots, the debates about her flare up and simmer down, but they are always present. Perhaps the best way to sum up the disparity of opinion about her is to quote two sources: a priest who told her that when he hears her sing he feels the presence of God, and critic John Simon, who explained her popularity as the American public's "collective will to live in ugliness and self-debasement." Filmgoers spent $100 million to see her 1976 film *A Star Is Born,* which Rex Reed chose as the worst film of the year and about which *The Village Voice* punned, "A Bore Is Starred."

Rarely has a public figure not in politics elicited such contradictory responses. It is far easier to catalogue Streisand's huge popularity and the often unrestrained vitriol she sometimes inspires than it is to explain them. Any attempt must begin when Barbra's career did, in the small New York clubs where she thrilled cynical connoisseurs with her stunningly beautiful voice and her utterly unique approach to singing. Streisand was unlike anyone else of her generation in 1961, and she created a niche of her own out of the growing dissatisfaction with soulless assembly-line singers like Patti Page, Connie

Stevens, and Debbie Reynolds; in an era when someone produced a record supposedly sung by the "Barbie" doll, Barbra Streisand was as fascinating as some strange humanoid from Mars.

Her voice, of course, would have set her apart no matter what her personal style. But it was what she did with that voice that made patrons at even her first few nightclub performances realize they were in the presence of someone very special. Her material was odd, eclectic, and surprising; her delivery was impassioned, bordering on frenetic. She sang a love song in a way that summoned up memories of first love; then she would launch into the outrageous contrast of "Who's Afraid of the Big, Bad Wolf?" with such comic abandon that many observers could scarcely believe that both performances were coming from the same girl.

It is indeed this intriguing duality in Streisand which comes closest to explaining her appeal. She is at various times sensual and funny, strong and vulnerable, independent and in need of a man's protection, sophisticated and naïve, elegant and a perfect klutz. She has described herself as "a cross between a washerwoman and a princess," and she supplied a litany of her contradictions in a *Life* magazine interview in 1970:

"I'm an adolescent who is very mature; I'm lazy and ambitious; I love fancy food, beautifully served, yet enjoy it most when it's simple, reheated and eaten out of the pot; I love rice pudding from a diner on 10th Avenue and the chocolate soufflé from "21"; in the movies I care about how I look, but would rather sleep the extra half hour than put on false eyelashes; I would like my figure to look great but wouldn't dream of refusing that extra piece of pizza; I have been on the best-dressed list and at the same time on the worst-dressed list; I have been called crude and I have been called elegant; I have been called ugly and I have been called beautiful."

These inherent contrasts and Streisand's unlikely background not only made her interesting, but inspired cultish adulation among many of her fans. After her extraordinary success on Broadway in *Funny Girl,* it was clear that Streisand was not only a popular performer but a *cause célèbre*, a symbol of hope to millions. She had risen from a deprived childhood in Brooklyn to the height of success; she was gracing the covers of fashion magazines after being ridiculed as ugly. Millions of young people in situations similar to Barbra's early years saw her as living, breathing, *starring* proof that hope was not lost.

And when critics, or friends, or relatives suggested to these adherents that Barbra wasn't beautiful, or that her voice was unpleasantly nasal, or that her theatrics were off-putting, they would jump to her defense—feeling that she, like they, still needed to be protected from the gaucheries of people with little taste and less sensitivity. There was still a battle to be fought, and Barbra and her fans were in this together. She might be a superstar, but she still needed them.

Once Streisand got to Hollywood, though, much of that ugly-duckling-to-swan, rags-to-riches aura had dissipated after years of gargantuan success. She arrived to make the movie version of *Funny Girl* amid a storm of publicity generated largely by a press which sensed that she might singlehandedly revive the terminal tradition of celebrity-hood. Now, the Streisand legend had a new facet: Barbra as the temperamental Hollywood prima donna. Her every move, every mood, every moment of anger was reported as though the affairs of state rested on it, and all of this simply added to an already formidable legend.

Streisand's success on screen could have been reasonably predicted, based on her prior conquests of stage, concerts, records, and television. But the *extent* of that success is enough to stagger the imagination. Barbra not only made the transition but became

Recording her first album, 1963

In *The Way We Were*, 1973

At a celebration of Columbia Pictures' fiftieth anniversary, 1975

Posing for Cecil Beaton, 1969

Filming *A Star Is Born*, 1976

On the set of *The Owl and the Pussycat*, 1970

In *The Owl and the Pussycat,* 1970

Another Cecil Beaton Portrait, 1969

With Robert Redford, 1973

Hollywood's biggest female star the minute *Funny Girl* opened. And she was, for years afterward, the only woman on the Top Ten Box Office Attractions list—and she remains one of only a handful of stars whose presence virtually guarantees a film financial success.

Streisand possesses those undefinable attributes that all great movie stars of the past had—screen presence, charisma, a larger-than-life quality, empathy. And her best film roles have highlighted the contradictory nature of her personality. In *Funny Girl, The Way We Were,* and *A Star Is Born*—not coincidentally her three most memorable films—she plays strong, talented, committed women whose vulnerability is brought out by their love of a man. Streisand's screen persona was perfect for the seventies—a decade in which many women were asserting their right to equal footing with men, and many men were feeling threatened by these female declarations of independence.

Barbra Streisand served as a role model for women who sought liberation, but she didn't threaten men in the process because the independence, force of will and brains of her characters were attractively packaged and sufficiently soft-sold. Streisand's message was clear: women can be strong and accomplished—but they still need men. Our more radical feminists may turn apoplectic at the very idea, but it was obviously what most of America wanted to hear.

Barbra's audiences also sensed—correctly—that her film characters were an extension of herself. Women's magazines portrayed Streisand as a lady who, despite her power, wealth, brains, and talent, longed for the love of a strong man. She said of one paramour in 1974, "I actually enjoy being subjugated to him. A man's career is more important than a woman's." She has made no secret of the fact that her attraction to her lover of seven years, Jon Peters, is based in part on the fact that he has never been intimidated by her. "Jon has always had women treat him like a king," she said. "He likes me in the kitchen."

Thus, in the arena of the seventies battle of the sexes, Streisand was a person for all seasons. So it is, too, in her appeal to broad ranges of people. Intellectuals and sophisticates can appreciate her intelligence, her musical mastery, her perfectionism, her Broadway roots, her experiments with albums like *Classical Barbra,* what she can do with a Harold Arlen tune. But the fact that she is not an intellectual, that she has a common touch and an unglamorous background, that her films are in no way highbrow, and that her music touches everyone's emotions with its universal romanticism—all of this makes her a heroine to millions of average citizens across the country. People over sixty might be listening to her first few albums with pleasant surges of nostalgia while their grandchildren disco dance to "Enough Is Enough" and rush to record stores to buy *Guilty.*

Streisand's many dichotomies are perhaps best embodied in her physical self. She has been described as "half street kid, half dowager empress," and the description is apt. She can look regal and imperious, her neck long and sleek, her face chiseled and aquiline, her cheekbones classic, her eyes coolly blue and piercing. A moment later—laughing, her face seen from a different angle—she can look like a sweet young girl with imperfect teeth whose baby fat has yet to disappear and whose features may have been molded out of silly putty.

Her voice, too, is chameleonic. She can sing a love song or classical lieder with enough elegance of diction to rival an aristocrat, then talk in a staccato Brooklynese peppered with "you knows" and gesticulation. Perhaps the real secret of Barbra's popularity is that the public is getting two celebrities for the price of one!

New stars are often subject to media hype, and Streisand was no exception. Early in her career, her reviews and magazine profiles were so full of glowing superlatives they were almost an embarrassment (and the pressure of living up to the expectations they generated put Streisand on a prescription drug to control her stomach). Her early interviews were alternately kooky, sullen, thoughtful, and theatrical; some were complete put-ons. Later, she would become elusive, rarely giving interviews to anyone. She has never guested on "The Tonight Show" or anything like it in eighteen years.

Her aloofness from the press infuriates some of its members and makes others all the more anxious to write about her. She is treated as American royalty when she does deign to be interviewed; Barbara Walters granted her unheard-of first rush approval of a 1976 visit with Barbra and Jon at their Malibu ranch—and ran the piece in a one-hour special along with an interview with President-elect and Mrs. Carter.

Other journalists choose to criticize her, villify her, mock her, belittle her, and question the taste of her admirers. Still, they write about her—and the public, adherents and detractors alike—read about her with a voracity that has every magazine editor in the country clamoring for a "new angle" on The Streisand Story.

New angle or not, the story is a fascinating one. Many legends of the past were created through embellishment by people who had never experienced the subjects of those legends firsthand. Not so with Streisand. She is there for all the world to see, and most of the world is riveted. "You don't fool anybody," she has said, "when your eyes are on a screen forty feet wide." She is a bonafide legend because of the *woman* that she is. One can only imagine what the woman she will become will add to the legend. When one realizes that her thirty-sixth album was her biggest seller in a string of Gold and Platinum records, her success enters the realm of fantasy.

And fantasies that come true are the stuff of legends, too.

PART ONE

STARTING OUT

1942-1963

Dreary Days in Brooklyn

She may well be the most famous by-product of the American dream, for it is likely that Barbra Streisand's successes would never have been achieved without her all-consuming childhood conviction that her life was, well, *just not what it should have been.* The childhood was not quite Dickensian, but to Barbara Joan Streisand it was all *Oliver Twist* and *David Copperfield,* with a little *Jane Eyre* thrown in. Her Brooklyn life certainly didn't measure up to the images she saw in glossy magazines and at Saturday matinees. "My mother hated it when I went to the movies, because I was always grouchy for a couple of days. After looking at all those beautiful clothes and apartments, to come back to the place where I lived depressed me."

Things might have been different if her father had not died at thirty-four, fifteen months after her birth on April 24, 1942. Little has been publicly known about Emanuel Streisand until now except that he was a well-regarded educator. The reminiscences of his brother and one of his colleagues, however, reveal that he was a likable man of singular intelligence, determination, and devotion to his family, who impressed all who met him.

He and Diana Rosen, the daughter of a tailor who occasionally served as a cantor in the local synagogue, were married in 1935, after a three-year courtship, at the height of the Great Depression. Their first child, Sheldon, was born later that year. Emanuel Streisand was a man who was not going to let the economic plight of the country defeat him. His dream was to be a teacher; he took great joy in motivating young people. His determination can be surmised by the fact that, after his graduation from college, he spent a year as a teacher-in-training, and another year as a substitute—all without any guarantee that he would find one of the scarce teaching jobs available during the Depression.

By the early 1940s, America was slowly recovering from its long economic nightmare and Emanuel Streisand was not only gainfully employed but, with a Ph.D. in education and a rare talent for his craft, was considered by all who knew him to be on the road to a distinguished career. Leonard Boyer, now a retired high school principal, met "Mannie" Streisand when he went to work at the Brooklyn High School for Specialty Trades, a vocational school. Such schools had proliferated during the Depression, because so many young people were leaving academic schools to seek work and bring their families more money. Emanuel Streisand taught English, history, and psychology—his ability to "double up" on his areas of expertise made him particularly valuable to the curriculum.

Leonard Boyer recalls that when he came to the school in 1941 Mannie Streisand took him under his wing. "He really made me a teacher," Boyer says. "He was a strong man, and a good disciplinarian. He helped me learn how to control the students." There were often discipline troubles at the school because most of the students were problem youngsters. "There was also a great restlessness among the young men," Boyer says, "because they knew that it wouldn't be long before they would go off to war."

Mr. Streisand was respected by the students, and well liked by the faculty, despite the fact that, according to Boyer, he was "something of a loner. He got along with everyone, even our terribly obnoxious principal."

At age five, 1947

16

Boyer estimates that Mr. Streisand made $4,500 a year at the high school, plus his pay for teaching at a Yeshiva school after hours. It wasn't a bad income for the time, and he and Diana felt secure in having another child. Manny was delighted when the child was a girl. "He used to show off Barbara's baby pictures," Boyer recalls, "and compare notes with the other teachers who had young babies. He was proud of both his children."

Murray Streisand, Mannie's brother, describes him as a man of medium build, with brown hair and intelligent eyes, who was "an eloquent speaker and a good writer He was a serious person, dedicated, determined and conscientious," Murray recalls. "He had his humorous moments, though—and he could appreciate a good joke." Obviously Mannie Streisand passed some of his personality traits along to his daughter as well as his looks. "Barbra looks a little like both of her parents," Murray says, "but she looks more like her father."

Emanuel Streisand died suddenly of a cerebral hemorrhage during the summer of 1943, while teaching at a summer camp. "It was a great shock," Boyer says. "I didn't find out until the next school year when the principal called the teachers together and made the announcement. Many of us wept openly. "One thing I must say about Mannie," Boyer adds. "He was a truly memorable man. I would have remembered him even if his daughter wasn't Barbra Streisand."

Her husband's death left Diana Streisand emotionally shattered, and she spent many of the ensuing months crying in bed. It also plunged her family into financial hardship. "The family would have had a small pension," Leonard Boyer offers, "but at that time it was nothing that could make a measurable difference in the financial setback that had been thrust upon them." Diana's brother sent home his army paychecks for a while, but when he was discharged from the service, Mrs. Streisand lost even that meager help.

Money was so scarce that, instead of a doll, little Barbara played with a hot-water bottle—and got spanked when she squirted water on the apartment floor. Diana was forced to move into her parents' home in a nearby section of Brooklyn, leave her children in their care, and take a job as a bookkeeper. Until Barbara Joan was seven, she was cared for primarily by her elderly grandmother.

As it does in every family in which the husband dies, Mr. Streisand's death left many voids—not the least of which was the one in his daughter's psyche. Not having had a father may have been the most important formative aspect of Barbra Streisand's personality. As a young girl, it made her feel both deprived and somehow special. "When a kid grows up missing one parent," she has said, "there's a big gap that has to be filled. It's like someone being blind, they hear better. With me, I felt more, I sensed more—I wanted more." And she has added, "For many years, I felt like the victim. Why did it happen to me? I wanted to be like all the other little girls who had their daddies come home. Mine never came home."

The little girl created all kinds of elaborate fantasies about the kind of man her father was, based on the glowing things her relatives told her about him. He became, in his absence, the most important person in her life. After she had achieved stardom, she would interrupt questions about herself during interviews and proudly tell the reporter that her father had been included in a directory of distinguished educators. In early 1981, she donated $500,000 to UCLA's Department of Cardiology, which established an Emanuel Streisand Chair in Cardiology. Barbra had earlier donated a large amount to the Pacific Jewish Center in Venice, California, which in gratitude was renamed after Mr. Streisand.

Her father's absence not only made the little girl "want more," but her mother's absence because of her work often made Barbara wonder if she was loved. She constantly longed for attention, and often refused to eat—a refusal her future stepfather would theorize was designed to win her mother's ministrations, which it often did. Little Barbara was mildly anemic, and skinny in the extreme. Her lack of interest in food drove her Jewish mama to distraction, and Mrs. Streisand packed her off to the first of a series of health camps when she was five. "Those camps were the most horrible experiences of my life," she said. "I'd get there, they'd dump me in a bathtub, and then put me into uniform. I hated it. I was homesick. Every day I would cry and the kids would make fun of me. I would say, 'I'm not crying, I have a loose tear duct that just runs.' From that time on, I always got allergies in summer anytime I went to the country. They were psychological in origin, of course."

When she was six Barbara was sent to a Hebrew health camp, but it didn't do much to fill her out: "The food was so awful I used to throw it down to the other end of the table." Her mother came to visit one day and brought along a man she intended to marry, Louis Kind. Barbara insisted that they were not to leave without her. "I was always able to manipulate my mother. I made her pack my bags and she took me home. With Louis Kind in the car. He hated me ever since. He was allergic to kids, as my mother said."

Louis Kind offered a different version of his attitude toward children in an interview he gave several years before his death in 1970. "I remember how worried Diana was about my reaction to having her children live with us. She suggested that they continue to live with her parents until she and I became adjusted to each other. 'No,' I said, 'I'm very fond of children and I want them to live with us.'"

Barbara wasn't nearly as magnanimous toward her soon-to-be stepfather. She saw him alternately as a usurper of the cherished position her father held in her mind and as a threat to her relationship with her mother. Louis Kind recalled, "I would call for Diana, wait for her in the living room, and then when she was ready to go out with me, I would take her arm and lead her to the door. Barbara, sensing that her life was to undergo some terrifying change, would hold on to her mother's skirts, pulling her back, fearful that this strange man was taking her mother away from her. 'Don't go, Mommy, stay with me,' she'd plead."

When Barbara was seven, Diana Streisand and Louis Kind were married and they moved with the children into an apartment in a six-story complex. Barbara was not happy with this new factor in the equation of her life. "I slept in the bed with my mother the first night. When I woke up in the morning, I had clicks in my ears. I told my mother, and she said, 'Well, sleep on a hot-water bottle.' She never asked me about it again. From that day, I led a whole secret life. Something was wrong with me—I had these clicks in my ears."

Louis Kind seems to have understood his stepdaughter's feelings. "She was forced to move away from her grandparents' home and begin a new life with a stranger—a man who had married her mother but wasn't her father. It's probably difficult for some people to realize what an unfortunate effect a situation like this can have on a sensitive child. Barbara, I truly believe, was starved for the kind of love that kids brought up with two parents take for granted."

As she grew older, Barbara became more and more withdrawn and unhappy. Louis Kind could not compete with her father in Barbara's mind. His career was in real estate, but later Barbra would dismiss him as "a used car salesman or something." In any event, he was unable to provide for the family in the same way her father could have.

A Streisand family album. *(above left)* At fifteen months, just before her father's death. *(above right)* At twenty months, with her mother. *(below left)* At four years, with her maternal grandfather, an amateur cantor with "a great voice." *(below right)* At age five, with her brother Sheldon

The apartment they lived in was small; Barbara slept on a cot in the living room. They had enough money for life's necessities, but there were few frills. "We weren't *poor* poor," Barbra has said. "We just never had anything." Things were made worse for Barbara by what she saw other people had—even friends in the same building seemed to her to be leading a much better life. Barbara found the environment of the apartment stifling and depressing and became more and more anxious to escape from it, but things outside weren't much cheerier. The section of Brooklyn she lived in was a drab procession of grays and concrete, store fronts and lower-middle-class housing projects. Later she would describe her birthplace as "the home of baseball, boredom, and bad breath." She was not received kindly by the neighborhood youngsters, who otherwise could have been her psychic cushion against the unhappiness at home. She was too different; she was emaciated and ungraceful, her nose was too big for her face, her eyes were slightly crossed. Her classmates called her "big beak" and "crazy Barbara," excluded her from activities and often frightened the frail little girl: "When I was nine years old," Barbra told *Playboy* in 1977, "sometimes the girls would gang up on me in my neighborhood, make a circle around me, make fun of me, and I'd start to cry and then run away. I'm still trying to find out why. What made them angry at me?"

Children rarely need a good reason for such cruelty and the fact that Barbara didn't "fit in" seemed reason enough. She looked odd, she acted strange. The clicking in her ears was joined by a buzzing when she was nine. "At first I wrapped scarves around my ears, but that only drove it in deeper. It must have looked pretty peculiar since it was 94° out. I think that's when people started calling me different. I never felt normal and I guess I walked around like a *forbiss*—which means kind of depressed. I felt totally abnormal." Louis Kind remembered, "She could be very depressed and very moody for such a little girl. I never knew what the child was thinking . . . at times she was impossible to reach."

And she was still, to her mother's great distress, often impossible to feed. "Diana would constantly worry about her," Louis Kind recalled. "One day, out of sheer desperation, she took Barbara by the arm, put her to bed, propped her up on pillows, and forcibly fed her with a spoon, as one does with an infant. I've never seen a happier look on a child's face. Not only did she lap up the food, but also the attention she was getting."

Striving for attention was a major theme that ran through young Barbara Streisand's life. The first hint of nonderisive notice from anyone outside of her family came when she was about ten and, as a sign of things to come, it was a result of her singing. "We used to sit on the stoop in Brooklyn and harmonize," Barbra says. "I used to imitate Joni James."

Louis Kind described the scene in detail: "I can see her now, singing songs she had heard on the radio in her little-girl voice, which even then was remarkably true and delivered with great feeling. The neighbors would stick their heads out of the window, clap loudly and yell, 'More, Barbara, give us more!' She was only too happy to oblige. Then, as a final encore (double-jointed as she was), she would lie down on the pavement, take both of her feet, wrap them around her neck and roll like a human ball!

"She was always play-acting, even when she was being chastised. Each time her mother or brother disciplined her by giving her a whack whenever and wherever they thought she needed it, she would pretend she was badly hurt." Barbra recalls that once her mother slapped her. "I pretended I was deaf for four hours and she believed it."

Around the time that Barbara began high school, her mother and Louis Kind separated, and her life took a turn for the worse. Her mother returned to work, but the family's financial situation further declined. Barbara had few friends and the little company she had at home came primarily from her baby half-sister, Roslyn, whom she cared for and, as Louis Kind remembered, took great delight in and sang to. But her dissatisfactions increased, and were compounded by the ostracism and tauntings of her classmates, leaving Barbara to wonder if she had been accidentally left there by a visitor from another planet.

But rather than try to conform, Barbara decided that if she were going to be thought of as different, then she'd give them good reason to think so. "I would take my brother's drawing pencil and put it on my eyes. Also, my mother had purple lipstick and I found this white stuff and mixed the colors so I had violet lips, blue eyes, and then I bleached the top of my hair blond, but I didn't like the color, so I put a rinse on. My hair, being porous, turned blue and green. I wore frilly clothes, because I wanted to be feminine, but I hung around with the smart kids, who wore glasses and oxfords and no makeup. I was this absolute misfit. I was in all honor classes, yet I looked like the kids who sat on the corner, chewed gum, and were always in the principal's office. There were the smart kids and the dumb kids, so can you imagine how peculiar *I* was?"

She spent a great deal of time alone, much of it sitting in the neighborhood movie house, watching beautiful people in glamorous environments. She would imagine herself as various movie heroines and being desired by handsome men. The movies provided her with a fantasy that sustained her. "Whenever I tried to imagine my future, I ran into a blank wall. I couldn't see kids or a husband or a home. I couldn't imagine any of the normal things."

Instead, she imagined great things—fame and fortune. And her fantasies were all-encompassing. She would be a famous actress, and the greatest star. "I became consumed with acting and used to go to the New York Public Library and look up all the plays by Dumas *fils* and other writers that Sarah Bernhardt and Eleonora Duse played. I read Russian plays, Russian novels, Greek tragedies. *Anna Karenina* changed my life."

After school, she would go up on the roof of her building and perform various parts from plays she had read. She wore different makeup and bought cheap thrift-shop clothes for each character, often playing all the roles in a certain drama at the same time. "I desperately wanted to become an actress," she says. "I wanted to express my *feelings.*"

When she expressed her feelings to her mother, Mrs. Kind was aghast. A deeply religious woman, Diana had strong reservations about the acceptability of the theater as a career. Beyond that, she looked at her daughter and was convinced that, in any event, she was setting herself up for heartache. "I didn't think she was pretty enough. There was no security." Mrs. Kind did all she could to discourage her daughter from these pie-in-the-sky ideas of hers. "All I heard," Barbra says, "was 'No, no, can't be done.' " Mrs. Kind wanted her daughter to be a school clerk—"all those paid vacations"—and bought her a typewriter so she could learn to type. Barbara resisted and grew her fingernails to extreme lengths to disqualify her fingers. But Louis Kind's reminiscences suggest that Mrs. Kind had her way: "Barbara finally learned to type, I understand, but hated it, even though, as it turned out, it was to be the means to keep her from complete starvation."

On Her Own

Shortly after her fifteenth birthday, Barbara decided to stop play acting and go for "the real thing": a summer at the Malden Bridge Playhouse in upstate New York. After much argument, Mrs. Kind relented and allowed Barbara to go, probably in the hope that it would finally get all of that nonsense out of her system. Of course, it had precisely the opposite effect. Happily toiling with scenery paint or a broom, Barbara lived for the few chances she got to appear on stage. When she did, she drove her directors to thoughts of homocide with outrageous hamming and improvisation; but she played a sexy secretary in *The Desk Set* with such *chutzpah* that the audience loved her. That sweet taste of large-scale public approval, the opportunity to let her inner self triumph over that questionable exterior—it was enough to make Barbara Streisand positively fanatical in her determination to succeed as an actress.

It also made her life in Brooklyn seem even bleaker when she returned, and her mother found it more difficult than ever to convince her of the joys of security and conformity. She became fascinated by Manhattan, which to her meant theater, independence, and escape. At first, she tried to convince her mother to get the family an apartment there: "Ma, look, it's only $105, why can't we afford it?" Mrs. Kind was unmoved, so Barbara began laying her own plans. She saved money from a job she had taken at Choy's Chinese Restaurant, worked hard at Erasmus Hall High School, and graduated six months early, in January 1959, with a 93 average. Once out of school, Barbara wanted to make her move. She told her mother she would live in Manhattan—alone.

Not surprisingly, Mrs. Kind put up a fight. "I thought it would be a fiasco," she has said. But she had learned nothing about her daughter in seventeen years if not that Barbara wasn't easily dissuaded. Mama relented, after Barbara found a "suitable" roommate, and allowed her to rent a tiny apartment on Thirty-fourth Street. It was not an easy thing for Mrs. Kind to accept, being left alone to care for Roslyn while having to worry about her older daughter's well-being. "Diana's heartbroken that Barbara doesn't live home anymore," a neighbor had told Louis Kind.

Mrs. Kind did not, however, allow her apron strings to unravel completely. She visited Barbara frequently, armed with jars of chicken soup, warmer clothes, and lots of advice and queries. She often arrived unannounced, and Barbara was very unhappy with these invasions of her new found privacy—so much so that later, whenever she moved, she wouldn't tell her mother where she was. But somehow, Mrs. Kind always found her.

Her life in Manhattan gave Barbara an exhilarating sense of freedom and a feeling of being truly alive for the first time. She plunged into acting lessons with two different coaches, and adopted a stage name she found in a telephone book: Angelina Scarangella. She had the name inscribed on matchbook covers and gave them out to her classmates.

She quickly established herself as an eccentric among eccentrics; when she was asked to do a scene, no one was ever quite sure what she'd come up with. She used the dramatic exercises to explore her subconcious: "I did a scene from *The Rose Tattoo.* I played this young girl; it was a scene of sexual exploration. All I did was pick a technical task, which was just physically touching the actor I played the scene with. At one point, he stood up and I stood on his feet; one time I jumped on his back; one time I pretended I was blind and while I was talking, I was touching his face. It was this awkward sexuality. I didn't know what I would do next. I was as interested as the people watching. It was a case of the conscious watching the subconscious self. I think it's what they call inspiration—which I've experienced very few times."

Both of her drama coaches saw potential in Barbara, and they suggested that she make the rounds of auditions to get some work. She excitedly embarked, but the experience soon turned sour. "I was humiliated—people looking at you like you're crazy. I was usually abruptly dismissed." Sometimes, she was not even allowed to read. Often she was told to fix her nose, change her name, dress more properly. Once, she auditioned for the walk-on part of a beatnik. She figured she had it made. "I used to look like a real beatnik. I wore black stockings and had this trench coat." Still, she didn't get the part, because she didn't have any professional experience. "We have to see your work," they told her. "Why do you have to see my work?" she shot back. "It's a walk-on; I don't even have to say anything. How are you going to see my work, if you don't give me a chance to do the work?"

It may have been no more than a convenient excuse to reject her without hurting her feelings *too* much. Barbara had so many strikes against her: she had no experience, she was not good-looking, she was totally unlike the ingenue roles her age suggested she play, she was highly ethnic, and thus limited in the number of roles she could play under the best circumstances.

She was frustrated, discouraged, incredulous. "How could they tell if I was any good if they wouldn't even let me *read?* That's when I got so angry and said, 'Screw you, 'cause I ain't coming back and asking you for no work.' I don't know how I would have gotten a job if I didn't sing. . . ."

She knew she could sing, but she *didn't want to be a singer.* She wanted to be an actress, to play Shakespeare and Chekhov. She didn't want to make any changes, either; she knew, somewhere deep inside, that if she were ever to succeed it would be because of her differences, not in spite of them.

She continued her acting classes, and her performances were often well received by her fellow students. One of them recalls, "Barbara was the only one in the class who argued with the teacher, who asked questions." Her confidence increased, and she invited her mother to a class in which she was scheduled to perform. Afterward, Barbara waited hopefully for her mother's reaction; perhaps now she'd see that her daughter's dreams were not all that misplaced. Mrs. Kind told her that she should find a job or some other outlet for her energies, because she would never make it as an actress. Barbara was crushed, but somehow found the gumption to renew her "I'll show her" attitude and keep trying.

Her financial situation became quite bleak. She took whatever job came along, went on unemployment for a while, and constantly struggled to make ends meet. Occasionally she visited her mother in Brooklyn and brought back some food, but that was the extent of the help she would accept from her family. "She was always of an independent, no-cry-baby nature," Louis Kind said. "She never asked favors. I would have been glad to help her, and so would her mother and brother, but she refused all offers."

"Finally," Barbra says, "I *had* to sing. I'd been working as a switchboard operator and was let go"—because she allayed her boredom by using different voices each time she answered the phone. "I went on unemployment insurance and got caught in a lie. I was supposed to be looking for work as a switchboard operator, but instead I went looking for work as an actress. The penalty was standing in line for five weeks before I could receive another check. How could I do that?"

Luckily, Barbara had a streak of realism in her as strong as her bent toward fantasy, and she realized that she'd have a better chance at theatrical employment if she sang. But she was unsure, afraid. She started practicing her singing tentatively with a friend who played the guitar. Her roommate at the time, Marilyn Fried, recalled the first practice session to author René Jordan: "I suddenly heard this remarkable voice coming out of the living room. My immediate reaction was to go to the radio and find out who was singing so marvelously. But the radio was not on. I realized there must be someone in this tiny apartment who had this magnitude, this power. I turned around and asked Barbara, 'Who was singing?' She said, 'I was.' That's the way it all started . . . I told her she should try singing. She said, 'I'm not a singer, I'm an actress.' Out came the sensitivity, the insecurity, the shyness. But next day she was singing around the house and asking me whether it sounded right and should she go for an audition."

She did go for an audition—for *The Sound of Music*. She ended up singing for three hours for Eddie Blum of the Rogers and Hammerstein casting office. Blum found her fascinating, took her out to meals, talked to her for hours. He told her there was nothing in *The Sound of Music* for someone so special, but that she would certainly make it as a singer someday.

That was just the kind of encouragement she needed, and she quickly saw that her singing could be the key to success. But she didn't need to rely on it immediately because she was soon cast in a makeshift production "slapped together", by a group of out-of-work actors, *The Insect Comedy*. She played four different parts, including a butterfly and a moth. Although the show lasted just three nights, it did bring Barbara her first newspaper, in The New York *World-Telegram and Sun;* mention.

The Insect Comedy was quickly assigned to oblivion, but it turned out to be extremely important to Barbra's career—it was here that she met Barry Dennen, a young Californian who was to play a very important part in her development as a singer. He also would become her first romantic involvement.

Dennen, known today for roles in *The Shining* and *Jesus Christ, Superstar,* first heard Barbara sing when he made a tape of her voice on his sophisticated audio equipment. "We spent the afternoon taping," Dennen has said, "and the moment I heard the first playback I went insane—I knew here was something special, a voice the microphone loved. I told her she had to sing, and she said, 'I'm an ehktress.' "

Dennen worked hard at convincing her to do something with her singing—to no avail—until one day he challenged her to take part in a talent contest at The Lion, a gay bar across the street from his Greenwich Village apartment. "If Barbara would actually walk in there and sign up, I would work with her on a set of songs, help her choose the material, and direct the act."

She accepted the dare—as much because the winner would receive fifty dollars a week and free meals as anything else—and showed up at The Lion, as did a singer of light opera, a comedian and another pop singer.

When her turn came, she stood before a noisy, boozy crowd of men for whom Thursday nights' talent shows were principally a chance to have fun at the expense of marginally talented performers with delusions of stardom. Watching this frightened, nervous, mousy girl standing at the piano, holding onto it for her life, her eyes closed in an attempt to summon up the requisite courage, The Lion's patrons expected little more than another embarrassing display of misplaced ambition. She started to sing "A Sleepin' Bee," the languid ballad by Harold Arlen and Truman Capote, and suddenly the audience quieted down. People started to listen. Coming from this frail, strange-looking creature was the most extraordinary voice. It was pure. It was lovely. She hit notes with a graceful ease that left one awestruck. The voice was big when it should have been, soft when it needed to be, and always beautiful. One third of the way into the song, everyone in The Lion was listening intently, and by its end they all wondered, "Who *is* she?"

Needless to say, she won the talent contest. Now, she had a one-week booking at the club, and an act to work up. It was at this point that Barbara began to rely on not one Pygmalion, but two: Barry Dennen and Bob Schulenberg.

Creating Barbra Streisand

Dennen, an ardent collector of vintage records, had thousands of tapes of legendary singers, including Ruth Etting, Helen Morgan, Ethel Waters, and Mabel Mercer. He knew a promising vocalist when he met one, but Streisand was like an amorphous mass of clay—undeveloped, unrefined, largely ignorant of the voices that had gone before her. Bob Schulenberg recalls: "Barry would say, 'Come on over, I've got some Helen Morgan.' And Barbara would say, 'Who's Helen Morgan?' Barry would play something for her, and you could see that she realized that Barry was somebody she needed. He really shaped her thinking in those days. You don't tell Barbra anything, but you *suggest* things, and she's sharp enough to know when you're right. Barry told her she shouldn't try to compete with Rosemary Clooney and Peggy Lee, that she had to be unique with her material. It was he who suggested that she sing songs nobody else was singing.

"At a certain point she got the key to his apartment, and she used to go over and study. Sometimes she'd listen alone, sometimes they'd work together: What is the point of view of this song? Who is this person singing it? How does the meaning come out?"

Barbara quickly latched onto the idea that singing a song was acting, and then her enthusiasm for singing became total. "We constructed each number as a set piece," Dennen recalled for René Jordan's Streisand biography, *The Greatest Star,* "evolving the character of the girl as she sang all through her moods. I would work with her phrase by phrase." Together they searched for songs that lent themselves to emotional interpretation, or material so strange it would cause people to sit up and take notice. Dennen claims credit for suggesting that Barbara sing "Who's Afraid of the Big, Bad Wolf?" in front of "New York's cleverest and sharpest audiences."

Barbara Streisand was a sensation at The Lion, each night gaining more confidence, becoming looser, trying out material she and Dennen had dug up from America's musical past. She was becoming so popular and was such an obvious drawing card that it was clear she could easily get more money and better exposure at a larger, classier club. But she'd have to improve her act, enlarge her repertoire. After two weeks at The Lion, she and Dennen set to work preparing for an audition several months from then at the Bon Soir, which was only blocks away from The Lion, but had a "big time" reputation.

Her appearances at The Lion gave Barbara her first look at her name on a marquee—or, more to the point, on a sign outside the club. She looked at it and wondered why Barbara, pronounced as two syllables, contained three *a*'s. Thinking back to the advice of casting people that she change her name, she decided to drop the second *a* and spell her name the way it sounded: Barbra. That was as much of a change as she'd ever agree to—if she changed her name to Barbara Sands, as someone had suggested, how would all those people who told her she'd never amount to anything know it was her when she became a star?

It was about this time that Bob Schulenberg, a friend of Barry's from UCLA, arrived from California and stayed with Barry while looking for an apartment. Schulenberg, an artist and designer, recalls vividly the first moment he saw Barbra Streisand: "Barry and I were coming out of his apartment building to go to the Pam Pam Coffee Shop for a midnight snack—I'd just arrived from L.A. I see running down the sidewalk this character, carrying two shopping bags in each hand; and out of the shopping bags is coming feathered boas and sequined fabric. She's calling, 'Barry! Barry!' and running toward us. I looked at her and looked at Barry and said, 'Barry, I think there's someone calling you,' but thinking it couldn't be *us* she wanted. She was wearing beautiful 1927 gold lamé-strapped shoes, a new cherry red velvet skirt about an inch above her knee-cap. That doesn't sound too amazing now, but in 1960 nobody did that. She had some chocolate brown nylon stockings and a gold and silver and cherry red brocade top with big, square-cut Elizabethan sleeves. She had a Venetian glass bead necklace on. Two, I think. She had drop earrings that were glass, and six Venetian glass bracelets. She had *everything* on. She was a walking Smithsonian!"

Barbra joined Barry and Bob at the Pam Pam, and Bob discovered that the young girl with everything on was as unusual as her mode of dress. "She was fascinated by the idea that I had just come from California—'You mean, you had lunch in California today and now you're eating here with us?'—and she kept asking all these *questions.* We didn't have a conversation; she just asked questions. And I was fascinated by her because this girl had a way of asking a question that didn't just ask a question, she wanted to *know* something, even if she didn't know exactly what it was she wanted to know. She was no light conversationalist. This is not an eighteen-year-old girl who is just an eighteen-year-old girl. You have to be impressed to meet someone like this.

"Barry and I got into a nostalgia trip about life in California, and Barry's family's house in Coldwater Canyon. She wanted a rundown on it—'What did the pool area look like? What was the patio like? What was it paved with?' I mean, she was like Barbara Walters. And she would be building this house in her mind and saying, 'Okay, now tell me, what would you and your brother do when you woke up in the pool house? Would you go into the big house for breakfast with your parents? Or would it be brought out to you by the maid?' She went through a whole fantasy thing about Barry's house."

Barbra and Bob soon became close friends—"I was like a big brother, I guess"—and while Barry gave her a crash course in show-business history and helped her work up her nightclub act, Schulenberg helped her develop the first of the "Streisand looks": "She really didn't have a good makeup job," he recalls. "She didn't do it well because she didn't know what she was doing. She had bangs down over her face because she had a little bit of teenage skin, and she had this little Dynel hairpiece that looked like a figure eight or a cheese danish on top of her head, with her real hair going down her back.

"I wanted to make her over, because I saw that she could be striking, but it was difficult to bring up. You want to be nice and not say, 'You look like shit. Let me do it for you.' But I got my opportunity when Barry was appearing in *Henry V* in Central Park, and we were supposed to go see him. I said, 'Let's surprise Barry when we go. We'll make you up like Audrey Hepburn in *Sabrina,* or one of those Richard Avedon fashion photos.' She was all for it. I know she wanted to look glamorous.

"So I brought over all sorts of theatrical makeup. I told her, 'Get all the makeup you can and we'll put everything on.' Barbra was really like undeveloped territory. Like a bare canvas for an artist. I looked at her and abstractly thought, Well, she's got fat cheeks. She's got no structure in her cheeks—we'll have to paint that in. But I saw that she could be stunning, even then. So it was like I was painting a picture."

Schulenberg applied deep shadow to her cheeks, to give them contour, extended her eyes with eyeliner so they would look bigger, and filled them out with false eyelashes. He teased her hair to add fullness and proper framing to the face, applied lip gloss, and covered her face with translucent theatrical powder. Then she dressed in a black leotard top, black slacks, black ballet slippers—and a cardigan sweater over everything. "Now this is a 140° summer night in New York," Schulenberg says, "and that's why we had to use all that powder—to keep her looking cool as a cucumber. The look was so striking. Nobody looked like that except models, and Barbra didn't look like a model, so it seemed real, if you can imagine it. She looked like a Modigliani painting. Like a dream, really. It was just some sort of illusionary thing. And we walked to Central Park and people would stare and you could see on their faces, 'Who *is* she?' Barbra *loved* it.

"However, we missed the performance. We got there so late the complimentary seats Barry had gotten for us were taken. He was furious. He wasn't even speaking to us after the show. 'How could you miss it?' he asked us. 'But doesn't she look *great,* Barry?' I said. But he didn't care, he was too angry. Barbra was very depressed."

Barry cooled off soon enough and continued to work with Barbra on her Bon Soir audition, and by the time the night came, Barbra had her eclectic collection of songs fully prepared. Still, some aspects of the act came up accidentally. "When I auditioned," Barbra says, "I forgot that I had gum in my mouth, and I took it out and stuck it on the microphone and it got a big howl." She would often repeat the chewing-gum bit later. "Then I started to sing. They liked it, but they thought I was going to be a comedienne. When I went off the stage, Larry Storch, who was the headliner there, said to me, 'Kid, you're gonna be a star.' Like in the movies! And Tiger Haynes's girlfriend, whose name was Bea, came over to me and said, 'Kid, you've got dollar signs written all over you.' I'll never forget it. I was wearing my antique twenties shoes with butterflies on them, and I just looked at her."

Bob Schulenberg has his own memories of the occasion: "It was the night to go to the Bon Soir, so she got dressed and did a lot of the makeup things I taught her. I knew that she sang, but I'd never heard her, because she didn't appear anywhere for a couple of months after The Lion. Peter Daniels was the pianist, and they'd never even seen each other. But she came out and Peter took the music, and it was just incredible. I mean, I started crying. I don't think she's ever, ever been recorded like she used to sound there. Afterwards, I was like melted butter on the floor. She said, 'How was it?' and I couldn't talk."

No one talked during Barbra's performances at the Bon Soir, where her weekly salary was more than double her pay at The Lion, but her audiences did talk *about* her to their friends. People began to come to the club just to see her, and many returned night after night because one could never tell just what she'd do next. As in acting school, she was experimenting—with her material, her interpretations, her clothes, her make-up.

The customers loved it. Musically, she was a creature from outer space. She was totally unlike the other pop singers of her day, whose white-bread interpretations had a sterile prettiness devoid of emotion. When she sang of love, one was reminded of one's initial fall; when she sang of betrayal there was bitterness and hate in her voice; sometimes she infused irony into a ditty no one had interpreted quite that way before.

It is basic to human nature to make comparisons, and that was one of the most startling things about this young woman: she was incomparable. The closest anyone could come to a parallel was Judy Garland, but that thought was followed lightninglike with another: Garland was a twenty-five-year veteran of show business with a great deal of full living behind her. This girl wasn't yet nineteen, could summon up as much if not more emotion in a song than Garland, and had a more beautiful voice with greater range. The audiences Barbra played to at The Lion and the Bon Soir knew they were witnessing the beginning of an extraordinary career.

Barbra's life was changing as rapidly as the shadings of her voice on a good night. Not only were her dreams of stardom becoming more real every day, but she and Barry Dennen had begun a romance. It was her first ever. "I never even had dates for proms in high school," she has said. She moved into Barry's apartment, and Bob Schulenberg recalls that it was a serious affair. "One night I went over to their place, and they were on the floor, and Barbra was resting her head on Barry's lap, and it was very romantic. They had that kind of glow that says two people have just been intimate. They started talking about getting married. I said, 'Are you serious?' And they said, 'Yeah, we're going to get married.' It was a sort of sacred, hallowed moment. It was very *intense*."

The relationship began to crumble several months later, however, when, Schulenberg remembers, Dennen started to treat Barbra cavalierly. On one occasion, Barry was visiting his parents in California and was scheduled to return on a certain day. Barbra prepared an elaborate feast to welcome him back. He didn't return for another week, and never bothered to call. Barbra couldn't call him because, he told her, his parents weren't to know about their living together. "It was very hard on Barbra," Schulenberg says. "She had planned this great welcome, and then this happened. It was her first taste of that kind of crap. I think it was then that she started to realize Barry no longer shared her feelings."

Schulenberg recalls another instance of Dennen's ambivalence about Barbra. "I was over their place one Sunday. Barbra was in Brooklyn and Barry had some friends of his over, guys. One of them went into her closet in the course of the evening and put on some of Barbra's clothes. He got up in front of everybody and started singing, 'Keepin' out of mischief now,' imitating Barbra. Barry was laughing and I thought, 'You schmuck! Those are *her clothes!*' I thought Barry should have gotten up and punched the guy in the nose. I should have punched Barry in the nose for not doing it. So I thought, 'Can this relationship survive?' And the answer I came up with was no."

The end of the affair with Dennen came several months later, and left Barbra bitter. Typically, she turned her sorrow inward and brought it out again in her work: "I knew the minute I heard her sing 'Cry Me a River,' " Schulenberg says, "that she was singing about Barry—all that bitterness and anger. 'Now you say you're *sorry!*' I mean, she's not acting in that song, she's *feeling* it." Barbra said somewhat later, "When I used to sing 'Cry Me a River,' I had a specific person in mind. I tried to re-create in my mind the details of his face. I don't sing it quite the same way anymore because I don't feel the same way about that person."

Schulenberg continues, "She always uses something to draw from in a performance. It's all that 'sense motivating' she learned in acting class. I once asked her, before the breakup with Barry, how she could sing 'Lover Come Back to Me' so emotionally when she'd never lost a love. She said, 'When I was a kid I had this wonderful bathrobe. I always used to love to come home from school and read movie magazines and listen to the radio or watch TV wearing this bathrobe. One day I came home from a terrible day at school, and like Linus' blanket, I couldn't wait till I got into that bathrobe. I looked around and I couldn't find it. My mother came home from work and I said, "Where's the bathrobe?" She said, "Oh, I gave it to the thrift shop." Now, every time I sing that song, I think of that bathrobe!' "

Her engagement at the Bon Soir, originally two weeks, was extended to eleven, and news of this wonderful new talent quickly spread across Manhattan. A young theatrical manager named Marty Erlichman went to see her one evening and immediately went backstage and asked her if he could represent her. She was, in fact, looking for a new manager—the one she had kept insisting that she change her name, fix her nose, and sing more conventional songs. Barbra asked Erlichman if he thought she should alter anything about herself. When he said "No," she told him he had a client, and a long-time association was born. Marty remained Barbra's manager for fifteen years—and never with a formal contract.

With Phyllis Diller backstage at the Bon Soir, 1961

"She looked like a Modigliani painting." Barbra in early 1961

Barbra informed her manager that his services were no longer needed (something that would cause her trouble and expense later), and asked Erlichman to help her get theater work. She still wanted to be an actress, and if she had to sing, better it be on a legitimate stage. After several months, Erlichman brought her to an open audition for an off-Broadway revue called *Another Evening with Harry Stoones*.

Stoones was an occasionally brilliant, often sophomoric collection of comic and musical sketches written by Jeff Harris, a soap-opera actor turned writer-director. Harris held auditions at the Gramercy Arts, the Greenwich Village theater where the show was set to open. He had already scored a coup in signing Diana Sands, a singer-actress who had scored a Broadway success in *A Raisin in the Sun* (and who later went on to create the role of Doris in *The Owl and the Pussycat* on Broadway). The rest of the cast was to be comprised of unknowns, with Harris' one prerequisite that they be "wildly talented."

The show was completely cast when one of the women backed out, leaving a vacancy that Louise Lasser, Linda Lavin, and Barbra Streisand auditioned to fill. "Barbra came to two auditions," Jeff Harris recalls, "both times with Marty Erlichman. I remember Marty wore the same suit to both auditions; it had a hole in the left sleeve. And Barbra was very impressive. I said to somebody after the first audition, 'You gotta see her.' She certainly was hot, clearly talented, and very different. But we were taking a chance hiring her, because most of the cast were familiar to me in one way or another."

The other cast members were Sheila Copelan, Virgil Curry, Susan Belink, Ben Keller, Kenny Adams, and Dom De Luise. Barbra stood out, even among a group of aspiring actors struggling to assert their individuality: "She was purposely unusual," Harris says. "You could sense that the insecurity was manifesting itself in the desire to do everything different. And she was different among a group of people who knew the importance of being different themselves. I remember Dom auditioned for a show once wearing nothing but a barrel."

Stoones was so irreverent, it is easy to see why Barbra wanted to be in it and why she was cast. "It was an anti-revue at the time," Harris says. "The title was a comment on all those 'An Evening With . . .' shows that were popular at the time. Here was *Another Evening* with a guy who never existed. The first act was called 'The Civil War,' the second act was called 'The Roaring Twenties,' which had nothing to do with anything. And all the sketches kind of made fun of everything."

Barbra appeared in nine sketches, sang three solos and a duet with Dom De Luise. One of her solos was "Value," which she later performed in Central Park, about the relative wealth of one boyfriend versus another; a second was called "Jersey." "Oh, God, it was wonderful," Harris says. "It was a full-blast jungle number right from a movie. She starts out by saying that her boyfriend went into Jersey, and she starts worrying about all the dangers that can befall you there, and there are native jungle rhythms behind her. Then she starts mentioning New Jersey towns: Matawan, Passaic, and worrying that her boyfriend went into the tubes and will never come back. Then she resolves to go in after him—even though she may die—and bring him out. Because it's better to die together in Jersey than be single in New York.

" 'Big Barry' was another of her sketches," Harris goes on. "It takes place in the boys' and girls' bathrooms in a high school. There's this big macho guy telling the other guys how he scored the night before, and there's a big bimbo in the girls' room telling about how she did this and that. The payoff is that a little mousy girl, played by Barbra, comes out at the end and meets this mousy little boy in the corridor, and she says, 'Harold, I'm pregnant.' "

Barbra's voice and comic abilities made a definite impression on the other cast members, Harris recalls. "Sheila Copelan came up to me at one point and said prophetically—prophetically enough so that I'd remember it—'This show will be remembered because Barbra was in it.' "

Barbra made another kind of impression, Harris says, because "she was having real problems during the show. She was being forced out of her apartment, she had no place to stay because her first manager—as I understand it—was trying to get paid and was going to take her clothes in payment because she had never paid him, and so she had to keep moving. She had no place to stay and I remember it was a problem because there was no phone in case rehearsals were changed, or what have you. I think he eventually got his money but lost her as a client. Marty treated her, from the first moment I saw both of them, as if she was the biggest star there ever was."

Bob Schulenberg recalls that Barbra indeed had to pay off her first manager, but says that was not the reason Harris often couldn't find her. "She got evicted from her apartment at one point, and she couldn't find another one, so she carried a cot around and slept in friends' apartments, wherever she could find to sack out. She wouldn't have been moving around to keep him from getting her clothes; you don't pull that sort of stuff with Barbra. But it did cost her something like five thousand dollars to buy out that guy. I'm not sure where she got the money, but there were people in those days who cared about her, who could have lent her money. Despite the homeless waif quality, she had some responsible people around."

Another Evening with Harry Stoones had fifteen previews before opening on October 21, 1961. "After opening night," Harris says, "there was going to be a party at my house and everybody came except Barbra. The party was a downer because the notices were not good. Everyone left and I got ready for bed. The doorbell rang and it was Barbra. She brought a loaf of bread, fresh rye bread, and she was so proud because it had been freshly baked and sliced. That was the level of affluence we all shared at that point. And I explained that the party was over—in more ways than one."

The first reviews of *Harry Stoones*—in the New York *Times* and *Herald Tribune*—were negative, and that was enough to kill the precariously financed show. Its opening performance became its closing performance, and when quite good notices appeared later in the week in *Women's Wear Daily,* the *World-Telegram and Sun* and *The New Yorker,* it was too late.

Barbra's notices were excellent, although many critics misspelled her name. *Variety* said, "Barbra Streisand is a slim, offbeat, deadpan comedienne with an excellent flair for dropping a dour blackout gag, and she belts across a musical apostrophe to New Jersey with facile intensity." *The Village Voice* critic noted, "Barbara Streisand can put across a lyric melody and make fine fun of herself at the same time."

Good personal reviews were not enough to lessen Barbra's disappointment at the failure of her first major theatrical venture. "Everyone was really hurt by the bad notices in the *Times* and *Tribune*," Harris says. "All it took then was a bad rap in the *Times* to kill a show. Everybody was so up for that show, because we thought it was so far ahead of anything else that had been done to that point.

"Every so often Dom De Luise, who has remained a friend, and I will joke around that we should revive *Harry Stoones* and see who emerges from it this time. But you know, so many people have come up to me and said that they saw it. And they say, 'Oh my God, it was so wonderful!' That many people *couldn't* have seen it. I don't know, but it seems that *Harry Stoones* is still alive for a lot of people.

"And it was certainly worth doing just to have met Barbra Streisand. Had I not known her, I could still say to you in all honesty that she's my favorite singer. She is just superb . . ."

"Indian nuts"—Barbra and Dom De Luise

A 1962 publicity still

A photo session for the back of the *Pins and Needles* album, 1962

Performing "Jersey"

Breakthrough

After *Harry Stoones*, Barbra began an engagement at the Blue Angel, a "classy" uptown club, where her act was seen by important record and theatrical insiders. The Streisand Legend has it that Arthur Laurents, preparing to direct a Broadway show for producer David Merrick, caught Barbra at the Blue Angel, was enchanted, and asked her to audition. Laurents, however, takes no credit for urging Barbra on to Broadway success: he first saw her when she arrived, along with dozens of other hopefuls, at an open casting call for *I Can Get It for You Wholesale.*

Bob Schulenberg recalls the events leading up to this momentous audition: "It was Thanksgiving 1961, and I had a dinner party. Barbra was singing at the Blue Angel, and she didn't get to my apartment until two in the morning, after everyone else had left. But she was dying for Thanksgiving dinner—things like that were really important to her because she didn't have a traditional home life. She ate, and we talked, and then it was four-thirty in the morning, and she had this audition at ten o'clock.

"So she slept over, and the next morning she didn't have anything to wear except what she'd worn at the Blue Angel the night before—a black evening dress and black shoes, and her twelve-dollar 1926 monkey-fur coat. And I'm making sandwiches for her while she's rushing to get ready and I put them in a shopping bag for her to take.

"The stories about that audition! Here she came carrying a shopping bag, with this big fur coat on that she wouldn't take off because she didn't want anyone to see what she was wearing because how can you explain—'I'm wearing what I wore last night because I didn't go home, but it wasn't sexual . . . it was a friend and it was Thanksgiving . . .' You don't want to go into all that, so she kept the coat on."

Arthur Laurents picks up the narrative from here: "It was all very cleverly done. I remember she had an enormous pile of music she put on top of the piano, and when she walked away with it in her hand, it just spread across the stage like an accordion and got a big laugh. Then she asked to sit down, and when the chair was brought to her she sat down, took a wad of gum from her mouth and put it under the chair. Now, she and I have had a running dispute about this, but I suspected that there was no gum, and after she left I had someone check under the chair, and there wasn't. She claims there was. But I think it was a ploy to make her stand out."

For Laurents, the "ploy" was unnecessary. "When she started to sing, I just flipped. I had her singing for sheer enjoyment. But I also had a problem: there was no part in the show for her. The only possibility was Miss Marmelstein, who was supposed to be a fifty-year-old woman. But I was determined to have this girl in the show; not only was she a marvelous singer, but there was something unconventional about her, particularly at that time. I thought I could take advantage of her unusual looks. I talked to the authors about having her play Miss Marmelstein, and I said, 'The way she looks, she will be accepted as a spinster, and the audience will have no idea of her age.' They agreed, and Barbra was cast as Miss Marmelstein."

I Can Get It for You Wholesale was written by Jerome Weidman with music and lyrics by Harold Rome. It revolved around Harry Bogen, a brash young man on the make who works his way up in the fashion industry by less than scrupulous means, using the people who love him to get ahead. Laurents chose Elliott Gould, previously a chorus boy in *Irma La Douce* to play the lead, and the cast also included Jack Kruschen, Marilyn Cooper, Lillian Roth, Harold Lang, Bambi Linn, and Sheree North. Just two members of the cast were Broadway novices—Barbra and Elliott.

Elliott was present at one of the four additional auditions Barbra was called upon to do before she won the role. He was fascinated by what he saw, and was offered a rare opportunity to express his interest. Barbra, after reading and singing, began handing out slips of paper with her telephone number on it, explaining that she had just had her phone installed and wanted someone to call her. Elliott never got one of the slips from Barbra, but intercepted one from a young man who was about to throw it into the trash. That night, Barbra got just one call. "You asked for someone to call you," the voice said, "so I called. I just want to tell you, you were brilliant today." There was a pause. "This is Elliott Gould." Then he hung up.

"When I saw her that first day," Elliott said later, "I thought she was the weirdo of all times. But when I saw her next, I offered her a cigar and we had a smoke together. She was always kind of a loner. The more I got to know her, the more I was fascinated with her. She needs to be protected. She's a very fragile little girl. She doesn't commit easily, but she liked me. I think I was the first man who ever liked her back. I found her absolutely exquisite. She was the most innocent thing I'd ever seen, like a beautiful flower that hadn't blossomed yet. But she was so strange that I was afraid."

Barbra: "I thought he was funny-looking. He gave me a cigar. One day at rehearsals I saw the back of his neck, and I just liked him. A couple of weeks later, we were walking around the skating rink at Rockefeller Center when he chased me and we had a snowball fight. He never held me around or anything, but he put snow on my face and kissed me, very lightly. It sounds ookhy, but it was great. Like out of a movie!"

The romance did take on storybook qualities. After rehearsals, they would walk the streets of Manhattan, see midnight horror movies, search for all-night diners with Barbra's favorite, rice pudding without raisins, play Pokerino in penny arcades and talk to each other into the early morning hours.

Their budding love affair made the pressures of their budding Broadway careers less difficult. Both were in for a rocky road to the Great White Way. Miss Marmelstein's age, however, was not a source of trouble for Barbra. "If the role was written for a fifty-year-old woman and could be played by a nineteen-year-old girl," Arthur Laurents says, "then the character couldn't have been written very strongly. So in that case what you do is use the performer's attributes, bring those out, develop them. What I tried to do was highlight that quirky, very offbeat humor that Barbra has."

Barbra's Miss Marmelstein was a harried, put-upon secretary, efficient at her job but ignored by men. Never called anything but Miss Marmelstein, she bemoans the lack of intimacy in the way she is addressed. Barbra's one solo musical number in the show, written by Harold Rome expressly for her, made her lament hilariously clear.

Wholesale went through out-of-town tryouts in Philadelphia and Boston on its way to New York. Laurents recalls that Barbra's inexperience sometimes caused him problems. "She didn't know very much about the stage. One night in an off-Broadway revue is not going to give you experience. She was very undisciplined. She's very inventive, but it never occurred to her that the invention should be for rehearsals and not for onstage. One thing she did—at the end of the first act, there was a fashion show, which was the equivalent I guess of an opening night in the theater. She'd fallen madly in love with the boss, Elliott Gould, who she really was in love with by then, and when the fashion show was a triumph, she suddenly jumped on his back, and then did this kind of

'Oh, what have I done?' walking away that she does so well. It was terribly funny, and all her own, but it did rather throw the other actors off cue.

"She didn't realize," Laurents goes on, "how disconcerting something like that could be for the other actors. My concern was—you plan certain things for certain effects, and if you let one person do as he or she pleases, it's only fair that everyone else does, and the result, of course, is anarchy. I had to be rather sharp with her just before we opened in New York. I was convinced she was going to walk away with the show. I thought then and I still think she's one of the most talented people I've ever encountered. But I finally had to do something I don't like to do—I called her down in front of the entire company and told her she must discipline herself more. There are various versions of that event. One is that she cried; hers is that she was planning the decoration of her new apartment during my admonishment and *pretended* to cry.

"She tries to project a real hard-shelled image, but I think she's very vulnerable. She'd like everyone to think my talk had no effect on her, but that night she was marvelous, and from that point on the performance was stable and solid."

According to Laurents, both Barbra and Elliott were in jeopardy of losing their chances at Broadway stardom all during the tryouts. "I had a battle every night with David Merrick. He wanted to fire them because he thought they were both unattractive, and he didn't think Barbra was funny. I thought she was funny—we kept giving her more to do in the musical numbers, taking what was a group number and highlighting her. Merrick wasn't that concerned with Barbra after a while, because she wasn't the lead. But Elliott was, and he wanted me to fire him. In Philly and Boston, Merrick kept bringing in every leading man in town. But when he finally said he was going to fire Elliott, I threatened to quit. Elliott stayed. I thought he was fine in the role. And they were absolutely adorable to look at together—they were very much in love and very sweet."

Once, just before opening, Barbra expressed unhappiness at playing Miss Marmelstein. "She came up to me," Laurents says, "and said, 'Why can't I play the ingenue? You don't think I'm pretty enough.' I said, 'Barbra, you're a smart girl, and you certainly should realize your part is much better, and you're gonna walk off with the show. And of course, she did."

When *I Can Get It for You Wholesale* opened at the Shubert Theatre on March 22, 1962, Barbra Streisand became Broadway's most acclaimed new talent. The show's reviews were decidedly mixed, but Barbra's were nearly uniform raves. Howard Taubman of the New York *Times* wrote, after a largely negative review of the show, "The evening's find is Barbra Streisand, a girl with an oafish expression, a loud, irascible voice and an arpeggiated laugh . . . a natural comedienne." Whitney Bolton of the *Morning Telegraph* said, "Especially to be noted (is) a shriek-voiced new comedienne who probably won't be out of work for the next eight years. Her name is Barbra Streisand, who is 19 years old and has packed 38 years of poise and professionalism into her still young life. Miss Streisand, singing or talking, burbling or walking, screaming or whispering, is a great, good friend to *I Can Get It for You Wholesale*."

Even John Simon, later a Streisand nemesis, wrote in *Theater Arts:* "Miss Streisand possesses nothing short of a Chekhovian brand of heart-breaking merriment. Gifted with a face that shuttles between those of a tremulous young Borzoi and a fatigued Talmudic scholar . . . she can sing the lament of the unreconstructed drudge with the clarion peal of an Unliberty Bell."

Barbra's "Miss Marmelstein" number stopped the show on opening night, and every night thereafter. Many people who saw Barbra in *Wholesale* remember that she

As Yetta Tessye Marmelstein

With Arthur Laurents and the *Wholesale* cast

With Jack Kruschen during rehearsals.   *(opposite)* "Miss Marmelstein"

(both pages) Barbra and Elliot at the Beverly Hills Hotel, later 1963

"took over the show." Arthur Laurents denies this. "She couldn't have, because the part was too small. The show was about Elliott Gould and his mother, Lillian Roth. Barbra registered, but the audience wasn't panting for her return every time she was off stage. If they had been the show would have been a failure, because it was too small a part. But every time she came on, there were fireworks. There's a difference between being dazzling in a small role—having people come out after the show wondering and talking about you—and taking over a show."

Audiences who did wonder about Barbra turned to their *Playbills* to read her biography, and found her even more intriguing afterward. Her biographical sketch indicated that "Barbra Streisand is nineteen, was born in Madagascar and reared in Rangoon, educated at Erasmus Hall High School in Brooklyn . . ." It was still another of Barbra's "ploys" to attract attention: "I used to read *Playbills* in the theater: '(He) attended this university. Was in this show, that show . . .' And most of the people would say, 'I am a member of the Actors Studio.' So I thought to myself, first of all, they've got to be more interesting than that. They're so boring. And two, I played this New York secretary and I thought, 'How interesting if people thought I was born in a foreign country,' and they'd say, 'Gee, this girl is actually putting on this accent.' Instead of thinking it was just me, you see? I thought it would be interesting for them as an audience. So that's why I did that. But then, you know, at first they refused to print it! . . . And I also said I am not a member of the Actors Studio, which *they* got incensed about."

A few months into the show's run, the places were changed to Zanzibar and Aruba, then Barbra finally owned up to her prosaic past. By then, it wasn't necessary for her to fantasize about her birthplace to attract attention; her career was gaining strong momentum. Articles about her appeared in *Time* and *Life;* she won the New York Drama Critics Award as Best Supporting Actress and was nominated for a Tony Award; she became a sought-after TV talk-show guest.

Almost all the excitement surrounding *I Can Get It for You Wholesale* was generated by Barbra Streisand and, on top of everything else, she had won the love of the show's leading man. Rumors abounded of deep resentment against this novice who was winning all the marbles and playing the game her way. Arthur Laurents denies this. "There's only resentment if people think someone doesn't deserve the praise or behaves badly. Barbra deserved everything she was getting and didn't behave badly at all."

Wholesale ran nine months on Broadway. At one point, Barbra was replaced for a few days by her understudy, Louise Lasser, over whom she had won the *Harry Stoones* role. Later, all Lasser would say about the experience was, "I was terrible."

During the run of the play, Elliott moved into Barbra's apartment. It was something he resisted doing for as long as he could, because Barbra lived over Oscar's fish store. Jeff Harris vividly recalls the place: "The odors! Fish, flounder, bass, whatever it was—all dead. It took a lot of getting used to. Barbra had decorated that apartment, and I'm here to tell you, there's never been anything like it. You could spend five hours in the bathroom alone—it was papered all over with cutouts from magazines, lay-over stuff everywhere. The rest of the place was just filled with *chotchkas,* little bits and pieces of things she had picked up at thrift shops. She had this one amazing thing that looked like a World War II oxygen mask—but to this day I'm not sure what it was."

Such as it was, Barbra's apartment became the lovers' nest. "We worked together, we lived together, we weren't apart for more than an hour," Barbra said. "We thought of ourselves as Hansel and Gretel." She wanted to learn Greek or Latin "so we can speak a secret language nobody else can understand."

There was an "us against the world" quality to their relationship, too. They could console each other over David Merrick's misgivings, and for every horror story Barbra told Elliott about her childhood, he could match it, from a totally different perspective. Both his parents were alive, but they fought so bitterly that their son welcomed their divorce. His mother pushed him against his will on to the stage; at eight he was appearing on the Milton Berle show, by eleven he was tap dancing at the Palace Theater. He hated it but finally accepted his lot in life. Barbra was intrigued by his unhappiness with a situation she would have welcomed as a child; their youthful dissatisfactions, although contradictory, helped form the bond that was growing between them.

Barbra was experiencing satisfaction for the first time in her life. The love affair with Elliott was idyllic; her career was beginning to take some shape. In an uncharacteristically sanguine interview during the *Wholesale* run she said, "They tell me I'll eventually win everything. The Emmy for TV, the Grammy for records, the Tony for Broadway and the Oscar for movies. It would be wonderful to win all those awards, to be rich, to have my name on marquees all over the world. And I guess a lot of those things will happen to me."

It was a prophetic musing, but Barbra's tendancy toward negativism ("I'm very Jewish in that respect") left her far less buoyed by the critics' praise of her talent as displayed in *Wholesale* than hurt by certain of their descriptions of her appearance: "an amiable anteater," "oafish," "a homely frump." They were, of course, describing Miss Marmelstein more than Barbra Streisand, but Barbra took the unflattering comments personally.

Along with the successes came disappointments. Streisand could not get a record contract. "For nine months," Marty Erlichman says, "I tried to get her a job. Every record company in the business turned her down: 'Change the clothes, change the nose, stop singing those cockamamy songs.' " Goddard Lieberson, president of Columbia Records, which was set to do the original cast recording of *Wholesale,* listened to Barbra sing and pronounced her "too special" to appeal to a mass audience.

Barbra feared at this point that her characterization of Miss Marmelstein would forever typecast her as an ethnic comic, and that was the last thing she wanted. Without a recording contract, the best thing she could do to avoid that fate would be to return to the nightclub circuit. She asked Arthur Laurents to help her put together another show for the Bon Soir, where she did late-night stints after performing in *Wholesale.* Later, Barbra would say she was extremely lazy—but at this point in her career she was willing to work as hard as necessary to achieve her goals.

"A Voice the Microphone Loved"

Columbia's Original Cast recording of *Wholesale* marked the debut of Barbra Streisand's voice on record. As in the show, the "Miss Marmelstein" number was the high point of the album. Not long after its release, Columbia decided to press a twenty–fifth-anniversary album of a show *Wholesale* composer Harold Rome had written, *Pins and Needles.* Originally a revue performed by members of the International Ladies' Garment Workers' Union, its songs celebrated the working man, unionism, and progressivism, and poked fun at reactionaries, conservatives, and imperialists. What began as an amateur show in 1937 became a Broadway hit that ran four years.

Barbra had done so well by his "Miss Marmelstein" number that Harold Rome insisted she perform on this new version of *Pins and Needles.* Columbia brass balked, suggesting a half-dozen alternatives they thought would be more suitable. But Rome stood his ground, and finally won out.

Pins and Needles developed into a delightful album of witty "message" songs. Barbra sang six of them, "Not Cricket to Picket," "Doing the Reactionary," "Four Little Angels of Peace," "Sitting on Your Status Quo" and her two best efforts, "What Good Is Love" and "Nobody Makes a Pass at Me." The former is a sullen torch song with a rather incongruous honky-tonk backup; Barbra's voice sounds quite immature here and lacks the shadings it acquired rather quickly thereafter. Surprisingly, she sings rather than acts the song, which detracts from it; perhaps she was intimidated by Columbia's "too special" edict. "Nobody Makes a Pass at Me" is the comically heart-tugging lament of a neglected young lady who, believing commercial pitches, buys every product on the market guaranteed to increase sexual magnetism and cannot understand why they don't work for her.

Barbra's rendition was funny and sad—and noticed by reviewers. John F. Indcox of *High Fidelity* wrote, "The original version of this, sung by Millie Wertz, was, until recently, available on the Decca label, but that rendition is now completely surpassed by a gorgeously funny performance by Barbra Streisand, a genuine comedy find. Here Miss Streisand sounds very much like a young Fanny Brice; again, in 'Not Cricket to Picket,' she sounds surprisingly like Beatrice Lillie."

Barbra's performances on these two albums and at the Bon Soir brought her bookings on television, where all the qualities that thrilled her nightclub and theater audiences could now be displayed on a massive scale. She was kooky and unorthodox; on one show she administered a psychological test to the other guests to determine if they were schizophrenic. On another, she warned of the dangers of drinking milk. Appearing with David Susskind, she listened to him praise talent, then interrupted to tell him that she had tried to see him again and again and when she finally did, he acted as if she weren't there. It was people like him, she continued, who were stifling young talent and hurting show business in the process. Susskind was so taken aback that Barbra felt she needed to lighten things up and cracked, "I scare you, don't I? I'm so far out I'm in." Barbra's impact on the home screen can be gauged by the fact that many people still remember these initial TV appearances.

Barbra's popularity on TV, accomplished by accenting rather than hiding her unorthodoxy, helped convince Goddard Lieberson of Columbia to take a chance on her.

She was signed to a record contract, and Lieberson waited to see whether he had made the deal—or the mistake—of his career.

Barbra launched into preparation for her first solo album. She hadn't liked the orchestrations on *Pins and Needles,* and asked Harold Rome to suggest an arranger-conductor she'd have a rapport with. Rome told her about Peter Matz, with whom he had worked in the theater.

After Matz was seen and approved by Marty Erlichman, he had his first meeting with Barbra. "I hadn't seen her perform live at that point," Matz now recalls, "but I had seen her on 'The Tonight Show.' I was immediately attracted to her when we met, and I realized this was a very special person. I had a strong impression that this girl knew exactly what she was doing; that, despite the public image, she was not kooky."

Matz soon learned that his first impression was correct. "She had a strong instinct about what was going to work for her, both in the larger sense, in the material, and down to specific things in the music. Frequently she'd suggest an alteration of some kind that at first you'd think was impossible. She knows exactly what she has in mind, and if you spend enough time you'll uncover it. Many of the ideas in arrangements that I've been credited with were really hers."

Matz worked to balance Streisand's voice and her orchestral accompaniments. "When a singer is very passionate or dramatic, it wouldn't do to have blandness in an accompaniment. When there's a lot of heat in the voice, you have to back it up with equal heat. But you have to draw the line at where it gets intrusive. That's a question of taste."

In trying to match Streisand's "heat," Matz was forced to make a small group of instruments go a long way, "We had very small combinations, just four or five instruments," he says. "The reason for that was not artistic at all. It was because Mike Berniker, the producer of the album said, 'Look, we can't spend a lot of money on this, we don't know if this woman is going to sell records.' It was a very precarious budget.

"And poor Mike, he was walking a tightrope between the upstairs guys, me, and Barbra. He would go upstairs and tell them, 'She's doing "Who's Afraid of the Big, Bad Wolf?" and they would say 'What!' and he would come down to me and say, 'Do you have to do that?' And she'd say, 'Yes, goddammit, it's on the album!' Mike's job was a hard one, but he was very supportive. He let her do what she was doing and fought for her to have her way. A lot of producers wouldn't have had the guts to do that."

Streisand and Matz hit it off well, because he understood her. He was extremely patient with what others saw as temperament. "What I saw and still see with her," Matz says, "is that her insecurity stems from the fact that she delivers so much when she performs. The only times I've seen her get uptight is when somebody else's part isn't working. She'll get impatient very quickly, if, for instance, she can't hear herself properly in the headset. But that's because she's operating on a much higher performance level, and energy level and emotional level. She's putting a lot out when she works and if she sees that someone is conspiring to keep it from being all that she wants it to be, she gets a little riled. That's absolutely appropriate."

Matz found it challenging to keep up with Barbra. "We would be playing something, and she would hear a string line, or an accompaniment, and she'd say, 'Hold it! Can we change that?' and she'd try to find the perfect line that would go along with what she was going to sing. Maybe she had made up her mind to sing something other than the melody, and she heard in her head what the violins should be doing. It was exciting, especially when you have very high-paid violinists sitting there.

Barbra and Columbia Records President Goddard Lieberson sign her first recording contract in 1962.

Recording *The Barbra Streisand Album*, 1963

"Of course, the schmucks among the musicians resent that sort of thing. A lot of people don't understand the adventure of doing this kind of work. Some guys are used to coming in, working for three or four hours, then going home and thinking about the stock market. They have no idea what she's up to, and they would resent it and make wisecracks. But to me, it was a challenge to try to understand what it was she was looking for. The cigar smokers don't care. I've had to literally throw out someone who was smoking a cigar. It's no use asking him to put the cigar out, because if he comes to a session where someone is going to sing and smokes a cigar, he just doesn't get it. All you can do is ask him to leave. It's people like that who give Barbra the bad mouthings she gets about her perfectionism. People who understand the quest for quality understand what Barbra's doing."

The Barbra Streisand Album turned out to be an eclectic collection of the unusual songs Barbra had been performing in her nightclub acts: the acid, Barry Dennen-inspired "Cry Me a River," the tongue-in-cheek "My Honey's Loving Arms," her wildly eccentric "Who's Afraid of the Big, Bad Wolf?" a risqúe "Keepin' Out of Mischief Now," the startlingly languid version of "Happy Days Are Here Again," "A Sleepin' Bee," the first song she ever sang in front of another person as an adult, and five others, including "A Taste of Honey," her one concession to the worried Columbia Records officials who begged her to include some current pop favorites in her repertoire. (Interestingly, that song holds up least well twenty years later.)

When the album was released in late February 1963, it was clear within two weeks that Barbra wasn't "too special" to sell records to a national audience—it took only that long for Barbra to become the #1 best-selling female vocalist in the country. The album established her as the most powerful, theatrical, and beautifully voiced singer in some time, and her choice of material and its delivery amazed and delighted residents of the Midwest as much as it had the sophisticated New York night owls.

The public became more and more fascinated by Barbra, helped along by Harold Arlen's positively clairvoyant album liner notes: after comparing Barbra to Helen Morgan, Fanny Brice, Beatrice Lillie, and a painting by Modigliani, he added: "I advise you to watch Barbra Streisand's career. This young lady (a mere twenty) has a stunning future. Keep listening, keep watching. And please remember, I told you so . . ."

The public did keep listening and watching. A single version of Barbra's cynical, downbeat rendition of the traditionally up-tempo Democratic Party rallying song "Happy Days Are Here Again" became a big hit and Barbra's first standard. Peter Matz recalls the genesis of Barbra's unique arrangement: "Doing the song slowly was Ken Welch's idea. He was working on 'The Garry Moore Show' when Barbra was a guest, and they used to do a segment on each show called 'That Wonderful Year.' On Barbra's show, the year was 1932 or whenever 'Happy Days' was a hit, and Barbra was supposed to sing that song. Ken suggested that she sing it slowly and sarcastically, conveying the opposite meaning from what the words were saying, and of course it was incredibly effective. I don't think Ken ever got any credit for that."

Barbra's first album was a critical as well as a financial success. It was named the Best Album of 1963 at the Grammy Awards, and Barbra was chosen Best Female Vocalist for "Happy Days." Barbra's position as a chanteuse was now sturdy, and she has reflected on the reasons for her acceptance by the public. "People were just ready for me. Music was predominantly rock and roll and there was no other major new artist around. So when I came along and did my esoteric, ethereal songs, I think people were struck by my audacity. The songs had quality, too—like Rembrandt.

"When I sing, I don't operate on the surface, so that emotions are slightly painful. That's why people like me, because I tell them the truth. But that is painful to me. It's not such an easy thing—you get up and sing the song and it's nice. No, there's many things attached to it."

Marty Erlichman: "I've had to figure it out as a man, not just a manager, and I think it's Chaplin. As the little fellow, people wanted to help him, and they were happiest when the worm turned. Barbra is a girl the guys never look at twice and when she sings about that—about being like an invisible woman—people break their necks trying to protect her."

People were also breaking their necks trying to *book* her; Marty found the phone calls coming in to *him* now. Barbra soon embarked on a national tour that took her to Mr. Kelly's in Chicago and the hungry i in San Francisco. Her salaries ranged from five thousand to seven thousand dollars a week, extraordinary sums for the period, and particularly for a girl who less than two years earlier was rejoicing at fifty dollars a week.

Nineteen sixty-three was turning into The Year of Barbra Streisand. After enjoying her appearance on "The Dinah Shore Show," President John F. Kennedy invited Barbra to sing at a White House Press Correspondents' Dinner. Barbra was instructed not to ask the President for his autograph, but when they were introduced, she was so taken with his dashing good looks that she muttered, "You're a doll," and asked for his signature. The legend has it that Kennedy, amusedly piqued at her chutzpah, signed his name after penning a choice obscenity.

Barbra returned to New York for a triumphant engagement at Basin Street East, then the top New York nitery. Columbia Records pushed her to record another album, now that the first was the number one best-selling album in the country on several sales charts. (Even her most loyal partisans were amazed at *that*.) Barbra and Peter Matz returned to the studio.

The Second Barbra Streisand Album contained more of the songs Barbra was doing in her nightclub act, notably "Down with Love," "Any Place I Hang My Hat Is Home" and "My Coloring Book," plus new material she and Matz constantly searched for. What did Barbra look for in a song? "I think she looks at a lyric first," Matz says, "but she's very responsive to a sound—the sequence of notes is very important to her, not in a technical way, but strictly emotionally."

"I really prefer songs that are universal in thought," Barbra said. "Pretty melodies. I guess I'm kind of a romantic. All the clever ones are fun but you really can't *feel* anything unless it's simple and basic."

"Easy listening" was not a term that could describe Barbra's second album. If she had been perceived, and sometimes criticized, as an "emotional singer," then this recording proved it. She sang most of the songs as though her life depended on it, biting into some of the lyrics like a cobra. Many of her fans loved it, but others, less smitten, found the dramatics off-putting. Critic John Indcox, who had raved about her first three efforts, expressed strong reservations about this one: " . . . her work here is pretentiously arty, overinvolved and overprojected, and made further intolerable by a vocal tone best described by the Irish word 'keening.' "

Peter Matz concedes the album has flaws: "I think most of the keys on the second album were too high—we were half a tone too high, from top to bottom. And she was not in the best voice. She was working very hard at the time. She went from the Blue Angel to a national tour and back to Basin Street East. That put a tremendous strain on her vocal cords. And she was a person who had come out of working in really rough situations, those little clubs with lots of smoke and bad amplification. She was just learning about microphones, and what happens in the studio to a voice."

Still, Matz thinks highly of the *Second Album:* "I think it's one of the best she's ever done. A lot of the people who didn't like it really liked the first album. But that

With Dean Martin and Bob Hope on a Hope special, 1963

With Mike Douglas on his show, 1963

Meeting President Kennedy after her performance at the White House, 1963

album always had a precious air to me; it was a bit special material-y, and Bon Soir-y. The second album was more of a record in its own right. We were able to open up instrumentally, because we didn't have the budget restraints once Columbia saw how well Barbra was selling."

Matz wrote one of the songs on the second album, "Gotta Move." "It came about in an interesting way," he says. "She was at the Angel, and she said that she didn't have a good closing song. I had been spending a lot of time on the first album and I was really getting into her speech patterns. I went home one night and got up at three in the morning, went to the piano and wrote that song in about twenty minutes. I had no idea if she would like it, but it seemed to me very much like her, the way she talks, the whole thing of 'Gotta get out,' that jagged emotion. When she used it on the album and in her act, I was delighted." The song also turned up on her "Color Me Barbra" TV special, and on her *Greatest Hits* album.

If further proof was needed that Barbra could appeal to the masses, it came with her first engagement in that microcosm of American consumerism, Las Vegas, in July 1963. Hard as it may be to believe today, she was the opening act for Liberace. He, in fact, was responsible for Barbra's getting to Vegas at all. After seeing her at the Bon Soir and on the Ed Sullivan show, Liberace wanted to use her as his opening act on tour but was dissuaded. But when he returned to the Riviera Hotel in Vegas after a five-year absence, he insisted that Barbra be on the bill with him. "The thing I most admired about Barbra," he wrote in his autobiography, "was that she was a perfectionist. When it came to her performance, her singing, it had to be 100% the way she thought it should be. Her arrangements, her lighting, her accompaniment, everything was just the way she dictated and that's the mark of a successful performer. Those who don't take the trouble, who don't care whether things are right or not, will soon find that their audiences don't care very much either."

Barbra's repertoire of songs varied little from those on her first two albums, but added "Value" from *Harry Stoones* and "Folk Song," both of which later turned up on her Central Park concert album. The reaction to her act in Vegas, however, was less generous than it had been elsewhere. Those audiences, then as now, preferred slick glamour and middle-of-the-road renditions of old standards and current top-twenty hits. "I must admit," Liberace says, "that the night we opened everyone didn't rush up to me and tell me I'd make a great new discovery. Many agreed that it looked like I'd made a great big boo-boo . . . the one thing (Barbra) hadn't discovered about show business was the value of glamour."

Her review in the *Hollywood Reporter* summed up the reaction of many veteran Vegas-ites: "Singer Barbra Streisand was a sharp contrast to the star. Her make-up made her look like something that just climbed off a broom, but when she sang, it was like the wailing of a banshee bouncing up and down on marionette strings. It isn't until she does three or four songs that her voice is even noticed as being very pleasant. Her outrageous grooming almost nullifies her talent."

Of course, there were many others who appreciated her. *Variety* commented, "Barbra Streisand, in her debut here, is a most pleasant nitery surprise. She has an interesting look and an interesting sound, which of course is necessary to set her apart from other canaries. She puts subtle excitement into a fluid voice with an excellent range; she has dramatic facial expressions for overall movements; moreover, she has a wonderful flair for low-pressure comedy patter . . . Patrons who are tired of assembly-line singers will be quite happy with Miss Streisand."

Miss Streisand, however, was not happy with Vegas; she complained that her audiences were more interested in eating and gambling than in hearing her sing. The

(both pages) Appearing at the Hollywood Bowl and the Cocoanut Grove during her West Coast tour in 1963

Three fashion portraits from the early sixties

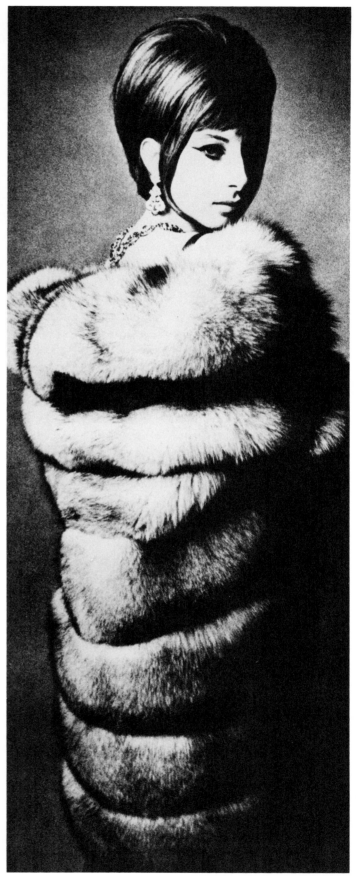

(opposite) With Judy Garland on Judy's show, aired October 6, 1963

Riviera Hotel was pleased enough with her one-month stint, though, to sign her for an "indefinite" pact. She put off returning for six full years, when she was a big enough star to command the full attention even of Vegas audiences.

While Barbra was making an impression in Las Vegas, Elliott was opening in a production of *On the Town* in London. He had asked her to costar in it with him, but her concert commitments were iron-clad. She did fly to London for the opening; since her visit was publicized and co-habitation was not as accepted in 1963 as it is now, Elliott intimated that they had been married the previous March in Miami.

They still weren't married after Barbra returned to the West Coast, but they soon would be. *On the Town,* despite favorable reviews for Elliott, was not a success, and shortly after Barbra returned Elliott rejoined her in Los Angeles. When Barbra flew to Lake Tahoe for a gig at Harrah's, Elliott went along. Secretly, with a few close friends as witnesses, they were married in nearby Carson City on September 13, 1963.

They honeymooned briefly in Las Vegas, but Barbra had a grinding schedule of concert appearances. Her performances at the Hollywood Bowl and the Cocoanut Grove grabbed headlines; Judy Garland, then doing a weekly television show, saw a Streisand concert and immediately asked her to appear as a guest. The teaming of the two greatest singers of their generations would become a milestone in television history.

Judy, it has been said, was apprehensive about working with Barbra, whose singing was being compared—favorably—to Garland's. Barbra joked about this at the beginning of the show, when Judy said she could do anything she wanted. "Can I replace you?" Barbra immediately responded.

Streisand's first two numbers were awesome. Against a field of black, with one spotlight trained on her face, she sang "Bewitched, Bothered and Bewildered," her voice purer, clearer, and more beautiful than it had ever been before and has rarely been since. Then the lights came up and she tore into "Down with Love," performing the song as high drama, complete with ironic laughter, clenched fists, bitter darting of the eyes and grimaces. The combination of Barbra lovely and Barbra theatrical resulted in high-pitched audience excitement. Garland looked at her after she finished "Down with Love" and said, her voice full of admiration, "You're thrilling." Then she added, "You're so good I hate you."

To which Barbra replied, "You're so good I've hated you for years."

Later in the show, Barbra and Judy sang a duet medley, each in fine voice and with a surprisingly natural camaraderie. Then they were joined by Ethel Merman, who came out of the audience and, calling Barbra "the new belter," held a contest to see which of these three divas had the biggest voice. Barbra was barely audible along with Merman and Garland; it seemed as though she conceded before the contest began. As Merman's voice got louder and louder, Barbra put her hand to her head in mock despair and, at the grand finale, mimed a *zaftig* soprano summoning up the last ounce of vocal strength. It was a funny, charming bit.

The entire show was a huge success, one of the few in the ill-fated Garland series. Streisand's performance, in fact, was nominated for an Emmy Award, the first time a guest appearance had been so honored. Streisand lost to Danny Kaye, but the Emmy Awards would soon be hearing from her again.

As Barbra's incredible year drew to a close, her position at the top of the list of female vocalists was supported by her selection as *Cue* magazine's "Entertainer of the Year." Things had coalesced very nicely for Barbra; her career was at a point most performers would envy. Before long, however, all the excitement and acclaim of 1963 would pale into insignificance—Barbra had been selected to star in an upcoming Broadway musical called *Funny Girl.*

PART TWO

ELEGANCE

1964-1969

"The Greatest Star"

It is one of the more fortuitous turns of show business fate that the musical play *Funny Girl* and Barbra Streisand developed at about the same time. As Barbra put it, accepting an Oscar for the movie version, "The first draft of *Funny Girl* was written when I was six. I'm glad it took so long to get it right!" If ever an actress and a role were made for each other . . .

Fanny Brice rose from a homely, gawky young girl in Manhattan's Lower East Side to one of Florenz Ziegfeld's funniest and most popular stars. The story of her success and her passionate, ill-fated love for dapper gambler Nicky Arnstein began as a screenplay by Ben Hecht, a friend of Fanny's son-in-law, press agent Ray Stark, who wanted to tell the Brice/Arnstein story on screen. Fanny, tough and witty, unable to remember names, wasn't pleased. "You write it a little fancy, kid," she reportedly told Hecht, "but at least you've got some of it straight."

Fanny then decided to tell the story herself, and dictated her memoirs before she died in 1951, at the age of fifty-nine. The autobiography was set in galleys when Stark—married to Fanny's daughter by Nicky Arnstein, Frances—bought the plates back from the publisher for fifty thousand dollars. He then tried to interest a studio in making a movie, but Hollywood executives were less smitten with Fanny's story than the denizens of Broadway, where she had enjoyed her greatest success. Besides, they told Stark, a thinly veiled version of the Brice/Arnstein story called *Rose of Washington Square* and starring Alice Faye and Tyrone Power had been released in 1939. It had not broken box office records, and both Fanny and Nicky sued Twentieth Century-Fox, settling out of court for different, undisclosed amounts. It was not a good track record, and Stark could not come up with much of a package to change producers' minds: the only star he could suggest to play Fanny was the unlikely Judy Garland. The project was shelved.

By the time Stark became a movie producer in 1960, he had decided that screenwriter Isabel Lennart's "affectionate" treatment of the Brice story, *My Man*, would work best as a stage musical. "It seemed wise to open it halfway as a trial before going the whole way with a film and also to be able to view a 'dry run' for a film," Stark said.

Lennart reworked her script and Stark sent it to Mary Martin, who indicated that she'd like to play the role. *Funny Girl*'s composer, Jule Styne, picks up the narrative from here. "Well, Mary Martin, number one star, it's money in the bank, so Stark arranged a meeting for Mary, her director, myself and Stephen Sondheim, who was to do the lyrics, but Steve said he was bowing out if Mary played the role. 'You've gotta have a Jewish girl,' he said, 'and if she's not Jewish she at least has to have a nose.' I said, 'Steve, we're not going to find any girl with a nose. Now, come on!'

"But he bowed out, and since nobody really wanted Mary Martin as Fanny Brice, the show was called off. Then suddenly it was on again—Anne Bancroft had okayed the script, and Jerome Robbins had agreed to direct." Bob Merrill took over as lyricist, and he and Styne worked up "People," "Don't Rain on My Parade," "Who Are You Now," "I'm the Greatest Star," and "The Music that Makes Me Dance." They brought the songs to Anne Bancroft. "She listened to them," Styne recalls, "and went absolutely pale, and said, 'You'll *never* find anyone to sing those songs.' More than that, she got up and walked out of the room. Now Bob Merrill confesses that he used to go with Anne Bancroft three years before, and that it ended terribly. 'When she saw me she had to hate the songs,' he said, 'but I wasn't going to blow this chance.' Jerome Robbins assured him the songs were brilliant, and that if it came to a toss between the score and Anne Bancroft, Anne would have to go."

After Bancroft's departure, Ray Stark and David Merrick, who was to coproduce, talked with Carol Burnett, Eydie Gorme, and Shirley MacLaine, among others, about playing the role. By this time, Jerome Robbins and then Bob Fosse had withdrawn as director and Garson Kanin was hired. "I was a great friend of Fanny Brice's," Kanin says. "I suppose I must have met Ray at Fanny's, the first time."

Kanin, Stark, and Merrick talked about other experienced stars who might play the role, and came up with no one. "And then," Kanin relates, "David Merrick said, 'Did you ever see this kid, Barbra Streisand, who works down at the Bon Soir?' And I said, 'Of course I have. She's absolutely sensational!'

"I had seen her in *Wholesale* as well, and of course she had just knocked everybody cold. But people who have theater experience know that it's one thing to come on and score in a number and another thing to carry a whole show. So we were all hesitant. Then David and I saw her at the Blue Angel. And it was after seeing that particular performance that I said to David, 'I think that it's folly to think of anybody else.' And I just plugged for Barbra Streisand."

There was opposition to Barbra's selection—from Fanny's daughter Fran. According to Jule Styne, Fran said, "This girl will never play my mother. She's sloppy, she's not chic. My mother was something special." And Billy Rose, Fanny's second husband, said in an interview in the *Ladies' Home Journal* late in 1963 that there was no actress of the day who could adequately portray Fanny Brice.

Even Barbra, at first, was unsure about playing Fanny. "I waited to say yes because I wanted to see the script. I was against the idea of doing anybody else's life. I didn't want to be compared to her. But the script was great. Even so, I thought it might be the worst thing for me to do. I might bomb."

Barbra was convinced to sign after heavy negotiations. Kanin remembers, "Her agents were David Begelman and Freddie Fields. Her personal manager was Marty Erlichman. Her business manager was Marty Bregman. And all of these people were involved, plus Stark and Merrick—so you can imagine. Finally, it was negotiated successfully and David Merrick called me up and said, 'Well, we've signed Barbra Streisand—and God be with us.'

"And I said, 'I think you've got the perfect girl for it.' There was never any question in my mind that she was right for the part. Not because she looked like Fanny, but she *was* like Fanny. She wasn't conventionally beautiful and yet when you were around her long enough, you began to see a certain classic beauty in her—in that respect, she was very much like Fanny."

At this point, the precarious *Funny Girl* package almost fell apart. Ray Stark and David Merrick had a serious disagreement, and Merrick removed himself from the equation. But there was a major complication. When a producer is preparing a Broadway show, he is required to place two weeks' salary into an Actors' Equity Escrow Account for every actor he signs. This serves as a guarantee that the actors will receive some sort of severance pay once the show closes. A veteran producer like David Merrick, however, is not required to post this bond. As Kanin explains, "They know that David Merrick is good for it. And since Merrick didn't have to put up that front money, it was he who signed the contract with Barbra. Well, when he called me to tell me he was out of the show, he said, 'I don't know what's gonna happen now because Stark has no contract with Streisand. *I've* got the contract with Streisand.'

"Well, for about five or six days, it almost looked like the whole show was off. I talked to David Merrick for three hours one night on the phone, trying to hold this thing together. Stark was, by now, terribly angry and unhappy about the whole thing. And apparently when Barbra's management found out about it, there was some question of upping the ante or changing the terms. Stark is a very proud man and a very, very good businessman and he wasn't going to give into a lot of pressure. So there was a time there that we certainly didn't know what was going to happen. Then apparently all got settled and we began further casting of the show."

Kanin recalls that his first meeting with Barbra was "a big luncheon at Dinty Moore's," and that "we talked generally about other casting. I remember Barbra saying, 'Whoever you get, be sure he's very tall. I love tall men. If they're not tall, I feel ridiculous.' I don't recall her ever making any suggestions, and I don't think she had approval. But, obviously, nobody was going to cast somebody opposite her that she didn't want."

Kanin wanted to cast Jerry Orbach as Nicky Arnstein, but was overruled, and Sydney Chaplin (Charlie's son), who had worked with Jule Styne in *Bells Are Ringing,* was given the role. "Other than that," Kanin says, "I don't think Barbra was interested in who the other people were going to be." Others cast were Kay Medford as Fanny's mother, Jean Stapleton as neighbor Mrs. Strakosh, Danny Meehan as Fanny's friend Eddie, and Roger de Koven as Florenz Ziegfeld.

Once preparations for the show began, Barbra had to decide how she would play Fanny Brice. "The first thing she asked for," Ray Stark has said, "was to see some pictures of Fanny. I told her it wasn't necessary, that she didn't have to look like her. She just had to have the talent to make her believable as a great star."

Garson Kanin explains, "At that point Barbra had never seen Fanny Brice, not even in films. So I told everyone that we had to take the position that Fanny Brice was a fictitious character. We discovered that most people had never even heard of her. So I said, 'The show can't lean on the old headlines and the old sentiment. It has to be a fully created character on its own.'"

Everyone agreed that this was the way to go. Barbra said at the time, "It's not an exact biography. What we have tried to do is convey the idea of the sort of person she was—a fiercely ambitious, hardworking, driving force of a woman who gave herself to audiences, was never lazy or slipshod about her material and very probably made it difficult for men she married to live up to her, or with her." In another interview, Barbra added, "*Funny Girl* is about me. It just happened to happen to Fanny Brice earlier."

Despite the fact that she was starring in a major show, Streisand was still little more than a Broadway neophyte, and Kanin remembers that this caused some problems, especially since her inexperience did little to temper her opinions. Kanin recalls the day Irene Sharaff, the costume designer, came to his house to show Barbra her portfolio of designs for the *Funny Girl* clothes. "They were laid out all over the room, and Barbra just went from one to the next and didn't say anything. She looked at every one and then came over to me and said, 'What am I supposed to say now?' And I said, 'Well, you're supposed to say which ones you like and which ones you don't think suit you.' She said, 'I don't like any of them much.' I said, 'Are you sure you know how to read a costume rendering? It's like reading a blueprint. It's just a mood, a sketch; until it has the contour and the materials and the accessories and all that . . . ' And she said, 'Yeah, well, I don't think I like them.'

"So I said, 'Well, Barbra, there's only one thing to do—speak your mind now before it's too late. These costumes are going to cost thousands and thousands of dollars for each one. So say exactly what you think . . . ' And she went to each one and told Irene what she thought. Now here was a girl, twenty-one years old, and Irene Sharaff was a woman who's designed a hundred Broadway shows, won Academy Awards. She didn't feel very good about this. It took a long time to reverse itself, but it eventually did. I think by the end of the show they were really great pals. But it was a rocky beginning because Barbra had extremely *definite* ideas about how she wanted to look.

"She had a very curious view of herself, you know. For instance, I think she has the most beautiful legs since Dietrich, but she *hated* wearing short skirts because she thought her legs looked so bad. Somebody somewhere gave her the idea that she had skinny legs, so she insisted on wearing long dresses."

If Fanny Brice was a "hardworking, driving force of a woman," the cast and crew of *Funny Girl* soon learned that Barbra Streisand was too. She was demanding, a perfectionist. She had strong instincts—usually correct—about what would and would not work for her, and she used all the professionals around her as teachers. She impressed hardened theater veterans. "Judy you felt sorry for," Kay Medford said. "This one you stand back in awe. I wish I knew how to make it more poetic, but . . . it's like when you have the cap off the toothpaste and it just flows free. God, she's so free . . . she's like the dancers. She's audacious. After Barbra, everyone else sounds old-fashioned."

Ray Stark remarked, "She'll drive you nuts with too much analysis. It's not arrogance but doubt. She is like a barracuda. She devours every piece of intelligence to the bone."

And Streisand was a very quick study. She had never danced professionally, and she would have to do some dancing in *Funny Girl*. Before the show began preproduction, Streisand asked that choreographer Carol Haney's assistant come out to Las Vegas. "While she was performing in Vegas," Garson Kanin remembers, "she was taking dancing lessons from this guy every day. And when she came back, I went over to the dance studio and saw her rehearsing with these dancers and I couldn't believe my eyes! I mean, she was dancing like a professional."

Because of Streisand's instincts and his own aversion to overdirecting, Kanin left Streisand pretty much on her own during rehearsals. "I don't think a real director comes with a preconceived idea of how a part should be played and then tries to make the actor or actress do it that way. Directing has always been based on marrying the actor to the role successfully.

"The first week or ten days we rehearsed, I think Barbra was dismayed because I wasn't telling her what to do all the time. Marty Erlichman and I went out for a drink one night and he said, 'When are you going to tell her more what to do?' I said, 'She doesn't have to be told what to do. She knows what to do. I'm only going to tell her what *not* to do.' "

One of the things Kanin told Barbra not to do was overwork. "It was up in Boston, and we had just played a matinee. I had to go back into the theater, and when I did I heard Barbra's voice. And I thought, Is this a recording? I looked down at the stage and there was Barbra, kneeling on the apron of the stage, with Peter Daniels in the pit, and she was doing "Don't Rain on My Parade." Full out.

"I went down to the footlights and said, 'Barbra, wait a minute—you've just played a whole long, tough matinee. In about an hour and a half you'll have to be in the theater to dress and makeup for the night show. This is the time you should be in your dressing room or back at the hotel having had a little food and resting.'

"And she said, 'Goddammit! I've got to get this fucking thing right! Jesus Christ . . . ' So I said, 'Go on, it's your life and your career. If you want to do it, do it.'

"When I came to the theater that night, she said, 'I'm sorry I blew up. I didn't mean that, but that whole number was getting so fucked up, and the tempo, I thought it was my fault, but it was somebody in the pit . . . ' "

Every Broadway show with large reputations and larger finances at stake has its share of horror stories, and *Funny Girl* is no exception. Gossip column items about troubles with the script, the scenery, the songs and the stars began popping up almost daily in the New York papers. The show reportedly "bombed" in its tryout in Boston, and Isabel Lennart began rewriting, Jule Styne and Bob Merrill began changing and adding songs, thirty thousand dollars worth of sets were replaced. There were absurd problems. In Boston, Barbra wore an apparatus to amplify her voice: a microphone hidden in her bosom and batteries taped to her derriere. During one performance, this hookup began picking up police calls that were audible to the first several rows. It was heartburn and headache time for Ray Stark and Garson Kanin, but Barbra says she enjoyed the craziness. She told *Playboy,* "When I started to rehearse *Funny Girl,* for several months it was great fun. I would eat these huge Chinese meals right before I would go onstage. The more they changed the scenes, the more I liked it. The more I had different songs to try out, the more I loved it. We had forty-one different last scenes, the last one being frozen only on opening night. Forty-one versions of a last scene. That was always exciting, stimulating."

It was a little less exciting and stimulating for the rest of the cast, however, and many of the changes favored Streisand over her fellow actors. Garson Kanin acknowledges that there was resentment toward Barbra over this. "More and more as the show went on, it was clear that it was a Barbra Streisand evening. So anything in which she did not figure importantly got dropped. Nobody wanted long interludes without Barbra Streisand on stage. And this caused tensions. The 'Who Taught Her Everything She Knows?' number with Kay Medford and Danny Meehan had to be shortened, and a wonderful gambling casino scene with Sydney Chaplin was removed all together. And Danny Meehan said, 'Gee, I haven't got a chance,' and Kay Medford raised hell. Jule Styne objected very strongly. He kept on saying, 'Jesus Christ, it's turning out to be *An Evening with Barbra Streisand.* And why should it be? It's about Fanny and Nicky and the Ziegfeld follies . . . ' And he lost every one of those battles.

"I could see certain values in some of the other numbers," Kanin goes on, "but a show can run only so long, and I thought if there were a choice between a big ensemble number and a Streisand number, you stick with Barbra, because she was the strength of the show. And I think, in the end, that most of the right decisions were made."

Some of the cuts needed to make *Funny Girl* more wieldy were detrimental to Streisand too, Kanin points out. "The show was hurt very much by the cutting of real *acting* scenes. I believed that Barbra was a terrific actress, a wonderful, instinctive, natural actress. Some of the other people connected with the production didn't think so. They liked her very much because she sang, but they were less confident in her when she was playing a scene. I thought the way she played the scenes just broke my heart. But many of the acting scenes were cut to make way for musical numbers, and I was sorry to see that."

Reportedly, Barbra showed little flair for drama or comedy early in the show's tryout period, but quickly picked up inflections and gestures that added much texture to her performance. It was she who suggested doing "You are Woman," originally played straight, as a comedy bit. She was experimenting, and she was learning. Garson Kanin feels he deserves credit for instilling in Barbra one of her most impressive characteristics. "She was very brash, very witty, very funny," he says. "But she lacked one quality that every great comic star has. And that quality is elegance. Buster Keaton had elegance. Chaplin. Beatrice Lillie. Fanny Brice. They all had elegance. Because if you don't have elegance, there's no dynamic between that and your clowning. There has to be that.

As Fanny Brice

With Kay Medford and Michael Craig

"You Are Woman"

"Private Schwartz"

"I told this to Barbra, and she said, 'I don't know what you're talking about.' And I said, 'I didn't expect you to. But think about it. Fanny Brice was an enormously elegant woman. And yet she was this low, low comedienne. And that's what gave her vitality. Barbra,' I told her, 'strive for elegance above all things.'

"Of course," Kanin continues, "you have to have the quality inside. But it has a lot to do with self-esteem, self-confidence. It can be gained. And I watched Barbra gain it, in the performance of 'His Is the Only Music That Makes Me Dance,' which she had been singing as a kind of one-on-one torch song, a real nightclub song. It took on much more. More feeling, more truth, more of a love song. She looked quite another way singing it. Her posture changed a little bit, and the way she held her head."

It is very clear, in fact, that from the beginning of rehearsals to the opening of *Funny Girl,* Barbra Streisand acquired elegance. Photographs of her taken during rehearsals and dress run-throughs as compared with photos taken in midrun (when Johnny Desmond replaced Sydney Chaplin), show a woman who had acquired tremendous sophistication and refinement, a better groomed, better-looking woman. Whether it was a natural maturation process or a conscious effort on Barbra's part may never be known. "But I kept stressing *elegance, elegance,*" Kanin remembers. "And it became a joke with us. One time I came to the theater after an all-night session with Jule and Bob and I hadn't shaved and looked terrible, and Barbra said, 'You know, you could use a little elegance yourself.'" It became such a buzz word around the *Funny Girl* theater, in fact, that it wound up as a song title in another show. "*Hello, Dolly!* was out of town at the same time that *Funny Girl* was," Kanin says, "and its producer David Merrick asked Bob Merrill to help them out with a comedy song, and it wound up as 'Elegance' in that show."

As *Funny Girl* made its way toward Broadway, the rumors about trouble increased. "You know," Kanin explains, "it happens in most great big musicals—the closer you get to opening in New York, the more tense and desperate and worried everybody becomes." The opening was rescheduled four times, and Barbra, by now bearing the brunt of the show, also bore the heaviest burden. She told *Playboy* years later, "That's what drove me into analysis, *Funny Girl* on the stage. No one knows the truth about it. I was on Donnatal to control my stomach. I was *so* frightened. I felt the pressure. Enormous pressure."

Barbra hid her fear from the other cast members very well. According to Jean Stapleton, "Barbra was an iron woman. There's a snake pit of opinion on Broadway. You have to win over critics and audiences alike. I was older and wiser than she, and I really understood what Barbra was going through. We all felt from watching her that first day of rehearsal what was going to happen to her. It was thrilling."

But the problems wouldn't go away. Finally, Ray Stark decided to bring in Jerome Robbins again to help the show. "By this time I'd given it every shot," Kanin says. "I had done just about everything I could do. I couldn't think of much more without *extensive* changes." Kanin agreed to have "a fresh eye," Robbins, come in, because he liked and respected him. But he rejected the suggestion that Robbins receive a codirecting credit. "I had been with the show for eight months and I didn't think that was fair." Robbins' credit wound up as "Production Supervised by Jerome Robbins."

"Even that wasn't strictly so," Kanin says, "but you had to find some respectable credit for the fellow." Kanin concedes that Robbins made some important contributions to the show. "They wanted more show stoppers. They wanted every number to stop the show. They just wanted it to be stronger and better. And who can blame them? I had no objection to that. Jerry Robbins felt that there should be an important sexy number that Barbra and Sydney do together, and Jule and Bob came up with 'You Are Woman.'"

And I think Jerry got the show paced a lot better, cut out little things that had crept in that probably some of us didn't even notice."

By the time *Funny Girl* opened at the Winter Garden Theater on March 26, 1964, it was clear that all the problems, all the last-minute changes, all the adjustments to accommodate Barbra were worth it. The show opened to cheering audiences and enraptured critics. Emory Lewis of *Cue* magazine wrote, "Magnificent, sublime, radiant, extraordinary, electric—what puny little adjectives to describe Barbra Streisand. After all, she is merely the most talented performer on the musical comedy stage in the 1960s." Whitney Bolton in the *Morning Telegraph* said, "Barbra Streisand . . . is talent, complete, utter and practicing. Vast talent, the kind that comes once in many years. That talent in *Funny Girl* flares and shimmers."

It was all overwhelming to Barbra. Elliott Gould has said, "Opening night was a disaster for Barbra. People were pushing her, sticking mikes down her bosom, telling her things she couldn't believe." If she was frightened before, she was more so now. As the word of her extraordinary performance spread, she felt pressure ever more acutely. "I was on the cover of *Time* and *Newsweek* in the same week, or something like that," she has said. "I thought, 'What do people expect of me?' They hadn't seen me, but they'd heard of me."

Actually, Barbra appeared on the cover of *Time* in April and *Life* in May, both magazines canonizing her as the greatest talent to hit Broadway since Sarah Bernhardt. It is difficult to overstate the excitement that Barbra in *Funny Girl* created. As Shana Alexander said in *Life,* "When Barbra opened on Broadway . . . the entire, gorgeous, rattletrap showbusiness Establishment blew sky high. Overnight critics began raving, photographers flipping, flacks yakking and columnists flocking. Thanks to such massive stimulation the American public has now worked itself into a perfect star-is-born swivet."

Barbra Streisand became America's Cinderella. The magazines and newspapers told the story of her unhappy childhood, her gritty struggle to succeed against all the odds. Streisand was the "born loser," as *Life* put it, who was now Broadway's biggest star. The legion of fans she had acquired through her records and concerts and television appearances grew geometrically with every *Funny Girl* performance and breathless magazine or newspaper recounting of the Streisand Story. Even without the benefit of a weekly television show or a film playing in local movie houses, Barbra's image, in words and pictures, was firmly implanted on the American consciousness. Suddenly, there was a "Barbra Streisand Look": pageboy hairdo, Cleopatra eye makeup, thrift-shop outfits recycled to stunning effect.

It had all turned around for Barbra. Everything about her that had been criticized, discouraged, even ridiculed was now being celebrated. She was being called "beautiful" in print; her clothes put her on the Best Dressed List. She still had a leftover image as a "kook," but she was no longer that. The kookiness was now considered savvy, an example of avant-garde thinking.

"Homely," "awkward," "terribly dressed" Barbra Streisand graced the pages of *Vogue* as a fashion model three times in 1964, and the Encyclopaedia Britannica chose her as one of two fashion trendsetters of the year. Barbra denied she ever was kooky: "To help set certain styles and certain fashions is not kooky, it's exciting. When I lived over the fish store I bought clothes for ten dollars, but it wasn't really kooky. I never wore white llama with black leather. That's kooky. I was really conservative."

The final word on the subject was had by fashion critic Eugenia Sheppard, who said, "She's only about as kooky as Gloria Guinness, C-Z Guest, the Duchess of Windsor or any of the all-time fashion greats when they had just turned 22."

Barbra: "I think that was a big compliment and I thank her so much for it. That kooky thing is so tiresome. Nothing that is kooky can really mean anything or stand up."

Her success, her impact, the adulation: it was all Barbra had ever dreamed of. But did the reality live up to the dream? "It hasn't come anywhere near it," she said. "The dream—you never achieve it. The excitement of life lies in the hope, in the striving for something rather than the attainment."

Not only was the reality of Barbra's stardom something of a letdown, but there were problems that came with the territory that she had probably never foreseen. One was a strain on her marriage to Elliott Gould.

In a sadly ironic twist, the Goulds's marriage began to mirror that of Fanny Brice and Nicky Arnstein—the wife's career was a phenomenal success while the husband's foundered. Gould's career had not lived up to the promise of *I Can Get It for You Wholesale,* and he was faced with the unpleasant position of "Mr. Streisand." And that was only part of the problem. "I had to realize," Elliott explained, "that Barbra is *my* woman, but everybody wants her. I have to be above it, because if I'm in it, I'm going to get stomped to death."

For Barbra, getting stomped to death was sometimes a literal fear. Peter Matz, working with Barbra one evening in his office near the Winter Garden, offered to walk her to the theater when her limousine failed to show up. "We approached the backstage entrance," he recalls, "and it was mobbed by those autograph people. They were just swarming about. I don't know if you've ever seen those people, but many of them are very weird. When they saw Barbra coming, they started screaming 'Here's Barbra! Here's Barbra!' and they started heading toward us, en masse.

"She dug her fingers into my arm to the point that blood was coming out. Her face was drained totally white. She was terrified of this assault. The doorman cleared the way and we got inside, but she was shaking and sweating. *I* was frightened. She's intensely vulnerable."

A cult had formed around Streisand: hordes of people who would wait outside the theater for hours to get a glimpse of her, or perhaps an autograph. There were reasons for the intensity of this devotion—the excitement surrounding Barbra's celebrity; her background, which gave hope to everyone who thought of themselves as different or inferior that they, too, could surmount the odds; her position as an enormous star who seemed, somehow, more accessible than the others. But Barbra could never understand the extent of the adulation. She told an interviewer who spoke to her in her dressing room that on the way up she had run into a fan who said to her, "Can I come up and watch the interview?"

"And I said, 'What did you say?' And the kid said, 'Can I sit and watch?' And I tell you, I couldn't answer him! It was so *sad.* I mean, can you imagine a kid saying that? If I let everyone *watch* me—it's just impossible, just so ridiculous. When they do it in the theater, I don't mind it, but when they do it in the street, you know, they follow me around, to my house, and they leave me presents, and it's frightening. When I was waiting for a cab the other day, this kid put his coat in the gutter for me to walk on—in the *gutter!* And, well, I didn't want to walk on his coat! I told him to pick it up. It happens often. It's insane. You can have people who love your work, have respect for you. But not your whole life. And anybody's human, who's a personality.

"Now, all of a sudden, the image becomes more important than the person; the symbol is more important than the flesh and blood, and it puts you on the spot. Everything you do can destroy the image, because I'm only human. I can never live up to their

In 1965, Barbra was named "Miss Ziegfeld" by former Ziegfeld girls.

72

symbol, and yet they pretend they want to get to know you. But if they ever knew you—well, then, you'd be like everybody else, mere flesh and blood, which they don't want.

"Like, I always wanted to meet Brando. I wanted to say to him, 'Let us speak to one another because I understand you. You are just like me.' So one night I'm waiting to go on at a benefit, and somebody comes up behind me and starts caressing my shoulder—you know—and nuzzling my neck. And I turn around and there he is! It's Brando! And he says—you know, kidding, 'I'm letting you off easy,' and I laugh and say, 'Whaddya mean, easy? This is the best part!' And then—I don't know—what the hell was there to say? It was kind of sad, because he wasn't just like me at all."

Barbra played *Funny Girl* for nearly two years. After a while, it began to bore her. "Once they froze the show, I felt like I was locked up in prison. I couldn't *stand* it anymore. I had a big calendar, I would cross off the days. After eighteen months, all I wanted was out, out, out. I played it 1,000 times, and along about the 944th time, I would come on stage, and I'd see the plastic flowers were dusty, and I'd wonder and worry why no one cleaned them. Then I'd wonder why they were plastic at all."

Before Barbra left *Funny Girl* in December 1965 to re-create the role in London, she had been nominated for a Tony Award as Best Actress in a Musical, but lost to Carol Channing in *Hello, Dolly!* Richard Burton, who had also been nominated for *Hamlet* and lost, called her with his consolations. "What a shame, love," he told her. "You deserved it."

When Barbra took the show to London in early 1966, it was amid a storm of prepublicity. Barbra was then the highest-paid singer in the world; she had scored an enormous success on television with her first special, "My Name Is Barbra," and her *Funny Girl* legend preceded her. London audiences and critics wanted to see for themselves whether this girl deserved all this hype she was getting. The *Daily Mirror* set the stage a week before the show opened: "Rarely in the whole bedazzled history of live and lusty entertainment has one box of assorted vocal cords been awaited with such pent-up, electrifying excitement. The reason is as plain, if not as prodigious, as the proud nose on Miss Streisand's delightful face. That pleading, passionate voice, soaring like the skyscrapers above her native Manhattan, is already setting the sky ablaze."

The opening night of *Funny Girl* was the social event of the season; celebrities arrived from all over Europe to attend. By the end of the evening, public and critics saw that Barbra did indeed deserve the buildup. Most reviewers forgot their typically British reserve. One wrote, "Barbra Streisand performed the daunting feat of living up to her legend. The girl and the myth are indivisible." Another said, "A star is a girl whose voice, face and talent are all familiar and who can still set the blood tingling by the impact of her personality. A star is a girl who can hush a thousand people into silence and a second later make them explode with joy. By these tests and any other you can think of, Barbra Streisand is a star, and *Funny Girl,* which had its official opening after the biggest build-up since D-Day, is her show."

Another critic asked, "Who will they get to play her when the time comes for a musical on her life?" And a fourth gushed, "For the next 14 weeks, people who visit the Prince of Wales won't be going to a theater. They'll be making a pilgrimage to a shrine. There, a goddess called Barbra Streisand makes every song she sings sound like a hymn and rouses her audiences to ecstasy."

The avalanche of press coverage Barbra received before the opening barely let up once the show opened; it had set box office records in advance bookings and was the hottest ticket in all of Europe. The Royal visit to the show made news; the presence of Princess Margaret and the Earl of Snowden kept the audience quite reserved. No one

At the height of her fashion influence, Barbra spoofs her prior image as a "kook."

74

Camping it up at a costume party during the *Funny Girl* run, 1964

Posing for a magazine layout of Rudi Gernreich fashions, 1964

laughed or applauded until the Royal party did so, and for that reason the energy level and timing of the show were way off. After the performance Barbra was introduced to the Princess, who told her how good she thought the show was. Barbra replied, "You should come back some night when you're not here."

Being complimented by British royalty was difficult for Barbra to handle. "Princess Margaret looked at me, almost like a fan, and told me she had all my records," Barbra said. "I didn't know what to say, so I just stood there and replied 'Yeah?' It was unbelievable, like a scene out of a bad movie." It would be just the first of a series of newsworthy meetings between Barbra and members of the Royal Family over the years.

During the British run of the show, rumors were rampant about Barbra's "difficulty." She was said to be distant and aloof from the rest of the cast; to have excluded members of the chorus from an opening night party, and to have sent critical notes to cast members she felt weren't carrying their weight. A month after the opening, her costar Michael Craig, cast as Nicky, was interviewed by the *Sunday Mirror*. He confirmed that Barbra was not easy to get close to: "I never see Barbra except in front of the audience. In fact, the only intimate conversation I had with her was once during rehearsals. I saw her looking upset as I passed her dressing room so I said, 'What's the matter, love?' 'It's not going right,' she answered, and so I told her not to worry, that's what rehearsals were for—to put things right.

"But she still looked miserable and said, 'Two and a half years ago when I started the show in Philadelphia it was such fun and everything was marvelous. Now it's all so difficult and I don't get any fun out of it anymore.' "

Craig went on to defend Barbra's lack of sociability. "Off stage, we have nothing in common. I'm fifteen years older than she is, so there's no reason why we should hobnob. I like to pop 'round the local [pub]—but if Barbra came with me she would be mobbed. Such fame is difficult to handle."

Craig also explained that the opening night party was thrown by Ray Stark—"He's entitled to invite whoever he wants to"—and that he didn't blame Barbra for criticizing people in the cast: "Most big stars do this when the standard of a show is their responsibility."

Generally, Barbra's press in London was highly favorable. She received glowing notices for a special benefit show she did at the American Embassy in Grosvenor Square. Two hundred British Government officials and figures from the world of the arts attended "A Very Informal History of the American Musical Theater: 1926–1966." Barbra performed songs from Gershwin's *Porgy and Bess,* explaining that she admired it because it combined elements of Negro spirituals, jazz, opera, and George Gershwin's Russian-Jewish background. "It sort of represents America," Barbra told the audience, "which is a beautiful mishmash." She sang, among other songs, "I Got Plenty of Nothing," "Summertime" and "It Ain't Necessarily So."

Shortly after the opening of *Funny Girl* in London, Barbra and Elliott announced that she was expecting a baby. The story was front-page news in America and Europe, and the press quickly dubbed the child "Barbra's million dollar baby" because she would have to cancel one million dollars in concert bookings as the result of the pregnancy. Theater audiences were very unhappy when Barbra missed several performances; on one occasion Michael Craig was booed and watched hundreds of people leave the theater when he announced that Barbra would not be performing that night. "I was very annoyed," Craig said. "But only because nobody had put a notice up outside the theater saying Barbra wouldn't be appearing. If I'd known that had not been done, I wouldn't have volunteered."

In London, 1966

Her pregnancy made performing very difficult for Barbra. "It's not like making a movie," she said. "You can't take a rest when you've got fourteen hundred people out there and they've paid a lot of money to see you. You've got thirty costume changes and all those songs and dances and what do you do when you feel like throwing up? I'm tired, I feel like sleeping all the time." Barbra didn't stint on her performances, though; all she did was cut out some of the gymnastics in numbers like "Cornet Man."

Barbra left London in late July to return to New York and await the birth of her baby. "All my life I've had an urge for strange foods at odd hours," she told an interviewer, "except now, that I'm having a baby!" She denied that she had wanted to get pregnant for three years. "If I'd wanted a baby before, I'd have had one. But I was too young, I was only a baby myself. Now, I'm twenty-four—an old lady!"

Barbra welcomed the change of pace her pregnancy dictated. "God has given me a perfect out. Now I can look forward to cooking." Elliott saw the impending birth of their baby as a way to settle down their marriage and remove all the distracting commotion surrounding Barbra's stardom. He told columnist Sheilah Graham that having a baby might make Barbra decide to give up her career. "I don't expect this to happen today or tomorrow, but one day she will be just my wife, quit the rat race and be content." Barbra seemed to confirm his domestic optimism: "A baby is the only thing that's going to give me roots again," she said.

Barbra took to motherhood the way she had to every other production—with gusto. She posed for a touching series of photographs in the *Ladies' Home Journal* modeling maternity clothes, and told writer Gloria Steinem that she was hoping for a little girl, whom she would name Samantha—so that if she turned out to be a tomboy, her friends could call her Sam. She prepared a pink bassinet, bought every accouterment a baby could possibly need, and waited for the birth, scheduled for mid-December.

The child didn't arrive until December 29—a healthy baby boy, whom Barbra named Jason Emanuel. Elliott Gould told the press, "He looks just like her, only he has a cleft in his chin and dark hair like me. But his eyes are the brightest, bluest, flashingest—just like hers."

Barbra still couldn't get over the fact that she had produced this "miracle." "My God," she said, "I'm a little girl myself and now I'm a mother."

When she *was* a little girl, Barbra couldn't imagine "any of the normal things: kids or a husband or a home." All the success, all the acclaim, all the wealth: they were wonderful, but they weren't *normal;* she had achieved a one-in-a-million lifestyle. Now, she had achieved something almost every woman in the world is capable of. Still, she wasn't every woman in the world, she was Barbra Streisand, and she was afraid the baby would receive undue attention from hospital visitors, She registered at the hospital under an assumed name. "To find him through the nursery window," Barbra says, "you had to look for the bassinet with the name 'Scarangella.' "

Later, Barbra would say of Jason to an English interviewer, "I think there are a million problems in front of him and it's going to be his problem to get himself out of it. No matter who I was . . . if I was a nothing he'd say, 'Oh, ma—why can't you be like the other mother who's famous?' or 'Why can't you be a famous movie actress?' or something. And if I am a famous movie actress, he'll say, 'Why can't you be just an ordinary person? So you can't win. But that's the nature of child/parent relationships, you know?"

With Jason, 1967

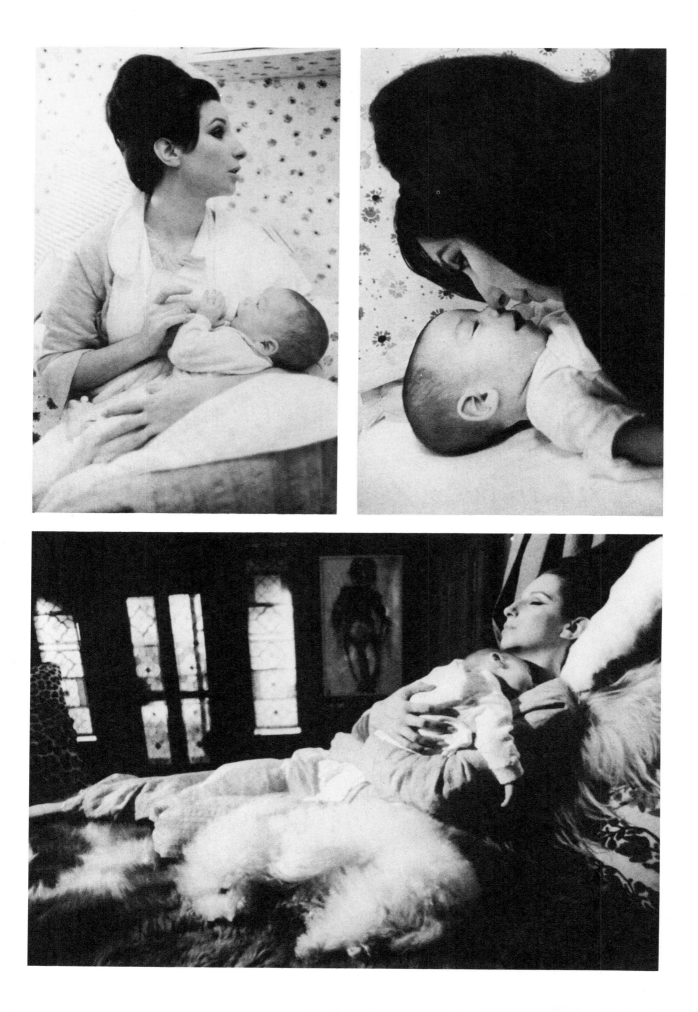

$5 million Baby

Barbra's enormous success in *Funny Girl* was accompanied by equal popularity on record. *Barbra Streisand/The Third Album* was as big a seller as her first two LPs, but its mood was dramatically different from the second album. On this one, Barbra was mellow and melodic, singing lovely ballads like "My Melancholy Baby," "Just in Time," "As Time Goes By" and "Make Believe." The songs were arranged and conducted by four different men—Peter Daniels, Sid Ramin, Ray Ellis, and Peter Matz—but the album's effect is one of gentle cohesion, and it has long been a favorite of Streisand fans as an accompaniment to romantic dinners or quiet reflection.

The original cast recording of *Funny Girl* was an enormous hit, reaching #2 on *Billboard* magazine's Top 100 albums charts and remaining on the list for fifty-one weeks. It was a highly unusual level of success for a Broadway cast recording, largely due to the fact that Streisand's fans purchased it as another Streisand album, a base of popularity few Broadway shows can boast.

Barbra's third 1964 release was *People*. It contained a new recording of her hit single from *Funny Girl*, "People." (With the show version, there were three different performances of "People" by Streisand available within five months.) The album was again low-key, but contained some unusual material: "When in Rome (I Do As the Romans Do)," "Suppertime," "Autumn," and "My Lord and Master."

The *People* album reached #1 in *Billboard* (the first Streisand recording to do so) and stayed on that chart for 84 weeks. During one week, *five* Streisand albums were in the top 100 nationally. *The Barbra Streisand Album* remained in the top 100 for *101* weeks.

Streisand's voice on the *People* album had reached a level of near perfection. The nasal qualities many listeners had criticized were barely evident; there was a strength and control that had been achieved only intermittently on her prior albums. Further, the theatrics that had singled her out earlier had been toned down considerably. Peter Matz, who arranged and conducted *People* along with Ray Ellis, thinks there were several reasons for the new maturity in Streisand's voice. "Obviously, she herself was maturing. She was only twenty when she made her first album. But also, she was performing every night in *Funny Girl*, and that forced her to take care of her voice and use it wisely. Rather than wearing her vocal cords out, having to sing that score every night strengthened them—it was like doing exercises."

People won Barbra her second Grammy in a row as Best Female Pop Vocalist, and Peter Matz was honored as well. The album was nominated as Best Album and the "People" single was nominated both as Record and Song of the year.

In mid-1964, it was announced that Streisand's fabulous success in *Funny Girl* and on record had won her the opportunity to conquer yet another medium: television. She was signed by CBS-TV to an unprecedented five-million-dollar contract to appear in a series of specials over the ensuing ten years. Despite Streisand's success on TV guest stints, most notably with Judy Garland, there was considerable press skepticism about CBS's wisdom in investing such a large amount (it was particularly large in 1964) for a relative newcomer. When it was later announced that Streisand's first show, "My Name Is Barbra," would be a one-woman spectacular, without the usual galaxy of top-

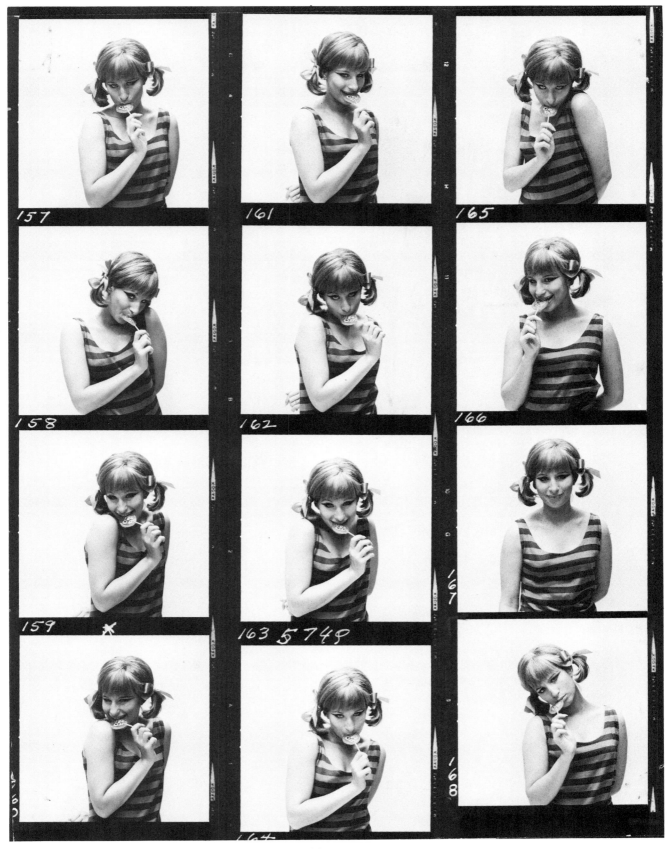

A 1964 photo session

name stars to assure ratings success, there were more than a few columnists wondering aloud about the sanity of CBS executives. The risk of the entire venture wasn't lost on Marty Erlichman: "Sure, she's a skyrocket on Broadway, but if fifty million people watch the show, thirty million will be watching someone they've never seen before."

Typically, Streisand was unbothered. "What do I know from TV?" she told a reporter. "I hire the best people in the business, then I let them do everything for me. I coulda got some big-name stars to clown around, just like everybody else does on their specials, but who needs it? I got complete creative control here, so I do it my way, right?"

The "best people in the business" included Barbra and Elliott producing (they had formed Ellbar Productions, Inc. a year earlier), Marty Erlichman as executive producer, Richard Lewine as producer, Dwight Hemion as director, production numbers conceived by Joe Layton and Peter Matz arranging and conducting.

The show was divided into three distinct acts. The first began with Barbra singing "My Name Is Barbra," and songs more or less about youthful discovery. Then she shrank down into a little girl and sang "I'm Five" and "Sweet Zoo" cavorting on an oversized jungle gym. Returned to normal, she sang a poignant "Where Is the Wonder?" ("Where is the wonder that years conceal, that a child can feel now and then?"). The segment ended dramatically with Streisand standing amid Peter Matz's full orchestra to sing "People."

Part Two began with a goofy monologue and then segued into a campy send-up of Barbra's well-known image as a thrift-shop devotee contrasted with her newly acquired reputation for haute couture. She pranced through New York's exclusive Bergdorf Goodman, trying on an assortment of items: ridiculous hats with feathers toppling over the brim, a sleek leather mini dress and a necklace so heavy it pulled her head halfway to the floor, and a sumptuous sable coat which she threw on the floor and danced a fandango on top of. All of this preening and posing was accompanied by ironic songs like "I've Got Plenty of Nothin'," "Brother, Can You Spare A Dime?" and "Nobody Knows You When You're Down and Out."

The Bergdorf segment proved to be the most memorable in Barbra's first special. "I hope we've brought a bit of theater to television," Barbra said while making the show. "We rehearsed long and hard on staging and choreography, even the Bergdorf sequence. It's funny—I used to browse through the store before I could afford to buy even a shoe buckle. Now they've turned the whole store over to me!"

Barbra may have tried to bring theater to television, but she found there were major differences. She had said she preferred working before a live audience because of the immediate feedback one receives. "I've switched my opinions," she said during the taping. "It's better without an audience. You have technicians, they're jaded, so if they like it, you know it works. The whole thing is so different. In the theater you sing and speak loudly—you wave your arms. You have to be theatrical. In television, if you wave your arms or take a step, they're photographing a closeup of your left ear. Or maybe you're off camera altogether."

Streisand was never off camera during the show's final segment, a concert filmed live in front of an audience of the most devoted fans available in New York. Dressed simply in black, against an elegantly spare set, Streisand delivered powerful performances of "When the Sun Comes Out," "Why Did I Choose You?" and a medley from *Funny Girl*. After "His Is the Only Music That Makes Me Dance," Barbra said, "Fanny Brice sang a song like that . . . " and sang "My Man." The special ended with a moving version of "Happy Days Are Here Again" under the final credit roll.

Three sequences from "My Name Is Barbra"

(bottom right) Accepting her Emmy for "Outstanding Individual Achievement in Entertainment"

"My Name Is Barbra" was an enormous success. It won high ratings and the kind of reviews few performers have ever been lucky enough to receive. The UPI critic wrote, "A pinnacle moment in American show business, in any form, in any period. She is so great it is shocking, something like being in love. She may well be the most supremely talented and complete entertainer that this country has ever produced." *Variety* said, "No young singer ever met a tougher challenge head-on and came off like at the head of a parade."

The impact of Barbra's performance can be gauged by the fact that the following morning, the New York *Journal-American* ran a front-page picture of Streisand with the headline, "Magnificent Barbra."

Literally overnight, Streisand became *the* most talked-about entertainer in America. Now all of those 50 million viewers Marty Erlichman spoke of had seen Barbra, and most of them loved her. Within days, high school girls were sporting the short-cropped new hairstyle Barbra had unveiled in the middle of the show. The debate about her looks became national, and even critics who had pooh-poohed her rather parochial New York success became slavish converts.

The dissenters, characterized by Ben Gross's New York *Daily News* comment, "Her voice? By no means a great one. Her acting ability? Fair," were distinctly in the minority. Barbra's considerable contributions aside, "My Name Is Barbra" was a highly innovative show. It changed the concept of what constitutes a television "special," and its impact on the medium was felt for years.

"My Name Is Barbra" won five Emmy Awards, including "Best Concept, Choreography and Staging" for Joe Layton and "Outstanding Individual Achievement in Entertainment" for Barbra. As an indication of the esteem in which she was held by the TV academy, Barbra's award was saved for last of the evening. During her acceptance speech, Streisand quipped, "When I used to watch these awards shows as a kid, I'd look to see who was drunk. Now I'm up here myself." She then related part of a note she had received from a very young fan: "Of all the people on your show, I liked you the best."

Barbra found television very satisfying. "It's there forever, unless the tape rots. So many times on the stage, you reach a moment of truth in a scene and then it's gone. You know it's so right, but you can't be sure of ever capturing it again. It's a very satisfying feeling to know that your work, your very hardest efforts, are preserved."

Columbia Records released the soundtrack of "My Name Is Barbra" in two parts—sort of. The first album, released at the time the special was aired, contained seven of the songs from the show and several others, and had a much stronger child-to-girl-to-woman theme. That album reached #2 in *Billboard* and earned Barbra her third straight personal Grammy. *My Name Is Barbra, Two (Too?)* was released five months later but contained only the Bergdorf medley. Its chief selling points were two hit singles, "He Touched Me" and "Second Hand Rose." "He Touched Me" was a highly dramatic Streisand performance. The song, originally titled "She Touched Me," was first sung by Elliott Gould in an unsuccessful Broadway show in which he appeared in 1965, *Drat! The Cat!* Barbra's recording of it is one of her classic performances. The sequel album also reached #2, and remained on the charts for forty-eight weeks.

Barbra's second television special, "Color Me Barbra," aired March 30, 1966, relied on the proven formula and personnel of the first. "This show is a bookend to the other," Barbra said during taping. "We're using a lot of ideas that couldn't be fitted in before but were too good to be thrown out."

One important element of this new show was the addition of color, still an unusual attraction in 1966 and a prerequisite for the show's opening segment: a romp through the Philadelphia Museum of Art. Barbra wafted in and out of the museum's rooms, stopping occasionally to admire—or "become"—several famous paintings. "Non C'est Rien" was passionately sung by a Modigliani portrait, "Gotta Move" became a living piece of pop art and "Where or When" took on reincarnation overtones as Streisand performed it in Egyptian royal garb.

The logistics of filming in the museum were formidable. Permission was granted only after assurances that shooting would be done after hours—meaning all-night weekend sessions for Barbra and the crew. The production hardware had to be gingerly moved about in order not to damage any of the priceless art pieces. Other assorted problems resulted in forty hours of tape having to be shot to capture eight minutes for the home screen.

True to the formula, part two opened with another wacky monologue, which served mainly to introduce Barbra's poodle, Sadie (a gift from the *Funny Girl* cast), and then a surreal circus setting stocked with various exotic animals. Peter Matz recalls going through picture books with Barbra and Joe Layton to decide which animals would be appropriate "props" for this whimsical segment. "Barbra would see an animal she'd like to use on the show," Matz says. "Then we'd think of all the songs that could be applied to that animal. Then I'd have to go home and link up all the songs in some reasonable way."

The songs were "linked up" cleverly: Streisand sang "What's New, Pussycat?" to a tiger and a kitten, soft shoed "Sam, You Made the Pants Too Long" with a group of penguins, and, rubbing noses with an anteater, sang "We've Got So Much in Common." Part Two ended with "Have I Stayed Too Long at the Fair?" and "Look at that Face"— sung to Sadie.

During the filming, Rex Reed, who was just establishing his reputation, was allowed on the set for a New York *Times* piece. When published, it proved to be something of a hatchet job, concentrating on all the problems and Barbra's short temper, often giving totally inaccurate impressions. In one instance, Barbra was very depressed by the death of one of the penguins under the hot studio lights. "She loves animals," Peter Matz says, "and she got so upset she couldn't work, literally for hours. Now, there's a heavy crew standing around, waiting for her to get back to work. I guess that might be interpreted as being temperamental if you don't like her."

Part Three was, of course, a concert, the taping of which was also fraught with tensions and misunderstandings. Streisand was unhappy with some of her material and her patience was frazzled after seemingly endless technical difficulties. It was reported that Streisand, after hours of takes, asked the studio audience to leave. Peter Matz denies this. "I don't remember her asking the audience to leave," he says. "What I do remember is her telling them, 'Look, it's getting late; if you want to leave I don't mind.' "

Rex Reed's article ("He just came in deciding to be very bitchy," Peter Matz says) helped establish him as a celebrity in his own right. A few years later, he sent Barbra a note apologizing for the piece. "Now that I'm famous myself," he told her, "I know what it's like to be descended upon by the vultures."

None of the chaos of production was evident in the finished show. The concert was electrifying; Streisand gave dramatic performances of "Any Place I Hang My Hat Is Home," "Starting Here, Starting Now," "Where Am I Going?" and a lovely, sexy version of "C'est Si Bon."

The strain she had undergone put Streisand in a cynical mood as she waited for "Color Me Barbra" to be aired. "I know this is a better show than the first," she said. "But *they* are waiting for it to bomb. They always are. People say, 'Go see this terrific

(above left) The circus sequence.   *(above right and below)* Scenes from "The Belle of Fourteenth Street"

(opposite) The concert from "Color Me Barbra"

girl,' but most of them come thinking, 'Nah, she can't be that great.' It makes me feel like they're the monster and I'm the victim."

Most of the critics agreed with Barbra about the show's superiority over the first, and also that she was as great as everyone was saying. John Wilson in the New York *Times* wrote, "Barbra Streisand's success on her first hour-long special was no lucky accident. She proved that last night . . . she did variations on the formula of her first show and, if anything, topped herself."

Leo Mishkin in the New York *Morning Telegraph* said, "It's difficult to see how any other television musical show can top it for the rest of the year. Unless, of course, a third Barbra Streisand program is to be scheduled."

"Color Me Barbra" was another ratings champ and garnered five Emmy nominations, but lost the major awards to Frank Sinatra's "A Man and His Music." The soundtrack album, including only the songs performed on the show, was a winner as well, topping the *Billboard* chart at #3. It won Grammy nominations as "Album of the Year" and for "Best Female Vocal Performance."

Barbra's next album, released seven months after the "Color Me Barbra" disk, was a radical departure for her. Entitled *Je m'appelle Barbra,* it was a collection of French songs, most sung in English, others in their native French. The arrangements by Michel Legrand were lush and a perfect accompaniment to Streisand's sensual voice on "Autumn Leaves," "Love and Learn," "Once Upon a Summertime" and "I've Been Here (Le Mur)," originally written for Edith Piaf.

The album was an excellent seller, reaching #5 on *Billboard's* chart, and it was well reviewed. Gene Lees in *High Fidelity* wrote, "It's true that Miss Streisand's success has set off an unpleasant melee of sobbing, shrieking girl singers. At the same time, she is associated with fresh material and superb orchestrations . . . her French is excellent . . . Among the best tracks are 'Free Again,' 'Martina,' 'Autumn Leaves' and 'Clopin, Clopant' . . . This was a powerful album idea and over-all, it's well executed. It's the best of the recent Streisand albums."

Je m'appelle Barbra is notable, too, for the fact that it contains Barbra's first musical composition, "Ma Première Chanson," a lovely, simple tune she sings in French. "I think I made a royalty of about thirty-seven dollars for that," she said later. "It was the most meaningful check I ever got."

When the time came to plan Streisand's third TV special, Barbra and her associates felt she had to depart from the formula of the first two. "We don't want to go to the well too often," Marty Erlichman said at the time. "The next special will have other performers. However, Barbra will never become just another hostess for just another musical variety show. Whatever we decide to do in future shows, she will dominate in a unique fashion."

"Unique" is surely the word for "The Belle of Fourteenth Street," which was broadcast on October 11, 1967. Promoted as a nostalgic look at the Golden Age of Vaudeville, the special was Barbra's least successful, both commercially and artistically, but it was hardly the disaster legend would have it.

Constructed as a turn-of-the-century revue (even the audience wore authentic costumes), the show highlighted several fine talents. Jason Robards was Barbra's main costar; vaudeville legend John Bubbles contributed a "Bojangles" dance turn; Lee Allen (Eddie in the London *Funny Girl*) offered comic support in several corny sketches; and rounding out the ensemble was the Beef Trust line, a grossly overweight group of chorines.

A purposefully hammy scene from *The Tempest* cast a bellowing Jason Robards as Prospero with Barbra both a coy Miranda and an airborne Ariel. An elaborate harness suspended on wires allowed Streisand to "fly"—after a trial run and a crash landing. Barbra was able to conquer her considerable fear of the "Peter Pan" contraption in time for the taping.

Another highlight of the show was Streisand, parasol in hand, turning "Alice Blue Gown" into a Victorian strip tease—with invisible wires pulling off sections of her pinafore during the course of the song—leaving her demure in tights and a Merry Widow. Contributing to her image as a show-off, Barbra performed a duet with herself as a German dowager with operatic pretensions and a young boy in the audience sweetly singing "Mother Macree."

Finally, in picture hat and Lillian Russell feather boa, Streisand served up a mini-concert of appropriate songs of the period: "My Melancholy Baby," "I'm Always Chasing Rainbows," "Some of These Days," "My Buddy" and "Put Your Arms Around Me, Honey."

"The Belle of Fourteenth Street" was not well received. It fared poorly in the ratings; most of Barbra's fans would have preferred another hour of Barbra solo. The critics found the show's "concept" an uneasy mix of elements. Jack Gould in the New York *Times*: " . . . an embarrassing outing, a concoction of deranged productions that not even the star and her major colleague of the evening, Jason Robards, could straighten out." Ben Gross in the New York *Daily News*: "Save for the time when Barbra held the stage alone and delivered a truly effective group of songs, the hour had a consciously coy and artificial air about it. This segment was the highlight of the show. For without gimmickry, it offered pure undiluted Streisand and showed her at her best."

As with her prior specials, Columbia prepared a soundtrack album of "The Belle of Fourteenth Street," but the show's lack of success (it was the first Streisand special not repeated), made them reconsider releasing it. One song from the show, "My Buddy/ How About Me?" eventually turned up, over seven years later, as part of Barbra's *The Way We Were* album.

Videotapes of Barbra's first two specials and her next one are currently available, but "The Belle of Fourteenth Street" is not. When and if it is marketed, Streisand fans who have never seen the show will be able to judge its merits for themselves.

In May of 1967, Barbra went to Hollywood to recreate her *Funny Girl* role on screen. On June 16, she interrupted the filming to fly back to New York for an admission-free concert she was giving the following evening in Central Park. She went directly from the airport to the ninety three-acre site in the Sheep Meadow area of the park, and into an arduous rehearsal schedule. The concert was to be taped for television and recorded for an album. Preparing the Meadow for such a complicated technical setup required extraordinary effort from the crew. The lighting and sound quality had to be up to the standards of previous Streisand specials and yet not interfere with the enjoyment of the huge audience expected.

With Mort Lindsey's orchestra Barbra worked out her program of songs (often just humming to save her voice) until the early morning hours. She tried various hairstyles and decided on the gowns that would be most flattering for the color cameras. A complex plan of lighting and camera angles took hours to set. Bearing all the technical snafus with patience, Barbra was relaxed and eager to perfect all the details of the concert. She cuddled Sadie, wandered across the stage (a series of Plexiglas levels), kibbitzed with the orchestra and traded quips with dozens of fans who had crashed the rehearsal. Rather than take the time to retire to her apartment or a hotel, she instead took brief rests in two elaborate ninety-foot trailers set up directly behind the orchestra seating. Elliott Gould joined Barbra as she prepared privately for the evening to come.

Fans began pouring into the park fifteen hours prior to the start of the concert.

By show time, 135,000 people had jammed into the Sheep Meadow and overflowed onto the Sixty-seventh Street entrance to the park. Additional thousands stood behind the stage. It was, to that date, the largest crowd ever assembled to hear a single performer.

Streisand seemed overwhelmed by the size of the audience but performed as if she were back in an intimate night club—involving the crowd in her comedy monologues and singalongs. In powerful voice, she sang her trademarks, "People," "Second Hand Rose," "Happy Days," and others, but she also drew on her *Harry Stoones* days for "Value" and introduced two haunting ballads, "Natural Sounds" and "Love Is Like a Newborn Child." In flowing chiffon, Barbra used the intermittent light breeze as a prop, adding a sensuous element to several numbers. She commented on the unexpectedly fine weather: "We're very lucky the night is so lovely, last night it was so humid . . . ," but it's doubtful that even a sudden downpour would have dampened the spirits of the rapt audience.

The entire "happening" was an unqualified success for Barbra and Rheingold beer, which had sponsored the evening. The only grousing came from the Sanitation Department when they were faced with the enormous cleanup the next day. Exotic items retrieved included a Russian-English dictionary and a Merry Widow bra.

The television version took over a year to hit the home screens, but "A Happening in Central Park" again won Streisand critical accolades.Percy Shain wrote in the Boston Globe: "It's not easy to sing your heart out before 128,000 fans and achieve a quality of intimacy under the stars in the stately wide open greenery of Central Park. But Miss Streisand managed it in a remarkable performance of spontaneity and assurance Sunday night during which she played that vast audience like a tuned-up violin."

Rex Reed: "Her material was tasty, her lower Second Avenue Kook City image was held to a minimum of adlibbing, and the television audience saw only the best of the evening."

Fans who had been put off by "The Belle of Fourteenth Street" a year earlier had Barbra just the way they preferred her—singing her heart out to an adoring audience. No guests, no elaborate sets, and, most refreshing of all, no overproduction.

The album, released to coincide with the TV airing, is fun primarily for the comic numbers, "Marty the Martian" and "Value," and the new ballads. It suffers from an inconsistent quality of sound, and there are several disconcerting clinkers from the orchestra, but generally it captures the excitement and power of Streisand's vocals and the interplay with that gigantic crowd.

The soundtrack album from "Happening" although containing much material Barbra had recorded before, reached a respectable #30 on *Billboard's* chart. Barbra's TV career had been a remarkable success. After "A Happening in Central Park," however, it would be five years until her next home-screen special.

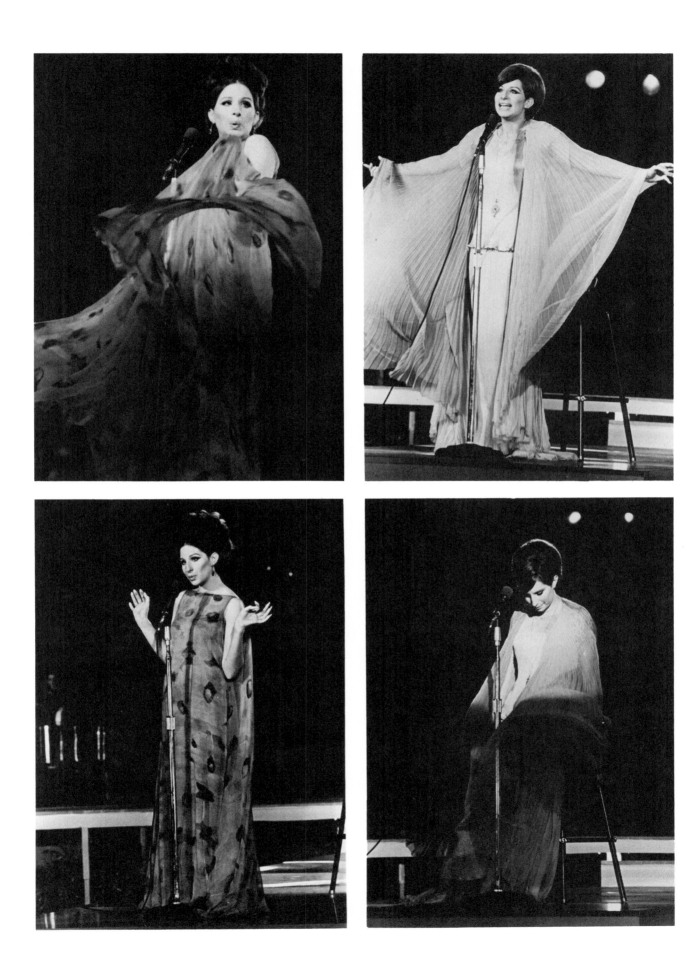

What Price Hollywood?

When Barbra Streisand stepped off the plane at Los Angeles International Airport in May 1967, she was accompanied by her husband, her baby, her dog, a half-dozen trunks, and reams of newspaper copy. Her arrival in Hollywood was the most heralded event since the Taylor/Burton love affair, and for a similar reason—Streisand was the most intriguing, glamorous, larger-than-life personality in Tinseltown since Elizabeth Taylor. The press panted in anticipation of her arrival, sensing that she alone could restore the American preoccupation with screen celebrity—a fascination that had waned with the eclipsing of the great stars of the thirties and forties, suffered a loss with the death of Marilyn Monroe, had its last gasp with Elizabeth Taylor's exploits and was then being carried on, such as it was, by a woman who had never appeared on the silver screen, Jacqueline Kennedy. Sheilah Graham, in her 1969 autobiography, summed up the feelings of the Hollywood press in regard to Barbra: "As long as we have a Streisand around, Hollywood will still be breathing."

For Barbra, the chance to re-create the role of Fanny Brice in *Funny Girl* was the last stop on her dream express. Whenever anyone had called her a star, she'd remind them of her childhood conviction that "being a star is being a movie star." That she would be a movie star was a foregone conclusion; on the day she arrived in Hollywood, she had contracts to film *Funny Girl, Hello, Dolly!* and *On a Clear Day You Can See Forever,* as well as three other films for Ray Stark in addition to *Funny Girl.* She had not wanted to sign a four-picture deal with Stark, but he had her in an uncomfortable position: "When I signed the deal in 1964 to do the movie, I only wanted to do *Funny Girl* and Ray refused to give it to me unless I signed a four-picture deal. I remember my agent saying to me, 'Look, if you're prepared to lose it, then we can say, sorry, we'll sign only one picture at a time.' I was not prepared to lose it."

Nor was Barbra prepared to fail in her first motion picture. Only the best talent was hired to surround her, starting with the director, William Wyler. A veteran of sixty-five films, he had won three Academy Awards and guided a dozen actors and actresses to starring or supporting Oscars. Wyler was known as a strict disciplinarian who had "tamed" the likes of Bette Davis, Margaret Sullavan, and Merle Oberon, and Columbia brass reportedly were seeking a director who could "handle" Streisand. "I am the only prima donna on the sets of my pictures," Wyler had been quoted.

Despite all of Wyler's qualifications, he had never directed a musical. Herb Ross, who had staged the musical numbers in *I Can Get It for You Wholesale,* was brought in to direct those scenes in *Funny Girl.* Each of these men had his own assistant director. Wyler's A.D., Ray Gosnell, recalls that Herb Ross was not autonomous. "There were very few things that were done away from Willy," he says. "Herb Ross choreographed and rehearsed a lot of things, all the musical numbers, but Wyler was always there, even when Ross was directing a sequence. Ross's presence made it much easier for Barbra to fit into the whole thing of making a motion picture, because she knew him, and being from the stage he could explain to Barbra what makes motion pictures different from the stage, that kind of thing."

Next in line was a leading man; Nicky Arnstein would not be an easy part to cast. Not only was the Arnstein role a relatively small one, and the picture obviously Streis-

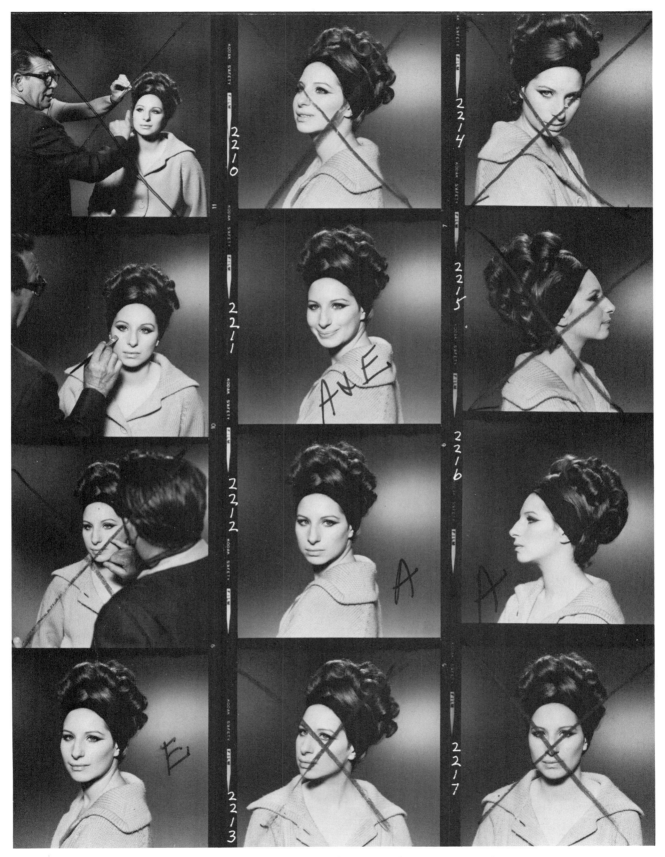

Make-up tests for *Funny Girl*, 1967. The markings are Streisand's.

and's, but Barbra was assured top billing. Both of these considerations doused negotiations with Marlon Brando and Gregory Peck. Jule Styne wanted Frank Sinatra in the role. "Sinatra as Nicky opposite Streisand, that would have been the collector's item of all time," Styne has said. "Imagine having four songs sung by Sinatra, imagine a duet by these two great people. He wanted to do it, but Stark said he was too old."

David Janssen was being considered when Wyler mentioned Omar Sharif, effective in *Lawrence of Arabia* as the Arab chieftain. It was odd casting, to be sure, and Barbra was ambivalent. She asked to meet Sharif, and Arthur Laurents has described the scene: "Ray Stark told me that Sharif came in, oozing Continental charm. Then Omar bowed elegantly, kissed Barbra's hand, and told her, 'In America, you are the woman I have most wanted to meet.' Naturally, he got the part."

Oscar-winning cinematographer Harry Stradling was entrusted with the job of committing Streisand's image to film. But Barbra was leaving nothing to chance, even in the best of hands. Ray Gosnell recalls that "Streisand had very definite opinions about the way she should look and how she should be lit. She had done TV before, so she had seen herself on film. She had slides that she brought with her of things she liked and didn't like about herself and she discussed with Strad how she would like to see herself photographed." Stradling didn't seem to mind what others called Barbra's "meddling"; he realized that she was someone who would have to be photographed a certain way and whose opinions about herself surely were valid. "I like the nose," he said. "You can't make Barbra look like Marilyn Monroe. But she does have a beautiful face—because she's got something back of it."

Despite Stradling's good nature, reports began making the gossip columns daily about Streisand's behavior on the set. She was, it was said, telling Stradling how to do his job and treating William Wyler like "a butler." Hollywood ate up the gossip, delighted that its preconceived notions of Streisand had been correct. Ray Gosnell recalls, "There was a major buildup about her that we all heard before she got here. We heard that she would be difficult in some areas. She came here with a reputation that has been perpetuated by gossip columnists ever since. But it doesn't really have any true foundation. She's no more difficult than any other actor or actress who's an artist."

But the press continued to paint Barbra as the reincarnation of Lucrezia Borgia, reportedly to the delight of the Columbia Pictures PR people, who knew the stories would only help box-office. Before long, however, Wyler came to her defense. He appreciated her input, he said. "What captivated me was, of course, Barbra, and my principal concern was to present her under the best possible conditions as a new star and a new personality. She was terribly eager, like Bette Davis used to be, to do different and new things. She wanted everything to be the very best. The same as I do.

"She fusses over things, she's terribly concerned about how she looks, with the photography, the camera, the makeup, the wardrobe, the way she moves, reads a line. She'll tell the cameraman that one of the lights was out—way up on the scaffold. If the light that was supposed to be on her was out, she saw it. She's not easy, but she's difficult in the best sense of the word—the same way I'm difficult."

Like Garson Kanin with the stage version, William Wyler directed Streisand minimally. "I don't like an actor or actress who says, 'Okay, boss, what do you want me to do?'" Wyler has said. "I say to them, 'What do you want to do? You've read the script and you know what's in it, so you show me.' I can't do it for him. I can guide his thinking—because if he *thinks* correctly, thinks like the character he is playing, there is very little he can do wrong. Barbra responded to direction very well."

According to Barbra, "I feel we had a great sort of chemical relationship. Willy can't dissect a scene for you. I mean, he would go, 'Oomph, a little more oomph,' and I'd say, 'Okay, I know what you mean.' And I would give it a little more oomph. A lot of people are not like that, but I couldn't have wanted a better relationship. He let me see the rushes with him, and I'm supposedly the first actress who's seen them. He knows I'm not destructive. I'm very objective about my work.

"We had a great creative relationship and I never told him where to put the camera. I would only, as an afterthought, offer an opinion. Naturally, I might feel in a scene, 'I would like to do it this way—maybe walk over there. What do you think?' And he would most of the time agree with me. Sometimes he didn't, so I would do it his way because he was the director; or as I learned later on, I'd say, 'Let's do it two ways.' But that's a very dangerous thing because then you have absolutely no control and I understand why certain actors would refuse to do it, although I wouldn't. I always thought that the actress' job was to fulfill the director's vision except if she really totally disbelieved in it and couldn't do it. Then it would have to be redone, rewritten, rethought-out.

"The whole idea of the movie medium is a challenge. It's so very different from the stage that it's like doing another story in a way. But I know *Funny Girl* so well—that's me. It's a different kind of acting involved—just being yourself. And Rod Steiger once said it took him twenty years to be himself. The movies are a very difficult medium. I'm always amazed when I see anything come out good, because it seems like it can never come out good because of all the technical facets of it."

Others on the *Funny Girl* set might have argued with Barbra's contention that she was "not destructive." Her closeness to Wyler led many to believe that she had influence on the film's final cut. When Anne Francis' role as Georgia wound up largely on the cutting room floor, she complained bitterly that her performance had been adjudged too good, too competitive with Barbra's, and that Streisand had had it removed. Ray Gosnell doubts this. "Some things work in a script and others don't," he says. "There may not have been enough time to play the character out. I cannot believe that if it was good for the picture as a dramatic entity, it would have been taken out. Wyler had final cut; I doubt that Barbra had much say in that."

Barbra's relations with the cast and crew were not friendly. She was an outsider who had arrived with a somewhat negative reputation, and whose many attributes did not include an overly gregarious nature. "She was a little bit distant," Gosnell recalls, "particularly in the early days, because it was her first experience out here. Everyone got along, there were no animosities or anything, but there were times that people felt she was distant. None of us got friendly with her. She's not a buddy-buddy type."

She did become rather friendly with her leading man. Sharif's casting at first had caused a furor because shortly after he, an Arab, had been signed to play opposite Streisand, the Arab-Israeli Six Day War broke out. When the first photo of Barbra and Omar kissing in *Funny Girl* was sent out over the wire services, a Cairo newspaper condemned Sharif in a front-page editorial for the association. Barbra thought it was all quite silly and quipped, "You think Cairo was upset? You should have seen the letter I got from my Aunt Rose!"

Once the brief war ended, so did the controversy, but reports quickly followed that Barbra (as if to complete her identification with screen greats of the past) had fallen in love with her leading man.

It was almost too pat, too cliché—but it appears to have been true. Sharif was quoted in *Life* magazine at the time: "When I first saw Barbra, I am thinking, 'This is not a pretty woman.' But in three days, I am thinking, 'This woman is beautiful,' and I am *lusting* after her."

Barbra reportedly said, "I am crazy in love with Omar and I have told my Elliott about it." In November, Streisand and Sharif attended a fashion show together, then dined alone in an elegant restaurant. To many, this was open admission of an affair. Elliott Gould talked to Sheilah Graham about it: "She's put herself in a very difficult position. The press doesn't like her, because she is uncooperative. I am a very secure person, but as a man I have certain reactions. I asked her why she had gone to that fashion show with Omar and she replied, 'Because the ticket would have cost me two hundred and fifty dollars.' She is just a terribly naive girl from Brooklyn." Then, as if to soften the bitterness of his comments, he added, "I love her and trust her all the way."

Many in Hollywood considered the whole thing a press agent's concoction—the attraction of opposites, the diva carrying the script's love story a little too far—but Omar Sharif, in his autobiography, offers an extraordinarily candid "confession" of their liaison: "I fell madly in love with her talent and her personality . . . Barbra's villa served as our trysting place. At the time, my own villa housed my family. We spent our evenings, our weekends at her place . . . we led the very simple life of people in love. Nobody could be more conventional, more discreet than a pair of lovers . . . We used to cook. When I'd used up all my Italian recipes—notably, ones for various pasta dishes which I can cook and season quite well—Barbra would heat TV dinners . . . Barbra and I would enjoy simple food, then, relaxed in our armchairs, we'd watch television."

Sharif says the affair lasted four months—"the time it took to shoot the picture. How many of my affairs seemed to last until the end of shooting! . . . How pleasant, how easy it is to fall in love with my female co-stars . . . whenever I make a movie I become one with the character I'm portraying . . . It's hard to play love scenes all day and then drop into apathy at night . . . because I'm in love with love."

Barbra and Omar *must* have been discreet about their romance, because Ray Gosnell says he wasn't aware of it until he read about it in the papers. Of course, his mind may have been distracted by all the exigencies of filming *Funny Girl*—one of which was getting Barbra Streisand to the set on time.

"She was always late," he says. "But I respected her on that, because I realized that she comes from New York and the theater, and theater people keep different hours than we do. On a picture you start at six-thirty in the morning and knock off at about seven at night. That was a big adjustment for her. But never, once she got there, did she ask me when she was gonna go to lunch or when she was going to go home—she was really a trouper once she was working."

She needed to be—many of the numbers took days to shoot, and the entire seduction scene which precedes "You Are Woman, I Am Man" had to be filmed twice, according to Gosnell, "because it just didn't work the first time and had to be completely restaged." Another headache for everyone involved was the problem of lip-synching. "Barbra wasn't experienced in that," Gosnell recalls. "And lip-synching is not something you learn easily. Imagine it—you record something, and then a few days later you're playing a scene, and you have to play the scene emotionally and still get the same lip-synching—that's not going to be easy. You could sit still and just mouth it, like you see on TV, but to really be involved in the scene and do it right is really tough. 'People' didn't work for that reason. Finally we had to do it the reverse way, synching the sound to the picture after filming."

Because of all these problems, Barbra asked to do the final number, "My Man," live, with no prerecording. Avoiding the lip-synching problems was especially important because the song was to be filmed almost entirely in close-up. Although it meant new problems and risks, Wyler liked the idea, realizing that the results would be far superior. Again, Barbra's suggestion disgruntled the crew, but she was resigned to that. "Wyler couldn't have been more pleased," she said, "but I suppose some of the people on the set could have seen this and said, 'She's making trouble.' They're not used to actors talking up in Hollywood."

"Oy, what a day I had today!" (With Omar Sharif)

"The whole world will look at me and be stunned!"

"Don't bring around the clouds to rain on my parade."

"Swan Lake"

"My Man"

Doing "My Man" live, in the words of Ray Gosnell, "paid off like crazy." It gave the number a reality and a spontaneity the others lacked; a split-second slip in synchronization can drive a thick wedge between audience and performer. But Barbra's emotion in the song was able to jump off the screen, and that final number left audiences in tears, silent for a moment before bursting into applause.

The premiere of *Funny Girl* at New York's Criterion Theater on September 18, 1968, was less a film opening than a coronation. The word was out—Streisand was fabulous in *Funny Girl,* she was going to be a *big* movie star, and things better be handled accordingly. Barbra, attired in a lovely, glittery gown and cape, entered the theater with Elliott on a red carpet as thousands of fans cheered her. It was the first opening night Streisand had ever attended at which she could see herself: "It was so exciting to go to an opening night and not be nervous and have to worry. I always envied my friends the fact that they could get dressed up and go to my openings while I had to worry and work. Now, I can go to the theater and *watch* myself work."

After the premiere, a huge party was held in a specially built tent constructed on a vacant lot across the street from the theater. The celebration was joyous; the audience had loved the picture, and some of the initial reviews were in. They were ecstatic.

Although criticism was leveled at the "overblown, irritatingly fake Hollywood production" and the miscasting of Omar Sharif, superlatives abounded when the critics came to Streisand. "All a show needs is Barbra Streisand," Barbara Spector wrote. "The Brooklyn-born talent dances, sings, jokes and beautifully acts her way through the nearly three-hour film." Rex Reed enthused, "I'll be damned if they haven't made her beautiful. In the most remarkable screen debut I will probably ever see in my lifetime, the toadstool from Erasmus High School has been turned into a truffle, and I, for one, couldn't be happier about the transformation . . . When Streisand is around, she turns *Funny Girl* from disguised Technicolor hokum into something bordering on art. With her voice, with her walk, with her emotion, and with the passion of her hydroelectric power, she makes tickets something worth buying." Pauline Kael, in *The New Yorker,* compared Streisand to Garbo.

If the critics were less enthralled with the vehicle than the star, *Funny Girl's* Broadway originators were downright unhappy with it. Garson Kanin was particularly displeased. "I thought Omar Sharif was terrible. A very poor choice. I mean, Nicky Arnstein was a Broadway guy—nothing to do with an accent or anything like that. And there were certain elements that I thought were a little overblown. After all, you're not talking about *War and Peace;* it's really a human, personal story. Fanny's real story was a personal one. And I think the picture suffered because they took out two of the best songs in the Broadway score: 'Cornet Man' and 'His Is the Only Music That Makes Me Dance.' I thought they could have had both 'His Is the Only Music' and 'My Man' in the picture, but their thinking was that 'His Is the Only Music' was put into the Broadway show as a replacement for 'My Man,' so when they could use 'My Man' in the movie, they didn't need it. I don't think that was clear thinking at all. They could have used both songs. They were two good songs . . . "

Jule Styne, on the other hand, was upset that "My Man" was included at all: "*Funny Girl* is the best movie that's ever been made of one of my stage musicals. My only disappointment was that in the latter portion of the film they destroyed Fanny's character. Fanny was a strong woman, nothing could affect her. Despite the many heartaches she had in her romantic escapades, she didn't fold up, she never needed an analyst, she liked herself and had many good friends. In the movie version they interpolated 'My Man' for her to sing at the end, and they made her self-pitying and timid, which was all wrong." Styne was also unhappy with the Sixties arrangement of a Twenties song.

Streisand arrives in style at the Hollywood *Funny Girl* premiere.

104

Despite all the reservations expressed about what was going on around her, *Funny Girl* was clearly a Streisand triumph. Movie musicals, it was said, were a dying breed. *Funny Girl's* huge success at the box office, coming so quickly after the failure of another blockbuster musical, Julie Andrews' *Star!*, could be attributed principally to Barbra's drawing power. At this point, all the controversy, sour grapes, and sniping at Barbra hardly mattered; she was bringing money into Hollywood, and if there's anything that town likes to hear more than hens cackling, it's the ringing of cash registers.

The soundtrack album of *Funny Girl* rose to #12 on *Billboard's* chart, and remained on the chart for 108 weeks, the longest charted period for any Streisand album, even to this day.

Barbra's career was at its zenith, but her personal life was not keeping pace. The publicity about Omar Sharif had put new strain on her marriage, already made shaky because her career was seemingly unstoppable while Elliott's had barely made a sputtering start. Clearly, Elliott's hopes for Barbra to settle down and abandon her career would never materialize. The announcement of their separation came with little surprise on February 13, 1969. "We are separating not to destroy, but to save our marriage," Barbra told a reporter hopefully. Barbra was experiencing another aspect of the Hollywood syndrome, and William Wyler was sympathetic. Referring to his stormy marriage to a temperamental and rising star, Margaret Sullavan, Wyler said, "Elliott handled these things a lot better than I did. Still they broke up. Those situations—right out of *Funny Girl* since Nicky couldn't handle Fanny's fame either—are very hard to cope with."

Publicly, Barbra was still gilded. The public waited to see if the ultimate certification of talent and success—the Oscar—could be hers. There was quite a bit of doubt—the winning of an Academy Award had been traditionally as much politics as performance, and Barbra was personally unpopular in Hollywood. And her fellow New Yorkers, in fact, had given their New York Film Critics Award to Joanne Woodward in *Rachel, Rachel,* with Katharine Hepburn the runner-up for *The Lion in Winter.* Streisand won the Golden Globe as "Best Actress in a Musical or Comedy," but the more prestigious Drama category was won by Katharine Hepburn. When the Oscar nominations were announced, these three women were joined by two other formidable challengers, Vanessa Redgrave for her portrayal of Isadora Duncan in *Isadora,* and Patricia Neal, for her comeback film, *The Subject Was Roses,* after a near-fatal stroke.

Barbra was a nervous wreck for days before the ceremonies, and she asked Elliott to escort her, despite their separation. She sat tensely throughout the seemingly endless announcements of Oscar winners—her category was the next to last. Finally, Ingrid Bergman opened the envelope to name the Best Actress of 1968. "It's a tie!" she said, her voice modulating with disbelief. The audience leaned forward in anticipation. "The winners are . . . Katharine Hepburn . . . and Barbra Streisand!"

Barbra rose to accept her award, revealing a daring see-through outfit designed by Arnold Scaasi for *On a Clear Day* and never used in the film. She tripped on a step on her way to the podium, and for one terrible moment it seemed as though the wispy material would come completely apart. After a thank-you speech was made for Katharine Hepburn, Barbra held up the statuette and said, "Hello, gorgeous!"—her opening line in *Funny Girl.* She then added, "It's an honor to be in such magnificent company as Katharine Hepburn."

She gave a gracious acceptance speech, but, as usual, controversy followed her—there was much criticism of her outfit in the next day's press. But it wasn't enough to mar Barbra's night of ultimate triumph. Could there be any question that the kooky kid from Brooklyn had *arrived?*

Ingrid Bergman looks on as Barbra emotionally thanks the Academy for her Oscar.

Dolly and Daisy

The announcement that Barbra had been signed to do the movie version of the long-running Broadway musical *Hello, Dolly!*—coming as it did before she had begun filming *Funny Girl*—did little to endear her to Hollywood. It appeared to many as though Streisand were taking the role—that of a middle-aged, widowed matchmaker—simply because it was an extravagant, expensive Hollywood version of a proven property, with little consideration of whether she was right for it. But the criticism didn't stop at Barbra—the producers were accused of hiring her because they felt they could make more money with her in the picture.

Many Broadway and Hollywood insiders had hoped that Carol Channing, who originated the role on Broadway, would be given a chance for movie stardom by repeating the role in the film. Its producer and writer, Ernest Lehman, in fact did want to cast Channing. But after seeing her in *Thoroughly Modern Millie*—a role, ironically, for which she was Oscar-nominated—Lehman felt that her Broadway personality did not translate well to the screen. "Carol didn't photograph too well," Lehman explained. "It had nothing to do with the fact that she was not as big a marquee name as Streisand."

Channing herself was very gracious, sending Barbra flowers when her signing was announced, and telling a reporter, "I'm really very glad Barbra Streisand got it. Obviously, with Barbra being so different from me, they're going to do a completely different kind of story and it should be very exciting."

Ernest Lehman publicly expounded on his decision to cast Barbra: "I'm not implying criticism of anyone else who has done the role previously, but I chose Miss Streisand because I'm convinced she's one of the most exciting talents to come along in the recent past and I know she'll be perfect for the role. She has a timeless quality, which means she could be the Dolly of 1890 as well as the Barbra of 1967."

At first, Barbra had been as skeptical as everyone else. "When they first offered me the part," Barbra told a radio interviewer on the set, "I laughed and said, 'This can't be serious—you can't want me!' I wasn't gonna do it. I tried to convince them that it would be more emotional if it were the story of an older woman whose time is running out and she has to make the most of it. I thought Elizabeth Taylor should play it because it would be her first musical and she's kind of at the right age, you know, but they didn't listen to my suggestions."

Taylor, in fact, expressed interest in the role to Lehman, who had once suggested to her that she do a musical. "I must admit I felt very guilty at having ever mentioned it to her," Lehman said, "because it was a thoroughly rotten notion of mine. At least I think it was. In this business, you can never tell until after the event."

Streisand had other reasons for thinking that *her* playing Dolly was a "rotten notion": "I was reluctant to show a part of me that is very Dolly Levi-ish—searching for bargains and all that. When I first saw the show on Broadway, I must say honestly, I didn't like it, and I never took it seriously. The audience, they couldn't wait for that one song, and it was such a simple song, really the most uninteresting in the whole score.

"Another reason I didn't want to play Dolly—I'd like to play glamorous, exciting women from the eighteenth century who had ten lovers at the same time. You know, I'm just fantasizing now. So in that way Dolly was an unglamorous character to me.

"But after I realized that I could bring something to it, I began to really enjoy using that part of me that I'd rather not show, because it really worked for Dolly. And the age thing is not a problem, because it's actually the story of one woman who has loved and lost, and now has to make the decision whether to live the rest of her life or just dwell in the past or memories. That's a universal problem for women of all ages. A woman of eighteen can be a widow."

Barbra liked Jerry Herman's score, and that was a factor in her decision to do it. "The score to me is lovely, and very underrated. They used to talk about *Dolly* as being a one-song show. But to me 'Hello, Dolly!' is the least effective song. The other songs were really unexplored on stage, but now I could do something with them in the movie. My favorite songs, though, I don't do—'Ribbons Down My Back' and 'It Only Takes a Moment.'"

There were a few other factors involved in Barbra's decision to play Dolly: "It was fun thinking about the jewelry that I'd wear, stuff that I had and loved that I thought would be good for Dolly. And I liked the idea of being able to laugh and smile a lot, which I usually don't do—I mean, I'm not much of a laugher."

Streisand's ambivalence about playing Dolly resulted in uncertainty about *how* to play her. "When I saw the first day's rushes," Barbra says, "I watched myself and realized that I was making a mistake—I was playing it a little too elegant for Dolly. Once I saw that on the screen, I realized that I would have to commit to me and to the part of me that I know could be right for Dolly. Once I decided to do that, I think everything was O.K."

Everything was not O.K. on the set, however. The tensions of making such a complicated, big-budget picture—a call went out one day for 2,500 extras—were becoming more and more palpable daily. Barbra's co-star Walter Matthau did not take kindly at all to her quest for perfection. He saw her as meddlesome, he resented her position of power and her billing over his—after all, he was an Oscar-winning veteran and she had yet to have a picture in release.

When tempers finally flared, the press reports made the gossip about *Funny Girl* sound like a Streisand fan club bulletin. After Barbra made another of her "suggestions" to director Gene Kelly, Matthau exploded: "Why don't you let the director direct?" Streisand hissed back: "Why don't you learn your lines?" and left the set. Matthau, not to be bested, called after her, "Everybody in this company hates you! All right, walk off! Just remember, Betty Hutton once thought she was indispensable!" Barbra stayed in her dressing room while Gene Kelly and Ernest Lehman tried to soothe the ruffled feathers. Matthau, it was reported, took to calling Streisand "Miss Ptomaine" and she to calling him "Old Sewermouth."

The problem for Walter Matthau, of course, was that Streisand *was* indispensable. Lehman and Kelly knew that the success of *Dolly* would hinge on the success of Streisand's characterization. Feeling he was being ganged up on, Matthau went to Richard Zanuck, head of Twentieth Century-Fox, and complained. "Do I need a heart attack?," he pleaded. "Do I need an ulcer?" He catalogued his complaints about Streisand and his chagrin at playing second fiddle to a twenty-six-year-old neophyte. Zanuck listened patiently to the diatribe, then responded. "I'd like to help you out," he said. "But the film is not called *Hello, Walter!*"

In a fascinating chapter on *Hello, Dolly!* in his book *Gene Kelly,* Clive Hirschhorn quotes Walter Matthau about a flare-up between him and Barbra on the day Robert Kennedy was assassinated in 1968: "Barbra kept asking Gene whether he didn't think it would be better if I did this on this line, or that on the other, etc., etc.—and I told her to stop directing the fucking picture, which she took exception to, and there was a blow-up in which I also told her she was a pip-squeak who didn't have the talent of a butterfly's fart. To which she replied that I was jealous because I wasn't as good as she was. I'm not the most diplomatic man in the world, and we began a slinging match like a couple of kids from the ghetto . . . the thing about working with her was that you never knew what she was going to do next and were afraid she'd do it. I found it a most unpleasant picture to work on and, as most of my scenes were with her, extremely distasteful. I developed all kinds of symptoms. Pains in the lower abdomen, severe headaches, palpitations: I was in agony most of the time. I wish I could figure out exactly what happened to me, but I haven't been able to yet. All I remember and know is that I was appalled by every move she made . . . I think Gene thought one of us was going to die of apoplexy or something, or that I'd belt her, or that maybe she'd scratch my eyes out— or worse, that we'd just walk off leaving twenty million dollars' worth of movie to go down the drain."

That fear was shared by Fox executives, who told the stars to be civil to each other for the good of the picture. Ernest Lehman tried gamely to patch things up publicly in an interview when he was asked about his feuding co-stars: "They quarreled and that lasted a few days. Now, they've kissed and made up. Walter's mother was on the set one day and asked Barbra, 'Why do you fight with my son?' and Barbra answered, 'He told me he fought with you, too. I guess he fights with everyone he loves.' "

Lehman would like us to think that Barbra delivered that line straight, but it's hard to believe she wouldn't have said it with just a touch of irony. Still, the personal animosities between the stars were resolved, on the surface at least, because of the exigencies of filming. "Before the Parade Passes By," the number requiring the 2,500 extras, was a nightmare, with incessant retakes necessary for reasons like the cameraman running over a cable. Barbra moaned, "But it was perfect that time." Kelly had to explain the situation. "The cable is just as important as I am," Streisand muttered.

Someone commented that Barbra seemed to have an affinity for parades, what with this number and "Don't Rain on My Parade" in *Funny Girl.* "I hate parades," she laughed. "I do. But I seem to sing a lot about them. I don't think there's a song about parades in *On a Clear Day,* though."

After the flare-ups with Matthau, Barbra kept to herself more and more. She ate all her meals in her trailer, although the reason for this was often not to avoid others but to spend some quiet moments with two-year-old Jason, a frequent visitor. "I don't like to take Jason on the set itself," Barbra said. "He came when we were doing the 'Hello, Dolly' number; there I was, his *mother,* in a red wig and a gold dress, with a strange man on each side of her, and he got upset. He didn't like it. I got embarrassed with him watching me. It was like having my mother watch me—because she *knows* I'm just pretending and it's not really me at all."

Despite the fact that Streisand felt the "Dolly" number to be the weakest in the score, she knew it was also one of the most popular songs in America. Asked how she intended to sing it, considering its familiarity, she replied, "I just looked for a way to do it that was in keeping with the character of Dolly. I always thought it should have been a little slower at the beginning, a little out of tempo, dealing more specifically and personally with each one of the waiters. That's the way I did it. Then, of course, it becomes a big thing when they have to sing back to me."

Louis Armstrong, who had had a #1 hit with "Hello, Dolly!" was brought in to share the song with Barbra. "Everyone thought it was an excellent idea," Clive Hirschhorn quotes Ernest Lehman, "except Barbra, who was dead set against it. She thought it was cheap and obvious, and accused us of exploiting him. But she changed her mind, and on the day we shot it, she was in a good mood and the sequence went very well."

Watching herself in daily rushes throughout filming, Barbra noticed something

As Dolly Gallagher Levi

else there was too much of besides elegance—herself. "I had three double chins in *Dolly.* I kept telling people it was because Dolly should be statuesque, but that was a cop-out because I couldn't diet."

Harry Stradling, working with Streisand again as cinematographer, came to the rescue. "Of course," Barbra said, "you can't see my double chins in the movie. It's a trick I learned from Elizabeth Taylor's cameraman. He told me that if you hold the camera up high and shoot down, you don't see the double chins."

Streisand may have been somewhat larger than usual in *Dolly,* but compared to the film's budget, she was Audrey Hepburn. By the time filming came to an end, more than $20 million had been spent, a staggering amount of money at any time, but especially so in 1968. Twentieth Century-Fox was a quivering mass of nervous executives, and Barbra wondered if her career in movies would be coming to an ignominious end—the movie would have to make an awful lot of money just to break even.

Walter Matthau said in a 1974 interview that Streisand was indeed worried. "She was just too young for the part and she knew it. That's why she made it so difficult for everyone involved. There's nothing more depleting for an actor than to feel he's playing the wrong role. You can be gallant about it, but she had too much at stake. I can see it now in perspective. She was a movie star, though none of her films had been released. She was insecure and she couldn't handle it."

Part of the tension between the two stars may have come from the fact that Matthau must have realized that if Barbra was miscast, so was he. Opposite Carol Channing, playing Dolly as a middle-aged woman, Matthau's characterization of Horace Vandergelder as a crusty, set-in-his-ways middle-aged man would have been entirely appropriate. But against Streisand's young, sensual, vibrant Dolly, Matthau's Horace seemed a little too old, a little too dull.

Fox's insecurities about the potential money-making power of the film were abated somewhat by the enormous success of *Funny Girl;* obviously, *Hello, Dolly!* had a drawing-card star if nothing else. Barbra's popularity was attested to at the *Dolly* premiere, where thousands of fans mobbed her car and a flying wedge of security officers had to be formed to get her into the theater. Plainly frightened, Barbra inched her way into the theater. Just as she got inside, the police barricades broke and mayhem ensued. Barbra was shaken, and Marty Erlichman suffered a bloody nose. Barbra's fear of crowds was obviously well founded.

The critical reaction to *Hello, Dolly!* was mixed. The show's strong points—a fun plot, hummable songs, and lots of razzmatazz—had made it a huge success on Broadway, but left many film critics unmoved. The film was criticized for its cartoon characters, "smirky dialogue," weak songs with "lyrics that make your teeth ache" and an unbelievable plot. But as with *Funny Girl,* Streisand's personal notices were better than the film's. Joe Rosen in the New York *Morning Telegraph,* wrote, "Barbra Streisand, the umpteenth Dolly, is magnificent as always in a role that apparently brings out the best in those who attempt it. And the best of Barbra Streisand has got to be the best there is." *Variety* said, "At a guess some may complain that Miss Streisand's title role, younger than the others and possibly more on the cool side, subtracts something of compassion. It is still a dilly of a Dolly on its own terms and she is, after the property itself, the big selling value." Richard Cohen in *Women's Wear Daily* described the title number: " . . . she is the champion female movie star of her time and she is poised for the most played, the most familiar, the most parodied song of the decade. We are expectant. Will she bring it off? Will she top all the toppers? Boys, the kid's a winner. The whole thing's a triumph. She was smiling that sly smile because she knew all the time that she was going to kill us."

Despite, or perhaps because of, the familiarity of the title tune, the *Dolly* soundtrack was not a big seller, peaking at #49 and staying on the charts thirty-three weeks.

Contrary to legend, *Hello, Dolly!* did not fail at the box office. It was grand family entertainment starring the most publicized actress of the day in a famous and beloved—if somewhat thin—Broadway musical. People did go to see it, and the film made $15 million, a sum any producer in Hollywood would be happy to enter into a ledger book. But because of *Dolly's* absurd cost, it has yet to make back the money spent to film, advertise and promote it.

Even Streisand's most vehement detractors were hard-pressed to blame her for *Dolly's* red ink. In fact, Hollywood insiders conceded privately that without Streisand the film would probably have brought in quite a bit less at the box office. Even though Streisand has since called *Dolly* "the worst mistake I ever made," she emerged from it with her aura of professional invincibility intact.

"I am a cross between a washerwoman and a princess," Barbra once said. "I am a bit coarse, a bit low, a bit vulgar, and a bit ignorant. But I am also part princess—sophisticated, elegant, and controlled. I can appeal to everyone."

Never was this strange and fascinating duality of Streisand's more highlighted than in her next film, *On a Clear Day You Can See Forever.* A moderately successful Broadway show in the mid-sixties, it starred Barbara Harris as Daisy Gamble, a nondescript New York college girl who goes to a psychiatrist to be cured of smoking. While under hypnosis, Daisy reveals a prior incarnation as Lady Melinda Winifred Moorepark Tentrees, an elegant, aristocratic Englishwoman of the nineteenth century.

Barbra was anxious to play the role; Melinda Tentrees was the kind of character she had "fantasized" about playing. And she couldn't have dreamed up better creative company: a score by Alan Jay Lerner and Burton Lane, direction by Vincente Minnelli, whose *Gigi* she greatly admired; contemporary outfits by Arnold Scaasi, period costumes by Sir Cecil Beaton, whose clothes for *My Fair Lady* had won an Oscar. Another of Barbra's fantasies was coming true.

Several actors, including Richard Harris, Gregory Peck, and Frank Sinatra, were considered for the role of Dr. Marc Chabot, the psychiatrist, before Yves Montand, popular French vocalist and dramatic actor, was signed. Montand had made his Hollywood debut opposite another "temperamental" superstar, Marilyn Monroe, in 1960's *Let's Make Love.*

Also in the cast were Larry Blyden, as Daisy's stuffy fiancé, Bob Newhart, John Richardson as Lord Tentrees, Mabel Albertson, and Jack Nicholson in a small role as Daisy's half-brother.

Clear Day's contemporary sequences were filmed in Hollywood and New York; period scenes at the grand Royal Pavilion at Brighton, England. (Minnelli was the first director ever granted permission to film in the building, one of England's most opulent structures, built by George IV as his personal "play house" while he was Prince and now a national museum.)

There were no reports of friction between Barbra and any members of the cast and crew; the *Clear Day* set appears to have been a happy one. Barbra was no longer an untried commodity, and her confidence had increased tremendously. By now, too, Hollywood was used to the Streisand quest for perfection and realized that, whatever her means toward being the best she could be on film, it was worth it: Barbra was the only genuine female superstar in Hollywood.

Barbra and Vincente Minnelli got along extremely well. She admired him tre-

With Jason during *Dolly* filming, 1968

mendously, and he respected her. Commenting today on her often strained relationships with her directors, Minnelli says, "The directors were at fault there. The director is supposed to be boss, but I didn't think that way—I saw it more as a collaboration, and Barbra likes that. Many directors have an instance in mind for a sequence, and if it doesn't go that way, they're unhappy. I'm not, necessarily. The chemistry of one person playing another is sometimes unfathomable, and the director has to be willing to give his actors some room.

"Many of Barbra's suggestions were very good, but I never agreed to anything that wasn't for the good of the picture. She wanted things explained. If I had an idea, I would explain it in great detail. Once she understood what I wanted and why it was important, she would go along. Not always, but usually."

One suggestion of Minnelli's didn't sit too well with Barbra. "I wanted her to go to a psychiatrist," Minnelli explains, "in order to understand the split personality better. I thought the psychiatrist could help her with the role, although I was a little afraid that she would wind up arguing with the doctor. But she never did go. She thought that she could do it fine on her own, and she did."

Barbra may not have talked to the shrink, but she did talk to Minnelli. "She has about ten ways of playing a scene," Minnelli says. "She'd talk at great length about it, and I love to argue. Sometimes she'd win, sometimes I'd win." Barbra took to phoning Minnelli at night to discuss the next day's shooting. "I got rid of that as nicely as I could," Minnelli laughs.

"I realized, working with her, that she could play anything. The surface hasn't been touched," Minnelli says. "I gave her a sketch of Sarah Bernhardt and told her, 'You will eventually play Bernhardt.' That made her very happy."

On a Clear Day's most beautiful sequence bears out Minnelli's contention about Barbra's versatility. In the Royal Pavilion, Lady Melinda Moorepark, gloriously clad in a white bejeweled gown and turban, toys seductively with a crystal goblet to entice a handsome man (her future husband) sitting across from her at a banquet table. Cecil Beaton went along with the company to England to supervise Streisand's wearing of his costumes and to advise on the sumptuous set decoration. In an interview given shortly before his death, Beaton spoke proudly of what one critic called "the most graceful Streisand moment ever put on film."

"Both our reputations were on the line," he said. "She had two previous musicals; this one had to be different. And I had done things like *Gigi* and *My Fair Lady,* so how could I top myself? We both topped ourselves visually. There is perhaps no more over-poweringly visual and sensual scene than the banquet. It was inspired—and both of our ideas, really—to wrap the Streisand features in a glorious white turban, to further accentuate her strong features. At the same time, she was totally feminine, beguiling, shamelessly sexual. I recall one of the reviewers found the Streisand performance as an English aristocrat reminiscent of vintage Joan Greenwood. I enjoyed reading that, because both women display a quality of cunning refinement. Barbra did an English accent to perfection; perhaps in an earlier life she was a landed lady with titles and royal lovers . . ."

"She just came up with the accent," Minnelli recalls. "I didn't help her with that at all. I wasn't even aware of any preparation on her part. She has within herself many great moments; she has a natural talent."

Beaton, one of the world's great creative minds, admired Streisand as well. "Barbra and I talked our way into everything, and I trusted her judgment, something I seldom do with any actor, especially a relative neophyte. She obviously thought everything out; I've never, to this day, met anyone so young who had such an awareness and knowledge of herself.

As Melinda Moorepark Tentrees

118

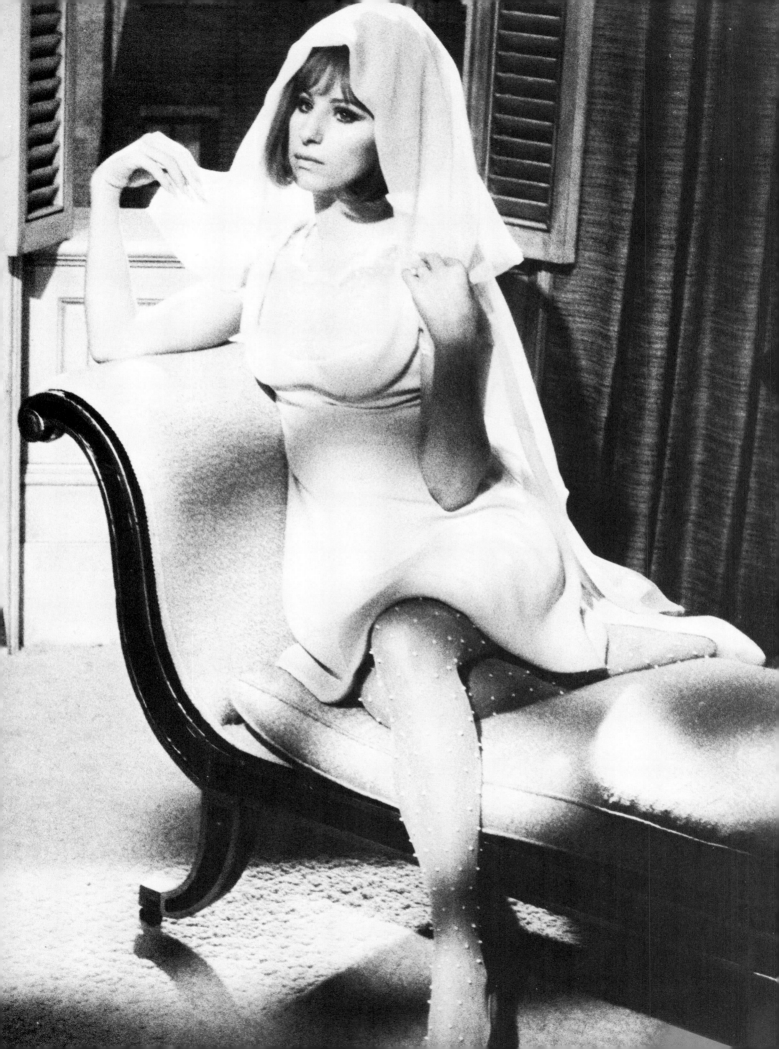

"She was charming to work with, almost literally. Like a hypnotist. Pleasing her was very difficult, but it pleased me inwardly, because I myself am extremely hard to please. I think each of us is ever aware of the name we've been given and, more importantly, what we've each done with it . . ."

On a Clear Day was Streisand's least troubled production, but it was not unplagued. The film cost $10 million to make and was originally supposed to be a three-hour road-show extravaganza. It was cut down to two hours, and several musical numbers were excised. Yves Montand complained that his role had been butchered. He told a reporter, "Streisand had the right to cut this film herself, so she cut me out so there could be more of her. Now I just have a supporting role in that film."

Vincente Minnelli vehemently denies Montand's contentions. "That's not true. Every scene Montand filmed is in that picture. No scenes with him were cut out. I did the final editing; the final print was mine."

When *On a Clear Day* was released, it was apparent that a pattern was emerging in Streisand criticism: reviewers again found her far superior to her material. *Newsweek* said, "Putting Miss Streisand in the dual role of Daisy Gamble/Melinda Tentrees was the movie's first, best and only inspiration . . . She flashes lightning-like between Melinda's airs and Daisy's earthiness . . ." Donald Mayerson in *Cue* wrote, "Barbra Streisand is the queen of the movie musicals. Unfortunately, as evidenced by this film version of the Broadway show, her kingdom has been reduced to a duchy. Vincente Minnelli has mounted an old-fashioned production which begins promisingly enough with a magical blend of charm and whimsy but soon collapses under the weight of a creaky libretto and a cardboard leading man. Streisand . . . is undeniably beautiful and absolutely enchanting."

Particularly negative reaction was reserved for Yves Montand. He seemed uncomfortable in the role, he was often difficult to understand, and there was absolutely no chemistry between him and Barbra. One critic said, "Montand doesn't destroy the movie singlehandedly, but almost." Rex Reed wrote, "When he's not standing on top of the Pan Am building with his arms outstretched, singing 'Bleest your hide, heer me cull, must I fight City Hull, cum buck do mee,' in his *boulevardier* style, he's announcing 'Daisy, somewhere in yoo is zee keey to all zis!' It's all Miss Streisand can do to keep a straight face."

Today, Vincente Minnelli still feels that the criticism of Montand was unfair. "People said that Gregory Peck or Frank Sinatra would have been better, but I think Montand was better than either of those two would have been. It might have been wonderful to have Barbra Streisand and Frank Sinatra in the same film, but the people who were advocating that didn't consider the play. According to the play, they met in a strange way; they were very different people, so there didn't have to be any chemistry between them. And I don't understand the criticism of Montand's accent; he was, after all, playing a Frenchman. I was totally satisfied with his performance."

Another criticism of *Clear Day,* and one that is even more valid with hindsight, is that Daisy Gamble was an unrealistic contemporary character. She was a college girl with no apparent income who had a fabulous high-fashion wardrobe and a glamorously decorated rooftop apartment. Not only was Daisy unbelievable as a college student, but she presented less of a contrast to Melinda than she would have had she been long-haired, dressed in blue jeans, and a little scruffy. "I think that's a valid criticism," Minnelli says. "Barbra didn't want to play Daisy that way. But the arguments went that way, and I agreed. We did, however, cut out a scene at the Central Park Zoo, because she was wearing a very high-fashion outfit. That was just *too* much."

On the whole, however, Minnelli has no regrets about *On a Clear Day.* "I saw it

As Daisy Gamble—too high fashion for a college girl?

again in 1979," he says. "I wouldn't change anything. I don't think that way—I get in and do it to the best of my ability, and once it's done, it's done."

The film was not a big box-office success, but it did make back its cost. The soundtrack album was Barbra's least successful ever, reaching just #108 on the *Billboard* chart.

Nineteen sixty-nine was an eventful year for Barbra, one of highs and lows. Her sorrow at her separation from Elliott Gould was blunted as much as it could be by the great acclaim she was receiving as an actress: an Oscar, the Friars Club Entertainer of the Year Award (she was only the second woman to receive that honor from the all-male theatrical association), a special Tony as "Star of the Decade," a second Golden Globe as "World Film Favorite," a second *Cue* magazine "Entertainer of the Year" designation and, interestingly, a Golden Apple Award from the Hollywood Women's Press Association for being "Most Cooperative" with the press.

Her burgeoning stardom, however, didn't always win her accolades: her attempt to buy an expensive Park Avenue cooperative apartment was rebuffed because she was "a flamboyant type." It brought back unpleasant emotions in Barbra. "My whole life I was always concerned with being looked down upon as an actress. I always felt that certain people thought, Oh, you're an actress. Ah, cheap. Vulgar. Loose. Immoral. Amoral. A kind of Victorian way of thinking."

She issued a statement echoing her feelings: "I have been criticized in Hollywood for not attending premieres or giving parties . . . I had thought that the mid-Victorian notion of actors as undesirables or second-class citizens was a prejudice which had gone the way of the bustle. I am an actress by choice; I am proud of my profession, and I am not prepared to accept an infringement of my civil rights because of it."

New York's Attorney General began an investigation into charges that Barbra's rejection and others were actually part of a widespread discrimination against Jews, but Barbra eventually found another apartment.

Later in the year, Barbra was back in the newspapers, being escorted around Ottowa by Canada's Prime Minister, eligible bachelor Pierre Trudeau.

Barbra attended a session of Parliament, and caused a stir when a member of the opposition party asked Trudeau to answer a question "if the Prime Minister can take his eyes and mind off the visitors' gallery long enough." Trudeau blushed; Barbra laughed.

There was a good deal of press speculation about the seriousness of the couple's subsequent dates and whether Barbra would give up her career to become Canada's First Lady. Their attraction ended long before Trudeau wed Margaret Sinclair in March of 1971. Barbra did not speak of her relationship with Trudeau until her *Playboy* interview in 1977, when she intimated that it was quite serious.

Q: Did he ask you to marry him?
A: I don't want to answer that. But he's an extraordinary man.
Q: Did you ever reflect on what it would be like to be the First Lady of Canada?
A: Oh, yeah. I thought it would be fantastic. I'd have to learn how to speak French. I would do only movies made in Canada. I had it all figured out. I would campaign for him and become totally politically involved in all the causes, abortion or whatever.
Q: What made you change your mind?
A: Certain realities.
Q: Would you ever have considered getting him to change *his* career?
A: No, I would never have wanted him to. His life was too important to a whole country, to a world.

126

In July of 1969, Barbra returned to Las Vegas after a six-year absence. She had left as Liberace's opening act, and was returning as the biggest star in the world, with the highest Vegas salary ever: $100,000 a week plus a sizable share of the new International Hotel's stock. She was the premier performer at the glamorous International, and her show was attended by a plethora of show business greats, including Cary Grant, Rudolf Nureyev, Peggy Lee, and Rita Hayworth.

Barbra's show, however, was panned. The *Hollywood Reporter* said, "Barbra Streisand is very fortunate indeed to be making a reputed $100,000 a week at the posh new International. Now she can afford to get someone to write an act for her. It would be money well spent. Her voice, a remarkable instrument about which enough has been said . . . comes through fine. But never does she warm to the people or they to her. The sameness of arrangements, the sameness of the treatment she gives each song, makes for such monotony you can't believe. A real live 'Barbie' doll."

Streisand was aloof, and barely talked between her songs. "I was kind of nervous," she admitted. "It wasn't stage fright—it was a thing called *death!* I would stand in the wings and my whole life would pass before my eyes."

Marty Erlichman further explained Barbra's reluctance to open up to her audience. "She was nervous about going back to the stage. Then we found out the hotel wasn't ready. There were no chairs, tables, or booths in the theater. She was rehearsing in an empty room. I took her around to some of the shows so she could get a feel of things. We were at the Dean Martin show and a kibitzer got tossed out by two security guards. Barbra said, 'If they do that to *him,* what'll they do to me?'"

Barbra was upset about the criticism, and she made some adjustments. Later performances were more warmly greeted. But Barbra perceived in Vegas that part of her problem was that she was working in a time warp. She felt that Vegas audiences wanted to see her in glamorous gowns with sky-high hairdos, singing her old standards. She was right, of course—but she wasn't happy. She was in a state of transition, desiring to try new things and contemporize her image. Vegas represented several steps backward for her. She was no longer content to sing the same songs she'd been doing for nine years. Her discomfort at this situation hindered the spontaneity of her performance.

Barbra was breaking new ground in her career and her personal philosophy. She was becoming more receptive to the new than ever before. Her next Vegas appearance, late in 1970, would reflect a looser, more contemporary Barbra. She would take the gamble that the tradition-bound town would accept this new Streisand persona. To her surprise, it did. And so did everyone else.

PART THREE

THE
EXPERIMENTAL
YEARS

1970-1975

"The Me That's Natural"

The start of the 1970s signaled a new direction for Barbra Streisand; she was now moving forward, not looking back. All her career, she had had an image considerably older than her chronological years. Most of the characters she had played were mature women; the songs she sang were the favorites not of people her own age but of their parents. Starting in 1970, Barbra began to contemporize her image, first with her appearance, then on records, then on film. By the end of the decade, as she neared forty, her greatest popularity would be with teenagers and young adults, a remarkable turnaround and one unique in show business history.

The change was not easy for Barbra, especially in her music. She wasn't at all sure that she would be accepted by young people whose favorites were The Beatles, Janis Joplin, Simon and Garfunkel, Bob Dylan, and The Doors. Nor was she secure about the public's reaction to her next film project. It was indeed a risky venture. Not only would she not sing a note, but she was playing a New York hooker in a very adult, very risqué sex comedy. All of her previous vehicles had been more or less "family entertainment"; this one was not only strictly for adults but very real life: no fantasy here.

Barbra may have been apprehensive, but she was also excited about the project. It was such a dramatic departure for her that she would be able to break down all barriers at one time and prove to everyone that she was not just a singer in wholesome, extravagant productions. "Now I can make a movie in ten weeks," she said happily. "No songs, like a normal person. I'm doing without wigs, hairpieces, dyes. It's just going to be me . . . the me that's natural and very today."

Barbra did wear a hairpiece in *The Owl and the Pussycat,* and her character of Doris Wilgus was far from "normal," but why quibble? It was certainly departure enough: the story of would-be writer Felix Sherman, a bookstore clerk, and Doris Wilgus, a would-be actress and model calling herself Doris Waverly/Wadworth/Washington (depending on her mood), a part-time prostitute. It had been a successful Broadway play starring Diana Sands and Alan Alda; originally producer Ray Stark had wanted to turn the interracial aspect around and cast Sidney Poitier opposite Barbra. "It will give it some social significance," Barbra said. "Make it a little more important." A script was prepared for them, but the idea fell through—that may have been *too* much for the image-conscious Barbra to risk.

Another script was prepared for Barbra and George Segal by Buck Henry, one of the funniest minds in Hollywood. He welcomed the assignment. "Having Barbra and George already cast made it a good deal easier to write in terms of dialogue," Henry says, "because I was a close friend of George's and everyone knew what Barbra sounded like. Lots of stuff in it was written for Barbra's rhythms and for that ingenious New York ear and accent which lends itself to certain patterns of speech that other actresses wouldn't sound good doing. There are few actresses whose rhythms are really pure, who you can construct for. It's been done badly for her from time to time, and when it's done badly it sticks out like a sore thumb."

Filming began in New York City in late 1969, with Herb Ross directing his first full motion picture, and Harry Stradling photographing Streisand for the fourth straight time. Barbra had insisted on Stradling, despite the fact that according to union rules he could not work in place of a local New York cinematographer. "Ray Stark got that settled," Buck Henry says, then smiles. "I hate to think how."

The Owl and the Pussycat script was peppered with more or less offensive expletives and very "in" sexual jokes. Streisand's character was street-wise and foul-mouthed, wore revealing outfits and a nightgown featuring two hands and a heart sewn over strategic areas. Buck Henry was on the set every day ("I use it as an excuse not to work") and says that much of this caused Barbra embarrassment. "There was a charming modesty on her part—but not an overwhelming self-centeredness—about doing the sexy stuff. I think she was quite shy and somewhat naïve about a lot of that stuff. I mean not unworldly, totally—God knows she wasn't that. I don't remember her using that kind of language except when in character."

Henry remembers one instance in which Barbra's commitment to total acting superseded her modesty. "There's a scene where she wants him to smoke a joint, and he won't. So she whispers to him that she'll do something for him if he'll try the pot. She asked me, being the method actress that she is, what it would be that she'd say to him. I'm reluctant to say what I told her, but I do remember because it was my own, private, twisted pleasure to whisper this line of filth in her ear. And she blushed and laughed in a way that made you know that it was something she would never, *ever* have said herself."

Barbra got along well with everyone on the *Pussycat* set except Ray Stark, with whom she has battled during every production of his she has starred in. "Barbra and Ray," Buck Henry says, "had an enormous love-hate relationship that you could taste sometimes. It's really palpable. But in some strange way, it was right. It's like one of those odd marriages that work almost because of the built-in hostility. I found Ray to be almost a perfect version of the mythic producer. He's always there when you need him and he knows how to bribe you perfectly to keep you working; and then when there's *real* trouble, he comes darting in and fixes it."

George Segal and Barbra had a warm rapport as actors, something that is quite evident on screen. "She's fantastic," George says. "I think there's Brando—and then there's Barbra. She has an unerring instinct—she's a natural phenomenon. She's the easiest person to work with. She's warm and even and a real professional. She knows *exactly* what she's doing. *I* was the troublemaker on that set. One time I got upset over working late hours. Ray Stark and I had a big screaming fight in my dressing room . . ."

"I can't tell you how marvelous she's been," Herb Ross said during the filming. "It all comes out sounding like platitudes, but she's so generous—willing to do it my way or George's way. She has a feeling not that everyone loves her but that she's one of us." Ross compared his star to Peter O'Toole, with whom he had just worked in *Mr. Chips.* "She isn't technical the way Peter is, a highly disciplined, highly trained actor. She has this ability to make right choices intuitively. But they're both alike in a way. They're never unprepared. They always know who they are and what they're doing. There may be areas within a scene that she's a little fuzzy about, and sometimes she gets hung up on a little thing, a trifle, but the essentials are always clear."

Barbra *did* get hung up on something, but it wasn't a trifle. It was her first nude scene. It was important to the script, and Barbra agreed to do it. But when the time came to film the scene, her feet were the coldest part of her. She didn't budge. Ross asked her what the matter was. "Herbie," she whispered. "I can't. I've got goose bumps and they'll show. Herbie, I just can't. What will my mother think?"

Buck Henry: "Ross said, 'But Barbra, it is a story about sexual passion . . .' And she said, 'Yeah, but I don't think I have that great of a body, and my mother will be unhappy . . . I don't think I'm ready for it.' Ross told her not to worry, she had a great body, and they went into a closet and she showed him why she thought she didn't have what it takes. Well, it happens that Barbra has a great figure. And he laughed and said, 'Well, you're nuts. You've got to trust me.' "

Ross finally convinced Barbra, who said, "What the hell, I'll try it once." He rolled the cameras, and Ross says, "Barbra threw off her robe and did her first nude scene. It was perfect. I yelled 'Cut and print. Beautiful!' But Barbra is the perfectionist. She wanted a retake. I think we were all shocked, because everybody burst into laughter, including Barbra. We did the retake."

"When she saw it," Henry says, "she said, 'No, I can't take my family looking at it. You have to fog the film.' And she had the right to have that done, so they fogged it."

Ironically, although Barbra's first nude scene cannot be seen on film, it turned up ten years later in the pages of *High Society,* a soft-core porno magazine, as a frame blow-up from the film. "I don't know where they got it," Buck Henry says. "They must have bribed someone in the vault to make it up from the original negative." In any event, Barbra threatened to sue the publishers, and received a court order removing the magazines from the newsstands. It was, however, still being sold in Hollywood months later.

The Owl and the Pussycat put to rest all of Streisand's fears about the public's acceptance of the "New Barbra." The film was a box office smash, and her reviews lauded her for the career move. "With *The Owl and the Pussycat,*" Jack Kroll of *Newsweek* wrote, "we can resume the inspection and the enjoyment of the real Barbra Streisand. In [her first three movies] she was forced to manipulate her personality and talent like some inspired Silly Putty in order to outface the elephantine exigencies of those big deals. But now . . . we have Streisand plain. There she comes, right where she belongs, in a real New York street . . . white boots scrambling, tote bag swinging, cussing out a departing bus in her interborough voice . . . That's the way girls used to come into our movies, and our fantasies, and it's about time we remembered that Streisand is the latest of our girls—our Normands, Lombards, Harlows, Blondells, Monroes."

Judith Crist wrote in *New York,* "Miss Streisand is as chameleonic as her face and she provides a variety of temperament and countenance that makes her role a delight—at last even for non-Barbra addicts."

Pauline Kael of *The New Yorker* said, "Streisand, self-conscious and self-mocking, is an intuitive actress who needs someone to play against . . . she and Segal have the temperamental affinity to make a romantic comedy take off. Their rapport has a beautiful, worked-out professionalism. Were Hepburn and Tracy this good together, even at their best, as in *Pat and Mike?* Maybe, but they weren't *better.*"

Buck Henry is pleased with everything about the film except the ending. "I wrote about ten endings," he says. "Herb kept saying—and rightly so—'Naw, you're forcing it, you're pushing it.' I mean, some of them were really elaborate, creepy and pushy and weird . ."

The ending is taken from the play, with some additions from Henry. "Barbra really wanted to play the dog thing at the end, where he makes her play dog, because she's an actress and it is a really playable moment for an actor to do. I was opposed to it, because I just think it makes George so unsympathetic that no one can recover from it."

Henry's contributions to the ending, in which Felix and Doris admit to themselves and each other that they've been deluding themselves, don't entirely please him, either. "I sometimes get a little embarrassed at the typewriter throwing. Even though the character George plays is half me and half the guy Alan Alda played on stage, I wouldn't throw my typewriter away . . . no one would. Of course, they'd take it and hock it at least. But the *point* is all right."

As Doris Wilgus/Wadsworth/Waverly/Washington

(*left*) Doris emotes in her first—and last—film, *Cycle Sluts*. Felix saw the film, but we never did. (*below*) "I'm a model and an actress"—and a go-go dancer.

(above) With George Segal.   *(below)* Streisand pours on the sex appeal—obviously thrilling her coworkers.

If *The Owl and the Pussycat* reflected the new frankness in movies, it was not destined to blaze a trail on television. When it was aired late in 1975, it proved to be one of the most butchered movies ever shown on TV. "I'm very fond of Ray Stark," Buck Henry says, "but he once said that he's got a great editor working on the TV version of *The Owl and the Pussycat* . . . even with network strictures, they could have done a better job. It's horrendous." Most of the spicier dialogue is missing, and in some instances so is Barbra: rather than show her suggestive "modeling outfit," the censors merely trained the camera on George Segal or fogged the film so it was barely possible to see Streisand. There were so many cuts it was very difficult for someone who had never seen the film to understand it. One viewer asked a friend after seeing it whether it was supposed to be a comedy. Despite numerous complaints, the film is repeated again and again in this sorry state.

Happily, the expanding home video market has made *The Owl and the Pussycat* available on videocassette, completely uncut.

While in New York to film *Pussycat,* Barbra took part in a benefit concert for Mayor John Lindsay. Her growing political consciousness had led to performances for Eugene McCarthy, Bella Abzug, and members of Congress opposed to the Vietnam War. Buck Henry remembers the Lindsay benefit with some disquiet. "George Segal and I played a banjo and sang a couple of songs, and Barbra was the headliner. People had told me about Barbra's reluctance to play in front of live audiences, how she was becoming more and more reclusive. I thought, like most people, 'Well, that's too bad and it's sort of selfish.'

"Then I saw why. During her performance, I watched a portion of the audience turn into dangerous animals. Kids fifteen and seventeen years old began to slaver and get bug-eyed and advance toward the stage like marauding night animals . . . Christ, I felt the terror from the stage! That's why I think Barbra puts a sort of wall between herself and the audience when she performs—to protect herself from that, and I don't blame her. At the end of the concert, they ran toward the stage, their autograph books held like weapons, and maybe even their weapons held like autograph books. Who knows, you know, who's got what? And the cops were there and the bouncers to keep them from ripping her to shreds, which I could easily see them doing."

Barbra had worked hard for three years, and decided at this point to take some time off to be with Jason and get in touch with herself. She told *Life* magazine, "I look forward to working less and simplifying my life, to fulfilling some of my potential as an individual and as a woman. My little-girl fantasy of being a recording star, a concert star, a theater star and a movie star is impossible to maintain; each of them suffers. There is so much else to learn, so much more to do . . ."

Barbra read, relaxed, mothered Jason, became involved in charitable work. She was named Honorary Chairman of the National Association for retarded children and filmed a television commercial on its behalf; she gave her time to a dozen other charities.

Although Barbra took more than a year off from movie-making, she was still recording, and her music career was going in a totally new direction, too. In 1969, her first attempt at a youth-oriented "pop" album, *What About Today?* was released. It was not successful. Streisand's choices were an awkward blend of message songs like "Ask Yourself Why," "Little Tin Soldier," and "The Morning After" with the fanciful "Punky's Dilemma," "With a Little Help from My Friends," and "Honey Pie."

What About Today? was arranged and conducted by Peter Matz, the last time they would work together for five years. "It's a hodgepodge album, a transition album," Matz says. "There had been a turnover of several producers for her, she hadn't been selling records like she used to. She had had a lot of contemporary songs brought to her by producers, but she wasn't comfortable doing them. *What About Today?* isn't a consistent album, it's just a bunch of stuff—some of it good. I love 'Punky's Dilemma,'—I think it's kind of an art song. 'Little Tin Soldier' was a Jim Webb song that never got popular, an antiwar song. Maybe it was a little premature. 'That's a Fine Kind of Freedom' I wasn't crazy about, but it was written by Harold Arlen for a civil rights fundraising thing, and she did it for him, I think.

"The breakthrough album for Barbra was *Stoney End.* Richard Perry managed to make her comfortable with this material; somehow he made it clear to her that there was nothing to be uncomfortable about."

Stoney End was indeed a watershed album for Barbra. It came about because Richard Perry, after two years as a staff producer at Warner Brothers, had gone independent and wanted to introduce Streisand to contemporary music. "She had such an older image," Perry says. "She told me she used to be asked to do benefits with Jack Benny. She was twenty-eight going on fifty-eight. Here was the greatest vocal instrument of our generation not at all relating to popular contemporary music."

When Perry got the *What About Today?* album, he thought he had "missed the boat—she's done it already. But when I listened to it I realized that, in my opinion, she really hadn't done it at all. It was merely picking up tunes by contemporary composers and singing them in the manner she had been doing."

Perry decided that he and Streisand should get together, and he spoke to CBS Records President Clive Davis. Davis told him to find some songs for Streisand and come back. "The first song I played for Clive was Nilsson's 'Maybe,' which kind of became the catalyst for the whole thing, because Clive agreed that it was a piece of Streisand material, and he moved to set up a meeting between us.

"When we met, it was obvious that she wasn't into any of the contemporary figures around.She didn't have a really good stereo in her home or anything like that; and just as a commentary on her, a mere two or three months later and I'd get calls from her late at night: 'I want the new Van Morrison, the new Joni Mitchell, Randy Newman, Marvin Gaye . . .' She had totally immersed herself in the pop culture."

Perry selected a group of songs for Barbra. "I didn't pick any song I felt was out of her realm. I knew that they were all songs that she could sing, and sing well—once she got her head into it."

Streisand, though, was uncertain. "The night before our first recording session—we were definitely going to cut an album—she called me up, freaking out. She said, 'I can't do it. This isn't me. I don't feel it.' So I tried my best to calm her down. I said, 'You've come this far, you gotta do it. Trust me that you're gonna love it . . . it's gonna blow your mind as soon as we get into it a little bit.'

"So the next day, the first song we did was 'Maybe.' Then we did Randy Newman's 'I'll Be Home,' then 'Stoney End.' All of Barbra's first takes are sheer excitement, listening to her sing the song for the first time with the whole orchestra, right? So, after she did the first take of 'Stoney End' we came in and listened to a playback. And she leaned over and whispered to me, 'You were right and I was wrong. But it's nice to be wrong.' It was certainly one of the thrills of my career."

That first recording session was the longest in the history of the Los Angeles American Federation of Musicians—it lasted from seven in the evening until five-thirty in the morning. The recording sessions on *Stoney End* were a visual mirror of the kind of middle ground Streisand was treading. "You'd have the rhythm section off on one side," says Perry, "which were musicians that she didn't normally work with at the time,

In 1969, Barbra's younger half-sister, Roslyn Kind, made her singing debut at the Persian room of New York's Plaza Hotel. Barbra and Mrs. Kind attended.

funky guys, you know, hippie types, guitar players with long hair, the hipper black musicians. Then on the other side there'd be the string and horn players, older, a little more conservative—it was really wild.

"Barbra was discovering her youth, among other things. At one point when we were rehearsing I brought Randy Newman in, and in the middle of rehearsal she suddenly realized that she was the oldest person in the room and it kind of blew her mind. That hadn't happened to her before. She was going through a metamorphosis, not just musically but in a lot of ways. And of course, now [in 1981], she's the essence of pop.

"Another interesting anecdote about the change in Barbra's life during this period is that I had made a mix of 'Stoney End,' the single, and sent it to New York, where she was living part of the time. A couple of days later I get a call from her and she says, 'There's no background vocals.' I say, 'That's impossible. They're there.' She says, 'I don't hear any.' So I say, 'Look, I'm coming to New York tomorrow. I'll come over and we'll listen.'

"So I go over to her apartment and listen. Then I say, 'Barbra, no wonder there's no background vocals—one of your speakers is out. And the background vocals are all on that speaker.' Right? So, three months later, back in L.A., she's got huge studio monitors built into the walls, complete professional tape deck, everything. When she goes, she goes all the way."

"Stoney End" was released as a single and entered the top ten nationally. "One great moment I'll never forget," Perry says, "is one night we went out to a dinner party and we were riding on Sunset Boulevard and the guy on the radio says, 'And now, the number one record in L.A. this week: "Stoney End." ' It was such a thrill for us, like a fantasy."

Until the release of the single, Barbra was still afraid to commit herself to a full album. But once the single became a hit, Columbia scrapped plans to release an album of more traditional music and rushed the *Stoney End* L.P. into release. The album rose to the Top Ten, and was reviewed very favorably. Rex Reed in *Stereo Review* wrote, "*Stoney End* is a lovely, listenable, often exciting album that does absolutely everybody justice . . . Barbra invests so much energy, discovers so many subtle and fragrant details, and displays so many lyrical attitudes in this program that almost every song sounds better than it ever has before."

Peter Matz was less impressed with the album. "They're all good songs," he says, "and it's consistent—*What About Today?* wasn't consistent. But I was bothered by the fact that many of those songs were just duplicates of other people's versions. I think she may have begun to fear she couldn't sell records anymore unless she did that, and that must have been a troubling feeling.

"I remember she called me and asked what I thought of the album. I wanted to be diplomatic, so I said, 'Well, it's #10 this week.' And she said, 'But how do you like it?' 'I'm thrilled for you, you haven't had a solid hit in a long time.' 'No, no, *how do you like it?*' Well, I *had* to answer. 'Well, Barbra, to tell you the truth, I don't care for it very much.' And she said, 'But, Peter, it's number ten this week!' "

When Matz's story is related to Richard Perry, he smiles and says, "That's Barbra!"

The success of *Stoney End* led Barbra back into the recording studio with Richard Perry. What emerged was *Barbra Joan Streisand,* an odd mix of material, some of it—like David Bowie's "Space Captain" and John Lennon's "Mother"—more real-life rock than she'd ever done before, and some of it—like "The Summer Knows" and "One Less Bell to Answer/A House Is Not a Home"—very much in the old Streisand mold. "I think it reflects the fact," Perry says, "that we were, on the one hand, experimenting further into the rock idiom, and on the other, there were still other songs Barbra liked. 'The Summer Knows' was kind of a concession I made to her—she liked it, her friends the Bergmans wrote it, it was a beautiful song. I knew it didn't work with the other material, but it was like, 'What the hell?' It was a give-and-take relationship."

This time, though, some of the "real-life" stuff came from Barbra. "I gave her the first John Lennon solo album," Perry says, "just for her listening pleasure, and maybe there'd be something she'd like to record. The next time I talk to her she says, 'Oh, by the way, there's a song on the John Lennon album I like.' And I say, 'Which one? "Love"?' 'No,' she says, 'What's that one—"Mother"?' And I said, ' "Mother!" You want to do "Mother!" ' I mean, here was the essence of the whole Lennon primal scream trip in that one song, and of all the songs for her to pick! I said, 'I can't believe that you want to do that song.' She says, 'Yeah. It has a nice melody to it.' That's so typically Barbra. You know—so unexpected that you never know what her next move is gonna be. And that's one of the many things that make her such a brilliant and creative artist."

Predictably, Barbra's version of "Mother" was ravaged by *Rolling Stone's* Stephen Holden: "An unqualified bummer . . . in which she 'belts out' the primal scream. A mechanized shriek that has all the humanity of a police siren, it makes an embarrassing mockery of a great song."

"Naturally, the purists would find it very offensive," Perry says. "They just missed the point by comparing it totally to the John Lennon record and not looking at it in another light. It was meant for a different audience. I know a lot of the most respected ears in our business who were completely blown away by that song."

Barbra Joan Streisand, like *Stoney End,* was well received, although it did not climb as high on the charts and its single, "Where You Lead," was not as big a hit as "Stoney End." But it was clear that Barbra was taking risks—and she was being admired for that. Morgan Ames wrote in *High Fidelity:* "To say that this is a 'new Streisand' implies that she has shed an old self. Yes and no—mostly no. What this album displays is an alive and growing Streisand. Because of that, she will appeal most to the young and to those with open and still-growing minds. Naturally, that means you."

After recording *Stoney End,* and with the single beginning to get good airplay, Barbra returned to Las Vegas. She completed her Riviera obligation with a two-week stint, then went directly to the Hilton for three weeks there.

This time, Barbra's reviews were wonderful: she was relaxed, down-to-earth, warm and friendly. There was none of the pretense and aloof sophistication of her previous appearance. Dressed in a pantsuit, she bantered with the audience: "Won't somebody please tell me the time? Have you noticed there are no clocks here? I go up to my room and the television set is broken, and the Bible has only five commandments. They're trying to tell us something!"

Streisand did many of her old favorites, but she included the new material she and Richard Perry had been working on: "No Easy Way Down," "I Don't Know Where I Stand" and "Stoney End," plus a rousing number she's never recorded—the gospel "Oh, Happy Day." The reviews were ecstatic: "It's possible to get so spellbound watching and listening to Barbra Streisand that at the end of one of 15 songs, one almost forgets to applaud," wrote the *Hollywood Reporter* critic. "Marvelously simple, uncluttered and unfettered by gimmicks, Miss Streisand is more than simply marvelous . . . she's uniquely brilliant, a natural comedienne and more than deserving of the adoration and ovations she received from the audience. She's a very hip performer and makes her material and bits charming and entertaining."

Barbra's last Las Vegas appearance to date was at the Hilton from December 24, 1971, to January 13, 1972. Here again, the show was wonderful and the reviews glowing. Bob Schulenberg, who had seen Barbra only intermittently since 1963, flew to

At the Las Vegas Hilton in 1972—and backstage with boxing champ George Foreman

Vegas with artist Richard Amsel (who did the ad campaigns for *Hello, Dolly!* and *Up the Sandbox*) to see Barbra perform. They stood and watched. "She was giving a dazzling show and everybody was on their feet cheering," Schulenberg says. "It was terrific, but I said, 'It's a brilliant show for anybody—Peggy Lee, anybody—but it's not a good show for Barbra.' I mean, she was giving them the best show they'd ever seen, but it wasn't the best she could do."

After the show, Schulenberg and Amsel left Barbra a note to tell her they were there. When they returned to their room, there was a message from Barbra that she had arranged for them to have good seats at the next night's show. "When she came out that next night," Schulenberg says, "I could tell she was looking for us—she kept peering into the audience, trying to make eye contact. Finally, she said something funny and I laughed—I have a big laugh—and she said, 'Oh, I hear my friend.' And she starts saying, 'Bobby?' and shielding her eyes so she can see beyond the lights and she spots me and starts going, 'That's my friend—ten years, eleven years friends. He used to do my eyes.' And I'm thinking, Oh, God, how embarrassing!

"But then she started the show, started to sing, and she was playing to us—after a song, she'd look to see our reaction. And she was terrific, so much better than the night before. And when we'd make eye contact, I'd indicate to her as best I could how good I thought she was. I was really touched, because even after all those years she seemed to really care what I thought of her performance."

A later comment of Barbra's, made to a British radio interviewer, relates to Schulenberg's remarks about the relative quality of Barbra's performances. "One night," she said, "I was at the National Theatre watching Olivier in *Othello*. And although perhaps some people—even myself—would quibble about certain interpretations, I felt he was absolutely brilliant. It was a staggering performance. I stood up to cheer and this boy on my right was booing him. *Booing* him. I got so incensed I went over to this kid and said, 'How *dare* you boo him!' And the kid said, 'He was off tonight.' I can understand his feelings as a possessive fan who knew Larry Olivier and his performance inside out. But what about the rest of us who were just blown out of our chairs by his brilliance?"

While Barbra was taking a rest from movies, Elliott Gould was becoming the hottest star in America. His films *Bob & Carol & Ted & Alice* and *M*A*S*H* had been huge successes, and he followed those up within a year with three others. *Time* magazine suggested that Elliott would become, and remain, a bigger star than his estranged wife. "I think our getting a divorce freed him," Barbra has said. "Freed his creativity, too. It also made him much more ambitious, which I felt was a good thing for him. It was fabulous, there he was on the cover of *Time* magazine. He became the antihero. I was very proud of him. I wanted it very much for him and for my son."

On July 9, 1971, this chapter in the life of Barbra Streisand came to an end: she and Elliott were granted a divorce in the Dominican Republic. It was no more than a formality; by this time Gould was involved with nineteen-year-old Jenny Bogart, who was five months pregnant with their first child. Gould and Bogart had no intention of making it legal: "She'll have my children," Gould said, "but she won't get married. She thinks it's more romantic this way."

Later, Gould and Bogart would marry, divorce, and remarry. He and Barbra remain good friends to this day, primarily through Jason. In 1972, Barbra told an interviewer, "Once you have loved someone, they become part of what you were and therefore part of what you *are*." Elliott responded to the comment in an interview of his own: "I recently read something Barbra said that pleased me very much. She said we would always be part of each other. She really is a remarkable person."

California Girl

While Elliott Gould was setting up housekeeping with Jenny Bogart, Barbra was in the midst of her own romantic involvement. For months, she and blond sex symbol Ryan O'Neal had been discreetly dating. O'Neal's healthy, earthy California surfer image was as right for Barbra in 1972 as Omar Sharif's smoldering sophistication had been in 1967. Ryan, famous for his role in the 1970 hit *Love Story,* was a perfect companion for the freer, fitter, tanned, long-maned Barbra. Their efforts to keep their dates secret failed when Ryan's younger brother Kevin came to blows with a Hollywood photographer in an attempt to prevent pictures from being taken of the couple outside a rock concert. The incident made all the tabloids and the story of Barbra and Ryan was out. Before long, newspapers were running photos of the couple at parties and premieres with headlines like, "A New Love Story?"

Barbra and Ryan wanted to work together, and the movie they eventually made began as an Elliott Gould film entitled *A Glimpse of Tiger.* That production was troubled. Gould fired the director one day; the next day Gould's partner rehired him; Elliott flew into a rage. It became clear to Warner Brothers that things on this film were not going to work out, and they halted production.

A few months later, *Variety* reported that Streisand had been signed to appear in *Tiger.* Ryan would costar, and Peter Bogdanovich, whose *The Last Picture Show* Barbra admired, was set to direct. Bogdanovich, however, wasn't impressed with *A Glimpse of Tiger:* "It was kind of a comedy-drama with a lot of social overtones, and I didn't like it at all." But he wanted to work with Barbra, and had an idea for a 1930s-style screwball comedy. He asked Robert Newman and David Benton *(Bonnie and Clyde)* to work up a screenplay.

Bogdanovich wasn't pleased with the script they submitted, and he called in Buck Henry. "The script was not very good," Henry says, "and there was just six weeks until they were supposed to begin filming. I thought, 'God, I can't do this in six weeks.' But Barbra was gonna walk off and so was Ryan—obviously, if one went the other would go too, and they were right. The script was in no condition to shoot. Peter asked me, 'Can you do something about Barbra's part?'

"I wrote steadily for six weeks, and I couldn't rewrite Barbra without rewriting Ryan. That's partially because I didn't want anything to be left of what was there before, because everyone wants to obliterate what's gone before him. But what happened was that in changing Barbra I changed so much of Ryan that I caught her up a little short. And when Barbra saw the script—like most actors—she counted the pages. And there's a long period in there where she doesn't say anything. Very long—the whole chase scene and the court scene, and all that stuff between Ryan and Madeline Kahn. And she—understandably, as a movie star—thought, 'Where am I? How did I get lost?'"

Barbra didn't feel much better after a read-through of the script with the other players—funny, eccentric character actors like Madeline Kahn, Kenneth Mars, Austin Pendleton, Mabel Albertson, and Liam Dunn. "Those guys were really hot," Henry says. "Character actors tend to be hot at read-throughs because they're carving out their territory. Barbra and Ryan were already nervous, and I think Barbra got really twitchy about it because all those other people were going to be very good."

Bogdanovich asked Barbra to trust him, and convinced her that she wouldn't get lost in the crowd. The script was, at its core, about Judy Maxwell, a zany, aggressive young woman who has been kicked out of dozens of colleges and universities because she tends to wreak havoc on anything she goes near. In San Francisco, she sets her sights on Howard Bannister, a prim, henpecked musicologist, and barrels her way into his life, at one point posing as his fiancée at a banquet. This basic premise is complicated thoroughly by four identical plaid suitcases, one containing Howard's rocks (he hopes to prove a musical theory using igneous formations), another carrying Judy's undies, one with stolen top-secret government documents, and the last with expensive jewels. The confusion and slapstick as various seedy characters try to steal and resteal the suitcases is sublime, and culminates in a lengthy, wild chase through the streets of San Francisco.

Ray Gosnell worked as assistant director again on this film. He echoes Bogdanovich's feelings about the importance of Barbra's role when he says, "It's an ensemble picture to a point, but Barbra was the sparkplug. Without Barbra, it would have been another type of picture. Barbra transcends the screen. Madeline Kahn can be very funny, but she doesn't come across on the screen the way Barbra does. The association between Barbra and Ryan was very important. If that didn't go right, the picture would make no sense. It was a fine line to work, because it wasn't just a comedy."

Filming began in late summer of 1971 in San Francisco. The first scene filmed was the last scene in the picture. "We had no choice," says Gosnell. "The actors didn't even know each other, and no one knew what their parts really were because they hadn't been in their parts yet. It's murder to do things out of sequence like that."

Barbra, Ryan, and Peter Bogdanovich got along very well. Both stars trusted Bogdanovich completely. "Peter spent more time with Barbra than with Ryan," Gosnell says, "because Ryan is more supple for a director to work with than is Barbra. He had to spend more time with Barbra explaining *why* these things had to be done. Barbra is stronger-willed as an artist than Ryan is."

Buck Henry: "Ryan was trying to do things he had never been called on to do. He was very un-self-serving as an actor. He let Peter place him, his body and his voice. He was playing Peter. And that's hard for an actor to do. Ryan isn't a comedian."

Several recurring Streisand problems arose during *What's Up, Doc?*—her lateness and her alienation from most of the crew. The latter wasn't helped by Warner Brothers, who supplied Barbra with an enormous trailer with velvet and crystal, resembling more a nineteenth-century railroad car than a place to relax between scenes. "Isn't it awful?" Barbra asked a reporter on the set. "I didn't ask for it and it makes me feel uncomfortable. It's not good for morale on the set." Ryan chimed in: "What's she gonna do in a situation like this? If she requests another trailer, the studio knocks her for being hard to please. If she keeps it, everyone here thinks she's strutting. She can't win."

Gosnell, for his part, had just about given up trying to get her to the set on time. But on one occasion, he told her she simply had to be ready to film at 8 A.M. because if they didn't get the shot by 11 A.M. they wouldn't be able to get it at all—the company could use the location only till 11 in the morning. "Barbra was there on time," Gosnell says, "but, wouldn't you know it, something went wrong and we couldn't get the shot. Barbra came over to me and said, 'I'm here. *You're* not ready.'"

Barbra may have regretted the fact that Gosnell *was* ready when the time came to film the lengthy chase which constitutes the better part of the film's last half. "The chase was totally written," Buck Henry says, "and Peter shot everything I wrote and I never expected anyone in the world to. I just sat down and wrote everything I'd seen or imagined. Some of it I just put in to amuse myself—like a guy runs around the corner and garbage cans chase him around the corner, down the street. I couldn't imagine how you'd do it, so I was amazed when I saw it and it worked. It cost a million dollars to shoot that sequence. That's five million today . . ."

With Ryan O'Neal

144

(*above left*) The final moments of the film. They were the first scenes shot.

The mood was light on the *What's Up Doc?* set.

Doubles were used for Barbra and Ryan for most of the chase. "The first double for Barbra broke her ankle," Gosnell says, "so we had to use a man as a double for Barbra in the scene where she and Ryan ride the cart down those steep streets. Fortunately he didn't have to walk, because that would have been a dead giveaway. But for the close-ups, we had to have the cart moving at the same speed as the long shots, and Barbra had to do those—she wasn't happy about it. It was a little cart going down a steep hill, and it was stressful for her, and a bit frightening. Ryan's 'Mr. Macho,' he probably didn't even think about it—and if he did, he wouldn't have mentioned it."

What's Up, Doc? was the Easter 1972 attraction at New York's Radio City Music Hall. It was an instantaneous smash, brought in more money than *Funny Girl,* and propelled Barbra to her first designation as *Box Office* magazine's "Box Office Champ of the Year." The reviews were mixed; some critics disliked Barbra's soft-sell in the film, preferring her at high-voltage intensity, but Vincent Canby wrote, "Not the least of Bogdanovich's triumphs is his success in scaling down Miss Streisand's superstar personality to fit the dimensions of farce. Although she never lets us forget the power that always seems to be held in uncertain check, she is surprisingly appealing, more truly comic than she's ever been before." Rex Reed commented, "When *What's Up, Doc?* is good, it is very fine indeed. Streisand is a nimble comedienne who is especially winning when she lounges atop a piano mimicking Humphrey Bogart and singing 'As Time Goes By' from *Casablanca* . . . the supporting cast is like a perfectly matched set of colored croquet balls bouncing off the stars in brilliantly diagrammed cameos . . ."

Streisand is so loose in *What's Up, Doc?,* she appears so slim, tan and lovely, and her rapport with Ryan O'Neal is so warm, that it comes as a surprise to learn that she was not happy with the film. "I didn't enjoy making it," she said afterward. "I thought it was a silly piece of material. I thought I would be dealing in something very personal and important at first, and what was it finally—a puff of smoke, a piece of fluff. There's room for both things, you know, but I didn't feel I was growing as an artist. It was a technical error on my part. I saw *The Last Picture Show* and I gave Peter Bogdanovich script approval. I made a mistake. The script wasn't ready until the day before we started shooting. I hadn't worked for nineteen months before that and then I had to try not to show my real feelings, my hostility, while we were shooting. The picture was trying to be 1940s. It's not. I just felt it wasn't good enough."

Ryan O'Neal has said, "Barbra was warning me all the time through *What's Up, Doc?* that, 'This is not funny, Ryan. I'm telling you this movie isn't funny.' She said, 'I know what's funny. Did you see *Funny Girl?* Wasn't that funny?' And I said, 'Yeah, it was funny.' And she said, 'Well, then I know what's funny. What we're doing here is not funny. *He* thinks it's funny, but it's not funny.' And I said, 'Oh—I hope it's funny."

Despite Barbra's reservations, the film was her biggest hit until *A Star Is Born* four years later. By the time filming ended, Barbra and Ryan were no longer dating, and Barbra and Peter Bogdanovich were. Barbra went through a series of romantic "flings" as she called them, including Warren Beatty, Kris Kristofferson, and several noncelebrities.

It was about this time that a rumor began circulating that Barbra had appeared in a pornographic film early in her career. It was being shown in cheap New York movie arcades for twenty-five cents every couple of minutes of film, and was offered for sale for home viewing. "I was gonna buy it for her," Buck Henry says, "and send it to her as a kind of perverted Christmas present. But I thought, 'No, no no. This is not something Barbra will laugh at.' You can tell it's not her, though. I put a couple of quarters in the machine and took a look at it and it's just a very vague look-alike."

Barbra told *Playboy* in 1977: "When I first heard the rumor, I thought it was a put-on. But these people you never can seem to find were selling a film and claiming it was me. I couldn't resist the temptation to see what the actress looked like—and also to check out her performance—so we got a copy. The film, naturally, is very blurred. The girl has long hair, like I did back in the sixties, although she was chubby, while I was very skinny. But the dead giveaway came when the camera zoomed in on her hands around the guy's you-know-what. There they were: short, stubby fingers! Definitely not mine. So all you would-be buyers, don't waste your money. Actually, the idea of me in a pornographic film is *preposterous!*"

Shortly after the opening of *What's Up, Doc?,* Barbra received one of the highest honors of her life: she was included on President Richard Nixon's infamous "enemies list." It wasn't that Nixon hadn't enjoyed her latest film, but she had done something that was clearly a threat to the security of the United States: she had publicly proclaimed her support for the presidential campaign of Nixon's opponent, George McGovern.

On April 15, 1972, Streisand took part in a McGovern benefit concert at Los Angeles' Forum. Eighteen thousand people came to hear Barbra, Carole King, and James Taylor. Seat prices ranged from $5.50 to $100, and ushers included Warren Beatty, Jack Nicholson, Julie Christie, Goldie Hawn, Gene Hackman, and Jon Voight.

Barbra was extremely nervous about the performance. "I was afraid that everyone would be coming to hear Carole King and James Taylor. I figured they'd walk out when I came on." Of course, no one did—Barbra was the star of the evening, and the audience was ecstatic over her combination of her standards ("Don't Rain on My Parade," "Happy Days Are Here Again") and her new music ("Sing/Make Your Own Kind of Music," "Sweet Inspiration/Where You Lead").

Originally, Barbra did not want to sing "Stoney End," although it had been her biggest hit in years. "The day of the concert," Richard Perry, who produced the album of the event, recalls, "I was going over her set with her, and 'Stoney End' was not on the agenda. I said, 'How could you not do "Stoney End"? This is a young, contemporary crowd.' She says, 'Oh, it's been two years since we did it. I don't remember the words.' 'Barbra, please. I beg of you. This crowd is going to want to hear it. I'll write the words on the floor of the stage for you.' So I'm on my hands and knees, right? And that song had a lot of verses to it."

Despite Perry's service (above and beyond . . .) Barbra still wasn't convinced she should do "Stoney End." She asked the audience if they preferred it or "Second Hand Rose." Expectedly, the response was for "Stoney End." Barbra sang it flawlessly.

During the concert, Barbra expressed another side of her new contemporary self. While discussing the various ways people conquer their fears, and saying that she hated the taste of liquor, she lit up a joint. As the crowd cheered, she said, "It's still illegal? Oh . . ." and continued to drag on the cigarette. "I think we should face our problems head on." After a few more tokes, Barbra interrupted her monologue. "What was that chord you just played?" (Nothing had been played.) "What *was* that, an F-minor seventh with a demented pinky on the fifth? It was really . . . *high.*"

"She came up with that on her own," Perry says. "It was a great bit. I don't know if you want to put this in the book, but that was one of the things of us working together. It was like the first time she seriously dabbled with getting high. I tried to incorporate it as part of the working process. I thought it would relax her in certain situations."

The recording of the Forum concert was another success for Streisand; a single of her "Sweet Inspiration/Where You Lead" cut was a moderate hit and won her a Grammy nomination for "Best Female Pop Vocal Performance."

The McGovern concert raised $300,000, but after the expenses of producing the show, McGovern's campaign was given just $18,000. This concert was the last live appearance Barbra would make on stage until March 1975.

"Just A Human Being"

After playing her first nonsinging role and making her first picture as part of an ensemble, Barbra's desire to experiment continued. "The characters I've played in the past," she said, "have been full of eccentricities, of idiosyncrasies. I wanted to play a part where I did nothing, where I was just a human being."

Fortuitously, producers Irwin Winkler and Robert Chartoff had bought screen rights to the Anne Richardson Roiphe novel *Up the Sandbox,* the story of down-to-earth Manhattan housewife Margaret Reynolds, for whom taking care of her husband and two children is no longer enough. Rather than leave the people she loves, she fantasizes herself in exotic adventures: challenging Fidel Castro at a press conference, working with Black revolutionaries to blow up the Statue of Liberty, telling her mother what she really thinks of her by pushing her face into her anniversary cake, traveling to Africa to learn the Somburu tribe's method of painless childbirth, and being saved from an abortion by her frantic husband.

Margaret's fantasies make her everyday life ever more unsatisfying, and she is ambivalent about the news that she's pregnant again. But the film ends with Margaret deciding against an abortion, telling her husband she's pregnant and simply taking a day off from her homemaking responsibilities.

The material was perfect for Barbra at the time: Margaret Reynolds was nothing if not "just a human being," the book dealt more or less with feminist issues, which Barbra was developing an interest in, and Margaret's fantasies intrigued her: "Fantasies can make a rich inner life," she said. "They can lead you places. If I never had a fantasy about being an actress, perhaps I wouldn't have become one."

Barbra decided that this would be her first film produced by First Artists, a company she formed in 1969 with Paul Newman and Sidney Poitier (they were later joined by Steve McQueen and Dustin Hoffman). She chose director Irvin Kershner, now famous for *The Empire Strikes Back,* because she admired his 1970 film *Loving.* They had met in 1968, in what Kershner calls "a peculiar way: I saw the movie *Funny Girl* and was so impressed, I sent her a letter and said, 'I think you're the hottest thing on the screen and I congratulate you on your performance.' I got a note back—'Why don't you come over to the house and have tea?' I did just that, and we had tea and talked. After that, we would go out to dinner sometimes, and when she had a party, she'd invite me, and we got fairly close gradually."

Still, when Kershner was asked to direct Streisand, he was wary. "I was apprehensive about *working* with her because I had heard all these negative things—how difficult she was for directors and the other actors and everyone. And once we started working, I realized that none of this was true. In fact, it was the opposite. She was absolutely cooperative. She questioned things, as every creative actor or actress should, which meant that it was up to the director to explain as much as possible what he wanted out of the character.

"She was absolutely easy—it was a shock. Each day was a pleasant surprise. She just did what had to be done and didn't stint on it—including things she didn't want to do, like flying in light planes and jumping out of windows and falling on mattresses, which she *hated* doing. I mean, she did everything—she rehearsed and knew her lines and she cared and she made the crew feel at ease, and the crew loved her."

The Reynolds clan—Barbra with David Selby, Ariane Heller, and Terry/Garry Smith

Kershner wanted to give Streisand a softer, gentler look to go along with her subdued personality in this film. "I wanted to make her look as beautiful as she was in my eyes, because I had this image of her on screen that I had never seen before. So I did lots of tests with Gordon Willis, the cinematographer, and we tried different lighting, different angles, we shot stills and studied them. Gradually we developed a way of shooting her that we thought would make her look absolutely wonderful."

Kershner and Willis decided on Streisand's best angles, used half-lighting and shadows, softened her hair with backlighting. "We wanted to keep her vulnerable," Kershner says, "because we felt that would give her a certain beauty. I think she's vulnerable and lovely in the whole picture."

Kershner wanted the rest of the cast to be unknowns, so that the problems of reducing Barbra's superstar personality wouldn't be compounded. He and Barbra chose David Selby, a young soap opera actor who had given an acclaimed performance in the off-Broadway play *Sticks and Bones,* to make his movie debut as Margaret's husband. "I didn't want a big, beautiful, handsome man who'd make you say, 'Oh, man, he's great, what is her problem?'" says Kershner. "I wanted just a guy who looks like he works, loves his family, loves her, and looks like the guy next door. He's nothing special. Love is not about special people, it's about ordinary people who feel special because they're in love."

Once filming began, Kershner saw that Selby was in awe of Streisand. "You can't blame him. To suddenly play opposite Barbra Streisand and be new to the screen is pretty overwhelming. It affected his work, in fact; in places he had to try very hard to just be there on the screen with her. It was tough on him."

Streisand and Selby got along well, Kershner recalls. "She got along with everyone. I'm telling you, there were no problems there. The only problem I had was in rehearsals. I was pushing a little too hard too fast, I guess, and Barbra sort of blew up and went off and said, 'I'm not going to do the film' and went home. The next day she was back and we continued. And that was it for the entire film. We never really had an argument. That doesn't mean we didn't have *conflict*—but it wasn't personal conflict. We had some artistic differences—it's hard to remember what they were now. But Barbra stands up for her rights, and I do mine, so we had to have conflict—but that's healthy, if it's not personal."

The similarities between Barbra's vision of what the film should be and Kershner's went a long way toward this harmony. She did not see the film as a "women's lib" picture. "I feel for Margaret," she said at the time. "Part of me wants to be a housewife—a mother and a wife, rather—and I feel for women who have this kind of predicament. I want to have them heard. There is something in between radicals and the women who go around proselytizing for women staying at home . . . we're against polarization. We're saying a woman should feel it's right to stay wherever she can be fulfilled."

Kershner was even more anxious, in fact, to steer the film against the revolutionary tide. "When I read the book, I thought, How nice, a woman who decides to have a third child. Why not? She's a good woman, she has good genes, her husband has good genes, they're in love. Why let those who may not be the best stock in the world, often, have all the children they want? All the people who are caring people, warm people, devoted people, intelligent people, who can do something for the children, they're the ones who cut themselves down. So we took an unpopular position at the time."

Kershner didn't have the anticipated problems with Streisand, but he did have problems with the script and storyline. He had, in fact, been reluctant to take on the project from the start.

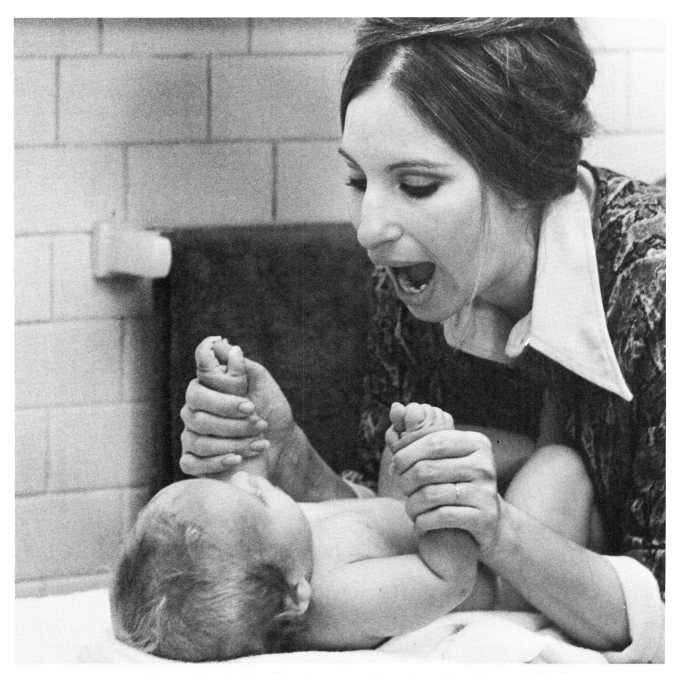

With Terry or Garry Smith. (The twins were used interchangeably as Margaret's baby.)

"I liked it as a book, but it wasn't the kind of material I would choose for a film. The book doesn't lend itself to dramatic treatment because of the arbitrary nature of the fantasies. But I took it on because Barbra wanted so badly to do it, and I wanted to work with Barbra, and I thought we could work through the problems in the story. The story did appeal to me; you certainly want to use that which is going on in society which reveals something about the human heart or the human condition. I thought this was something that could do that."

Paul Zindel, who won a Pulitzer Prize for his play *The Effect of Gamma Rays on Man-in-the-Moon Marigolds,* was hired to turn *Up the Sandbox* from a book into a movie. Kershner did not feel, when the time came to begin filming, that the script was ready. "There were problems," he says. "The fantasies were unclear; there wasn't enough drama in the main story. All the drama was in the fantasies, which didn't work because you knew it wasn't really happening. I was quite unhappy going with it. But I had been warned not to tell Barbra that I was unhappy with the story because she would just walk off the picture. I followed the advice that her agents gave me—'Don't ever let her know that you have any doubts about anything, or you'll be off the picture, or the picture will be canceled, she'll walk off.' And so I said, 'All right, I'll have to work this out.'

"Now, once we were working and we got to know each other in a professional capacity, I revealed to her one day that the reason we were struggling every day and every night was because we never made the story work as well as it should. She said, 'Did you know this before we started?' I said, 'Of course I did.' 'Well, then, why did you start?' 'Because I was being pushed, and I was told that if I didn't start, and made you aware of my doubts about the material, I'd lose you.' She said, 'That's ridiculous. We just would have kept on working until we got it right—that's what our lives are about.'

"And that's really true, you see. Nobody read her correctly—everybody was afraid of her, intimidated by her. Well, I was very sad when I heard that because I realized that I had been bamboozled and I had weakened. I thought I was being strong by starting, but I was really weak to start. I should have called her and said, 'Barb, you're running this show as far as I'm concerned, because they don't need me, they don't need the producers, they need you—without you, they don't have a picture. Now, here are the facts'—I could have done that, but I didn't. Gross error."

Despite the script problems, Kershner was confident the film would work because of Barbra's contributions. "She brought so much to the film and to the character of Margaret. First of all, to take someone who's bigger than life like Barbra, and to pull her down, reduce her to ordinariness, automatically gives you an edge. It gives you a dimension that you don't have with just an actress.

"And if there was any chance for humor, Barbra went right to the heart of it— she got it. And when she had to be bitchy, she could be *very* bitchy. When she had to be playful, she could be wonderfully playful. In other words, she understood the emotion we were trying for each time, and gave us that. I thought her contribution was enormous—in fact, the picture was her—the way she treated the children, the way she treated her husband, her mother, the terrorists in the fantasy. The picture would have been a totally different picture with another actress. But she was so powerful she took over every scene, and of course I wanted that, because it was her story."

Kershner very much admired Barbra's acting technique. "She's a thinker, and I think the key to really fine acting is to be in control and make it look like it's just happening. To me, the best acting is not improvisational, where you let it happen and hope it works. It's easier to improvise than to think through a performance and follow a line that is very precise. When you follow a line, you have to know what you did

In Africa, Barbra posed for Steve Schapiro in native costumes.

Barbra was fascinated by the natives, and they quickly adopted American customs.

before, what you're doing now, what you're building towards. You have to have a trajectory for your performance, and Barbra can do that work—she keeps it in mind very well."

Still, there were aspects of the performance and the film that were spontaneous. "Barbra didn't have much input into the script," Kershner says, "but she did have in individual scenes. I encourage ideas—can we make this better, can we make this more intense, more emotional—this is where she had lots of suggestions. Her instincts in drama are fabulous. She has a great sense of truth. Even when she's funny, she's very real with her humor. It's not one-liners, it's not gags. It's the character saying what has to be said, which is what makes it funny—but not trying to *be* funny."

The anniversary party for Margaret's parents, probably the film's best scene, was the first time an incident from Barbra's own life ever sparked an idea for a film sequence. She had just been to her own family reunion, and it had not been a comfortable experience—the family members did not feel particularly close to one another. Her brother Sheldon, who takes pictures of everything, was too busy snapping away to be a part of the experience. "You know, you're not here," Barbra said to him. "You'll be here when you develop those pictures." She told Paul Zindel and Kershner about that day, and it was written into the film.

The cinematic version appears as a 16-mm film within a film. "The actors had to look into the cameras like nonactors would," Kershner relates. "Barbra was the only one who wasn't afraid to look smack into the lens. I thought that scene really worked well."

After filming in California and New York, Kershner decided to go on location for the African fantasy. "We could have done it in Hollywood, but it didn't cost that much more to go over there, and I thought we'd get something authentic—you get a feel of the clouds and the sky, and it was a real village. When I first went over there, they had sent art directors ahead and they built me a village. I hated it! It looked just like a Hollywood village—like Tarzan. So I had them tear it all down and we found a real one."

The village Kershner found housed the Somburu tribe, and there was some difficulty at first. "We were suspicious of them," Barbra says, "and they were suspicious of us." But Kershner had brought along interpreters who convinced the tribespeople to let the company film there. "We made it like a game for them," Kershner says. "They made some money, naturally, and we built them a schoolhouse."

Barbra was fascinated by the native people, took pictures of them and with them, exchanged clothing and makeup ideas with the women, and learned as much as she could about their culture. "These women are not permitted to experience pleasure, nor are they permitted to show pain," Barbra related with amazement. "They can't even scream when they have a baby. They seem happy, but wow! Who am I to say anything, to preach?" For Barbra, the African trip was a revelation. "It teaches you the absolute lunacy of possessions." But the natives fast absorbed Western culture. Wealthier than before the Americans arrived, they were also more interested in convenience. As Barbra explained it, "It's funny . . . these people are used to walking five miles a day. But only yesterday, after three days with us, they asked for a bus to take them back to their villages."

After completing filming in Africa, Kershner and Barbra made a trip to Israel. "Neither of us had ever been," Kershner says, "so we went to Jerusalem and Tel Aviv. That's when Barbra got really sick, sick as a dog—some kind of stomach problem. You can't go to the equator and not come back with *something*."

Once back in the states, Kershner began editing his film. When he showed his final cut to the producers and studio executives, he was told to shorten it and revise the ending. "I had originally shot the ending so that it was a fantasy within a fantasy within a fantasy. It was three fantasies removed from reality, so you didn't know where you were anymore. Everyone got scared and at the last minute it was redone so it was clearer. But I wanted the ending to be totally ambivalent, totally unreal, because we're talking about the interior life of a woman, not the exterior. The exterior is just to have something to photograph."

Kershner cut twenty minutes from the film and reshot the ending, and everyone then felt confident the film would be a hit. "I remember sitting with the agents and producers and we all thought, Well, this is sixty million dollars! At that time that was a lot of money. We were all very surprised when the audience was mostly indifferent."

The film opened at Christmas 1972, and despite some excellent New York reviews, fared very poorly at the box office, taking in just $4 million, a very small amount for a Barbra Streisand picture. One of the reasons may have been that although it was a thoughtful film with a sensitive Streisand characterization, it was advertised as a zany comedy, and since it followed *What's Up, Doc?,* audiences expecting another screwball comedy left disappointed, and word-of-mouth was bad.

The material, too, Kershner feels, worked against the film. "The story was never solved. It didn't have that strong line that a story needs. The fantasies themselves destroyed the line. You know in a fantasy that there is no danger because it really isn't happening to the character. Instead of creating more tension, the fantasies released the tension, and yet all the *action* is within the fantasies. It taught me a lesson, all right."

Kershner feels as well that the film may have been too sophisticated for many of today's audiences. Many viewers complained that it was difficult to tell when the action was indeed a fantasy. "The fantasies were easy to spot," Kershner says, "because of the way people acted. It was all cliché—is this how people who are going to blow up the Statue of Liberty act? Of course not. But I guess it was too subtle for the audience. You see, they take seriously the cliché—that's what television has done for everybody. Therefore, to use the cliché for humor doesn't work—it's taken literally."

Kershner blames himself for the film's failure. "I should have spoken up at the beginning and expressed my doubts about the story. You don't start a picture without as perfect a script as you can develop."

Despite the financial failure of *Up the Sandbox,* it is well regarded by Streisand fans because of her performance and its highly unusual—for a Streisand film—look and feel. "The film does have an underground following," Kershner says. "That isn't going to put any money in my pocket, but it's nice to know. I love the film. I think it's so unusual for her, I think she's wonderful in it, she shows the full range of what she can do. I think it's an intriguing American film—no one's made a film like it, especially with a superstar. I'm very glad I made it, even though as a result I didn't work for two-and-a-half to three years. Hollywood thought, He must be crazy, he doesn't know how to make a film, he didn't solve the story, he makes a Streisand film that's unsuccessful—how can you do that? So I ended up taking the rap. Barbra didn't know that; she went on to another film that made a lot of money, and another after that. I just couldn't get another assignment for the longest time. I never told Barbra, but I went broke on account of that film."

Kershner smiles and sits back. "But I don't regret doing it. If I hadn't done it, I would have missed the experience. And it was a wonderful experience. I would love to work with Barbra again. She's my favorite actress, and I've had some good ones. But she's a joy."

Katie and Hubbell

Barbra was extremely disappointed in the commercial failure of *Up the Sandbox*. She had agreed to a rare publicity tour to promote the film, explaining, "I care about *Sandbox*. I think it is a provocative film and I want to help it." When the box-office receipts dwindled after the first few weeks, Barbra feared that the cause was an unwillingness on the part of the public to accept her in a character part. Would she have to play glamorous, larger-than-life characters for the rest of her career in order to remain successful? The possibility disturbed her, especially since she was about to begin another movie in which she would have to create a genuine character.

The release of *The Way We Were*, less than a year after *Up the Sandbox*, put Barbra's fears to rest. It was an immediate smash hit, Streisand's biggest money-maker to that date, and proved to her that she could submerge her superstar personality for the realities of a role without losing her public.

She played Katie Morosky, an intense, activist, politically passionate Jewish coed of the 1930s who both abhors and desires the campus golden boy, WASPy Hubbell Gardiner, whose interest in politics is limited to fraternity elections. She is contemptuous of his "America the beautiful" friends, played by Bradford Dillman, Suzie Blakeley, and Lois Chiles, but longs for his attentions. Her interest in him is heightened when she learns he is a talented writer, and he is intrigued by her ardent convictions and individuality.

Later, during World War II, they meet again and begin a romance. After a brief idyll, her politics cause strife with Hubbell's friends, many left over from college, and he tells her the relationship cannot work. She pleads with him not to leave her, telling him that no one will ever love him as much. He realizes this is true, that Katie's feelings for him and interest in his writing are not the superficial kind he has known with other women. They marry and move to California, where Hubbell, against Katie's advice, plans to turn a novel of his into a movie.

The marriage disintegrates in Hollywood, where Hubbell is forced to prostitute his work and the blacklisting of the 1950s threatens to destroy his career because of Katie's previous Communist sympathies. These pressures force him back into the arms of Carol Ann (Lois Chiles); when Katie finds this out she realizes the marriage is irreparable and agrees to a divorce after the birth of their child.

The final scene of *The Way We Were* is played in New York City, where Katie and Hubbell run into each other again after years of separation. There is great tenderness in their embrace, a knowledge that they both still love each other but could never succeed as a couple.

The success of *The Way We Were* took everyone involved in it by surprise. The upper echelon at Columbia Pictures, in fact, was convinced it had financed a disaster. The film's director, Sydney Pollack, thinks it ironic that the film was such a hit because "it was the straw that broke the back of management at that time. The president of the studio, Stanley Schneider, hadn't had a hit in a long time, and the Board of Directors forced him to resign because everybody at Columbia felt we were making a disaster, we were having so much trouble."

The film was plagued with difficulties from the outset. It was obviously a star

With Robert Redford

160

vehicle, revolving as it does around Katie and Hubbell. It had one star from the beginning—Barbra Streisand. Arthur Laurents wrote the screenplay as a vehicle for Streisand, using a girl he knew in college and another woman he knew in Hollywood as prototypes for Katie. "These girls were not like Barbra," Laurents says. "Although Barbra's slightly involved politically, she's unsophisticated politically. The connecting tissue between those women and Barbra is her passion and her sense of injustice."

But Laurents recalls that Barbra felt that much of the Katie Morosky character was modeled after her. "We were talking about the script, and Barbra mentioned a certain part and said, 'How did you know that?' It was the fact that Katie never used four-letter words, which Barbra never did. There's something rather prudish about her, even now, underneath all that. When Katie goes to Hollywood, she is using four-letter words and everyone is swinging around, and Barbra thought I got it from her. It's simply something that happens to everyone who goes out there, especially if you become a star."

Streisand clearly saw other similarities between herself and Katie; in the film she begins as a skinny, unfashionable, unpopular girl with convictions that make her more substantial than the prettier people around her. Later, she evolves into a striking, well-turned-out woman who has lost none of the passion which Hubbell Gardiner found so attractive even in college. The parallels with Streisand's own development are obvious. "I fell in love with it instantly," she says.

Barbra and Ray Stark asked Sydney Pollack, whose *They Shoot Horses, Don't They?* both admired, to direct, and he immediately agreed. "I was very moved by it," he says. "I thought right away, Gee, this would be great for Bob." Pollack had directed Robert Redford twice before and was a close friend. He mentioned it to Redford, who said he had read it in treatment form and did not like it. Pollack persisted. "When I'd see Redford I'd drop little hints, 'You know, this could be really terrific . . . you and Barbra . . . really odd chemistry.' " Pollack sent a script to Redford, who declined again. "I just couldn't see doing it without him," Pollack says. "As a matter of fact, I was at the point where I was going to try to get out of it if he wouldn't do it.

"It wasn't that there weren't other actors who could act it, but they didn't look like Bob. You had to have a WASP, all-American, blond, blue-eyed. Newman was too old, really. There was just Bob and Ryan O'Neal in terms of stars. And I like Ryan. He's a good actor in certain things. But he'd worked with Barbra in *What's Up, Doc?,* and he was good, but she was just too strong and she overpowered the picture."

Barbra and Stark wanted Redford, too, after ruling out Dennis Cole and Ken Howard, but Stark did not appreciate Redford's stubbornness. After months of haggling, Stark told Pollack, "I'm going to give him one hour. I'm not going to chase my life around Robert Redford. Ryan will do it, what do we need Redford for?" Pollack met frantically with Redford and finally convinced him to do it, almost as a personal favor. "I called Ray Stark," Pollack relates, "and told him we got Redford. He said, 'Oh, terrific Sydney, congratulations. That's really wonderful.' There was this whole turnaround."

Then, Pollack says, "the nightmares began. Bob and I were really worried about the script. We brought another writer in, another two writers, to fix things up." Rewriting the script, in fact, was a prerequisite to Redford's agreeing to make the movie. "The reason I finally decided to do it," Redford says, "was that I had faith that I and Pollack and David Rayfiel and Alvin Sargent could make something more of that character than was in the original script. As it was written, he was shallow and one-dimensional. Not very real—more a figment of someone's imagination of what Prince Charming should be like."

Dancing with Frankie McVeigh at the prom, Katie stares across the floor at Hubbell.

HUBBELL: "You're beautiful." KATIE: "You are."

Arthur Laurents disagrees that there were problems with his script. "I don't think Hubbell Gardiner was a one-dimensional role. The picture was about Katie, and it was intended to be. When they started mucking around with it, I said to Pollack that no matter what they did, the picture was about Katie."

From Redford's point of view, the rewrites weren't designed to take the story away from Katie, but to make for a more well-balanced film. "What emerged out of the rewrites," he says, "were glimpses of the darker side of this golden boy character—what his fears were about himself. The idea was to create a supposed Mr. Perfect but then give little hints along the way that everything wasn't so perfect—or that he, more importantly, knew it wasn't."

While all of these behind-the-scenes machinations were taking place, Barbra had her own frustrations. She wanted to meet with Redford and get acquainted, a customary practice before actors begin a film. Redford wasn't responding. "He wouldn't meet with Barbra for the longest time," Pollack relates, "till she began to develop a complex— 'Why can't I sit down and talk to Bob Redford? I'm going to act with him in this movie.' But he still wouldn't see her. Finally, it started to get destructive. I said, 'Bob, you've got to see her because she's starting to take it personally.' So he agreed, but only if I went along. So the three of us sat down to dinner at her house and talked, and we had like three meetings before the picture began—that's all."

Pollack feels that there was a method to Redford's apparent madness. There is a charming awkwardness, a tentative discovery of one another between Streisand and Redford in the film's opening scenes, and Pollack thinks Redford stayed away from Streisand initially in order to heighten the realism of those scenes. "I think it helped," he says. "Here they come on the set the first day to play scenes and the fact that they didn't know each other inside out worked for what was supposed to be going on."

Arthur Laurents has said that a great deal of the sexual chemistry of those early scenes was quite real. "She was simply mesmerized because she found him so beautiful." Pollack confirms that Barbra was taken with Redford—but it was his acting that most impressed her. "She would call me at night and say, 'How does he do it?' And she would see the dailies and think that he was wonderful and she stunk. But they're very alike in that respect, because he would see them and think that she was wonderful and he stunk."

Marilyn Bergman's comment rather sums up Barbra's reaction to Redford: "He's the best-looking leading man she's ever had, and she knew it. We sat next to her when she first saw the movie. She kept nudging me and saying how great *he* was."

Redford has nice things to say about Barbra, too. "Barbra . . . I can't explain it. Her femininity brings out the masculinity in a man, and her masculinity brings out a man's femininity, vulnerability, romanticism, whatever you want to call it. It's a crude way of putting it, but that's what it boils down to. She has a very good sense of herself as a performer, and I enjoyed working with her very much. She's also very pretty."

Despite this apparent mutual-admiration society, there were some instances of friction between the two stars during filming. "I don't remember a single *fight* that they had," Pollack says. "I had fights with Bob and I had fights with Barbra. Not fights where we disliked each other but fights because everybody was uptight about how to make it come off. Considering that they are both strong-willed people and very different kinds of people, it's amazing they got along as well as they did. Everything about them is opposite—their lifestyles, the way they work. Bob is a very athletic sort of outgoing guy who loves the outdoors. Barbra is a typical New York City Jewish girl who if you say horse to her—she doesn't understand from a cabin in the mountains: 'You really ski down a slope? Aren't you afraid you're going to break your legs?'

"Also, she likes to rehearse and talk a lot about everything. Bob is a very impatient guy that way. He likes to do it—just do it and see what happens—'If it doesn't work, we'll try it again. But don't tell me what the scene is about every ten minutes.' "

Pollack smiles and recalls, "Barbra would call me up every night at nine, ten o'clock and talk about the next day's work for an hour, two hours. Then she'd get in there the next day and want to talk and Bob would want to *do* it. And Bob felt the more the talk went, the staler he got. She would feel that he was rushing her. The more rehearsal we did, she would begin to go uphill and he would peak and go downhill. So I was like a jockey trying to figure out when to roll the camera to try and get them to coincide."

"She'd talk and talk and talk and drive me nuts," Redford says. "And the amusing thing was that after she'd talk and talk and talk, we'd get down to doing it and she'd do just what she was going to do from the beginning. There comes a point where you're ready to go, and then you're better off expending your energies in front of the camera trying things—films are made up of pieces and you might get something usable. But you learn too much in rehearsals. Things start to get pat and film is a medium of behavior and spontaneity."

Streisand did offer some improvisation, however. "The three of us would go onto the set," Pollack relates, "and send everybody away for an hour and we'd talk about how can we do this? And she'd say, 'Well, you know what I'd like to do . . . I'd like to be feeding him grapes or something.' And he'd say, 'Yeah, that's kind of a nice idea. Let's try that. Call the prop man and let's get some grapes.' And they would break each other up. Whenever he said anything Jewish, she would get hysterical. There's one scene that's almost all improvised in the beach house where he was trying to learn some Jewish words and she was breaking up. A lot of that we photographed and tried to keep in."

Pollack is quite pleased with the acting of both his stars. He's quite adamant in his view that Redford is very underrated as an actor. "Redford is considered a selfish actor, a cold actor, an actor who walks through his roles. All of these things I violently disagree with. For me, and for most people I trust with taste in this business, he's a superb actor, a surprising one, and very, very subtle."

Subtlety was a quality Pollack worked to help Barbra achieve. "I wouldn't let her perform the way she performed in the other pictures, nor would she have wanted to. That was a mutual objective we set out for, because it was not a performer role. It was not *Funny Girl,* and I couldn't have two different movies going along. I couldn't have *Funny Girl* meets *Downhill Racer.* So all of us worked for that. Obviously, she was influenced by Redford's work, too."

Arthur Laurents thinks that both Redford and Streisand were wonderful in the film, but that Streisand was at her best in several scenes which were cut out, including one in which Katie, while in Hollywood, sees a campus demonstration and begins to cry, and another in which she happens upon Hubbell and Carol Ann in a compromising position. "I think Pollack did her a disservice, even in some of the scenes not cut," Laurents says. "She could have been even better. Like the telephone scene, which was a terrific scene—she's got her hand in front of her face and you don't see how well she was acting it."

Once *The Way We Were* was ready for release, no one expected it to succeed. Redford was convinced he had made a mistake, Laurents thought his script had been hopelessly muddled, and Pollack, according to Laurents, apologized to him for botching things up. Barbra wondered if the public would accept her in this character role.

When the film opened in late October, 1973, however, it became quickly apparent that this unorthodox love story had struck a nerve with the American public. Millions were able to identify with Katie's quest for the seemingly unattainable Hubbell, share her joy at winning him and her sorrow at losing him. It was still another example of Streisand's message: you don't have to look like Lois Chiles to be capable of being loved. Audiences were profoundly touched by the failure of Katie and Hubbell's relationship despite their deep feelings.

The film received mixed reviews, mostly because of its failure to adequately deal with the blacklisting period in its second half. Pollack's biggest script problem, along with trying to keep Hubbell's character on an even keel with Katie's, was how to integrate the film's politics with its love story. He does not feel he succeeded. "I don't think it's a very good movie from a director's standpoint. It's a successful movie in that it reached an audience. People who see the film are satisfied by it. They're moved. It's a film that is made totally by the performances of its two stars . . . totally. It's not a film of ideas, which it could have been and should have been. In that sense, it's a failure. I don't think it successfully mixed the politics with the love story except in the beginning. In college I think that worked because the politics advanced the story dramatically. In the end, it was tacked on. We were sort of attaching ourselves to ideas to make the film more serious and it just didn't work. I had an idea, but I couldn't use it. I wanted to make him an informer, and have that break them up. I mean, if he was really a bad writer he would have gotten desperate. But I wanted him to be a sympathetic character, too. So it wouldn't have worked."

Redford agrees. "That's a movie. But it's a different movie. That's a cold, hard look at what happens to people in that kind of situation. This was a love story. The love story was the most important thing."

Arthur Laurents feels that this kind of thinking worked to destroy his original script. "Ray Stark said we had to choose between the love story and the politics. I think that's balderdash—they're constantly underestimating the public. The original ending was this: because of the witch hunt, he comes home from the studio and says, 'They're gonna fire me because you're a subversive. If you don't inform, I'm out of a job.' She says, 'There's a very easy answer; you won't have a subversive wife—we'll get a divorce.' They shot that scene and several others about informing, and Barbra was marvelous in them. And if you know how much principles meant to this woman, you can understand how she could divorce a man she loves rather than betray those principles. In one scene they cut, Katie is listening to an agent who had informed, and he's saying, 'I guess I won't know for years whether I've done the right thing.' It was a long speech and Katie just listens, picking at her food. Then he's finished and she looks up and says, 'Well, I can tell you right now, you're a shit.' It was telling the audience that no matter how you rationalize it, an informer is a shit.

"By cutting that scene, they undercut the character, because unless you really knew how passionately this woman felt, not intellectually but emotionally, about it, and to see her husband going along, then you don't justify her leaving him. The way it is now, it looks like the marriage breaks up because he goes to bed with another girl, which is not only cliché but also untrue. Marriages don't break up because of that, it's always something deeper. Here, it was the character of a woman. Maybe it was too early in the feminist cycle to show a woman who had not only intelligence but political passion and principles.

"I'm glad the picture was a success," Laurents goes on. "The thing I regret about it is that if the political section had been better, it could have been a really good picture. But there's a line in *Gypsy*—'If you've got a really strong finish, they'll forgive you for

168

anything.' And I knew that last scene was a killer, that no matter how much they fucked it up before, that scene would save the picture. Which it did—they were both marvelous in it, just beautiful."

The Way We Were was able to transcend its shortcomings as cohesive film-making and become one of the few memorable love stories of the 1970s. Pollack speaks for many viewers when he says, "I'm still moved when I see the picture. I'm moved by the final scene. I'm moved way before the final scene. When they start to break up . . . in the hospital. I love when Bob tries to get his job back. I love him in the sailboat with J. J. going nowhere. I love the Roosevelt party where she blows up. And I love Barbra's phone call when she asks him to be her friend. And their first night together. I'm very proud of that love scene because it didn't cheat anybody and it was in excellent taste, I thought, and yet I didn't have to cut away to the rain on the window and all that.

"What I basically like about the film is what attracted me to the material in the first place. When I read it I cried. And I managed to get that on the screen. But I didn't manage to do the other things I would have liked to do with it."

Barbra received generally excellent reviews for *The Way We Were,* and the film re-established her as a potent box-office attraction. She was mentioned in the balloting for the New York Film Critics Best Actress Award, which went to Joanne Woodward for *Summer Wishes, Winter Dreams,* and was nominated for a Golden Globe, which was awarded to Marsha Mason for *Cinderella Liberty.* She won the "People's Choice Award" and Italy's David di Donatello prize as "Foreign Actress of the Year."

At Oscar time, *The Way We Were* was nominated for six Academy Awards—Best Actress, Cinematography, Art Direction, Costume Design, Original Score, and Best Song.

Barbra and Joanne Woodward were considered the favorites, and there was some surprise when the Oscar went to Glenda Jackson for what many considered a lightweight performance in *A Touch of Class.* "It was Barbra's unpopularity in Hollywood that cost her the Oscar," Arthur Laurents says. "She plainly deserved it."

The film did win two Oscars, for scoring and song. Barbra's recording of the title tune became her first #1 single ever, and won a Golden Globe and a Grammy as well. The song, with music by Marvin Hamlisch and lyrics by Marilyn and Alan Bergman, was actually the second written for that title—Barbra wasn't happy with the first and asked that it be redone. The rewritten version became a standard; the original wasn't sung publicly by Barbra until a benefit concert for the Bergmans in 1980. Barbra, calling it "The Way We Weren't," performed it touchingly, but it was clear why she preferred the second version: this one lacked the haunting, evocative melodic and lyrical qualities we have come to know so well.

The Way We Were left Barbra's admirers highly satisfied: she had acted beautifully in a moving, successful movie; she looked lovely in the period fashions and makeup, and it seemed more and more that she was prepared to stretch herself as an actress.

Whatever the original terms of Barbra's contract with CBS may have been in the mid-sixties, she had somehow avoided producing one special per year for ten years. After "Central Park" in 1968, it was a full five years before "Barbra Streisand and Other Musical Instruments," taped in London, was televised on November 2, 1973. Lacking the crisp style of its predecessors, the special was an exercise in overproduction.

As the title implied, the gimmick was the versatile Streisand voice woven through a travelogue of exotic instruments and ethnic sounds. The opening was deceptively sim-

Scenes from "Barbra Streisand...and Other Musical Instruments"

ple. Barbra sprayed her throat as members of the orchestra tuned up. Dressed in a low-cut gown with a bow tie at her throat, Streisand sang a lovely version of "Sing/Make Your Own Kind of Music." After she dabbled at the piano with her eleven-year-old accompanist, Dominic Savage, the first act's pièce-de-résistance got underway.

Barbra and company then sailed through a fifteen-minute medley of Tin Pan Alley standards built on a framework of "I've Got Rhythm" and set against unexpected musical motifs. India supplied the rhythms for "Johnny One Note/One Note Samba." "Glad To Be Unhappy" was given the Kabuki treatment, while "Second Hand Rose" became a clumsy, comic flamenco turn, and "Don't Rain on My Parade" was offset with Indian tom-toms. Streisand of course wore appropriate international costumes—many of her own design—and seemed to thoroughly enjoy the worldly romp. The segment ended with a full throated reprise of "I've Got Rhythm" (backed with African drums and then bagpipes). The song's final note was held so long, Barbra reportedly passed out from lack of oxygen.

Part two began with a garish montage of computerized effects and Streisand singing a frantic "Come Back to Me." A short monologue was witless, completely wasting Barbra's comic flair. Fortunately, the show was elevated by several levels with the introduction of Ray Charles. He offered a lively version of "Look What They've Done to My Song" with Streisand scat singing as part of his backup. "Cryin' Time" became a memorable duet, with Ray and Barbra's voices blending perfectly. A short segue got Streisand into a tame version of "Sweet Inspiration/Where You Lead."

Not surprisingly, the special's final act was a concert. Opting for elegance, Barbra wore turn-of-the-century lace and a Gibson-girl hairdo. Stately palms and the orchestra in full dress added to the old-world atmosphere. Barbra belted her individual treatment of "On a Clear Day," and playfully led a sing-along of a Schubert aria, but the highlight was "I Never Has Seen Snow" from *House of Flowers,* Harold Arlen and Truman Capote's early fifties Broadway show. Streisand's version of the song was touching and exquisitely sung. Going from the sublime to the ridiculous, the show ended with an embarrassment: "The World Is a Concerto," in which insipid lyrics were performed gamely against a cacophony of household sounds: washing machine, vacuum cleaner, juice blender, sewing machine.

Redemption came with the final credits over a dreamy Barbra with long silky hair singing a tender "The Sweetest Sounds." In spite of the show's inconsistency, it did fairly well in the ratings and earned five Emmy Awards.

Critics were quick to point out the problems with "Barbra Streisand and Other Musical Instruments." John O'Connor in the New York *Times* said, " . . . it is overproduced, over-orchestrated and overbearing to the point of aesthetic nausea." Other reviews were kinder, but the show was not one to garner the kind of effusive notices her first two did.

The soundtrack album is surprisingly listenable considering the erratic pace of the special and the many distractions inherent in its format. Most of the "I've Got Rhythm" number is enjoyable and "I Never Has Seen Snow" becomes lovelier with repeated listenings. The album was not a sales success, peaking at only #64 on *Billboard*'s chart. Fans were just getting used to Barbra's new command of the pop-rock genre and the Broadway approach of the "Musical Instruments" songs seemed a regression to earlier, more traditional albums.

For Pete's Sake—*and Jon's*

It is difficult to fathom why Barbra decided to make *For Pete's Sake.* If she thought *What's Up, Doc?* was a "piece of fluff," what could she have seen in this story: housewife Henrietta ("Henry") Robbins, concerned about her husband's bad financial luck, borrows money from the Mafia so he can act on a tip to buy pork-belly futures. When the futures fail to pay off quickly, the Mafia men threaten to collect in their inimitable way. Rather than risk that, Henry agrees to sell her debt to Mrs. Cherry, a madam, and she rationalizes that her prostitution is all right because she's doing it for her husband. She has zany experiences; when a judge suffers a heart attack in her closet, she gets out of the business by having Mrs. Cherry sell her contract to two "businessmen." They dress her in a blond wig and have her deliver a package. Interrupted by police decoys and chased by a police dog, she manages to get back with the package intact. Too bad: it contained a bomb. Her contract is next sold to cattle thieves, and she winds up transporting a truck full of cows and riding a bull through the streets of Brooklyn.

Barbra may have felt the film would turn out better than its premise suggested. The project was developed specifically for Streisand by Marty Erlichman working with Stanley Shapiro (who won an Oscar for writing *Pillow Talk*), and Maurice Richlin. "We had to develop it from scratch," Marty said at the time, "because there just weren't scripts being written for women stars. Writers tell me that's because, aside from Barbra, there are no bankable women stars—so it's foolish wasting time writing scripts for women. But people will come to hear Barbra laugh or cry or sing."

Peter Yates, renowned at the time for *Bullitt* and *The Friends of Eddie Coyle,* and now best known for directing *Breaking Away,* was selected to direct. "*For Pete's Sake* was the very best of packaging," Yates now says. "It was put together as a showcase for Barbra, to show all the most attractive sides of her. She wanted to do a film in which she didn't sing, because in this period she was trying to prove to people that she could be successful without singing. I'm delighted she proved that and went back to singing again, because she does have the most incredible voice—even though I don't think she can quite understand it herself. I remember she said to me during the filming, 'I don't see what all the fuss is about singing. All I do is open my mouth and it's just like talking.' And I answered, 'Well, if everyone else was able to talk like you sing' . . ."

Like many of his predecessors, Yates was wary of working with La Streisand. "I wanted to meet her, you know, and find out whether the stories were true. And I found that they weren't, and indeed throughout the whole picture I found they weren't. She was a strange, strange girl. She has a sort of unusual attraction about her. It's not only her talent—which is enormous—but she has this extraordinary personality which comes through, even when you first meet her and talk to her. I think that she's far more friendly than her reputation would lead one to believe."

Yates wanted to socialize with Streisand a bit before the film opened as a way of breaking the ice. Barbra was then dating a "businessman," rumored to have been married at the time, whose name has never become public knowledge. Yates invited them to East Hampton to water ski with him. Barbra had never tried skiing, but as part of her experimental period, she was attempting to pick up some of the athletic skills that had always been anathema to her and, in the words of Sydney Pollack, "know from a cabin in the mountains." Yates describes the experience: "The first day, her boyfriend and I were fussing over her. The next day we had an instructor who said, 'You get in the water on your own, put your own skis on, or you don't do it from my boat.'

"I'll always remember Barbra saying, before she was supposed to go out and try it, 'What do I need this for? I can *sing,* for Christ's sake! I think one of our people already did this walking on the water!' And when she did it, she got up on the skis in one try. It was incredible. But that's very typical of her. She can do almost anything she sets her mind to."

By the time rehearsals began, Michael Sarrazin had been signed to play pliable, accommodating Pete to Barbra's Henrietta. "It's very difficult to cast somebody in a film opposite Barbra," Yates says. "Because unless you have a major star, you're gonna have problems of balance. But no major star wanted to play it, because the part didn't warrant it. It was like playing the girl's part in almost every other film. Instead of the girl following two paces behind the guy, it was the other way around. So we had to find somebody who was a strong personality who could act and stand up with and get along with Barbra. Especially get on with Barbra."

And Michael Sarrazin did, Yates says. "Barbra was extremely generous to him. By that I mean, it's possible for a major star to be very tough; there are certain ways that they can make someone feel uncomfortable. If a star is selfish, he or she can do things to cut down on the time spent shooting the other person. But Barbra wasn't selfish. If it was his scene, she would give it to him and help him with it."

Yates's preparations for the film included a little reshaping of Barbra. "I wanted her to lose weight, because I think she looks wonderful when she does; she looked great in *What's Up, Doc?* I was determined that she should lose weight. And I wanted to change her hairstyle because she virtually had the same hairstyle ever since she started. And I had a feeling she might look marvelous in a short cut.

"She wasn't at all sure about it, but you know, I always claim that I am entirely responsible for her meeting Jon Peters. Because one night she called me up and said, 'I've just seen an incredible short haircut that would be perfect for me. Maybe I could get a wig made up like that.' So I said, 'Whose haircut was it?' 'Well, I asked the person who was wearing it and she said it was cut by somebody called Jon Peters.' So I said, 'Look, why don't we contact Jon Peters? Maybe we could arrange for him to come to your house and talk and we'll see what we can evolve with him.'"

And of such things are great romances born. Jon Peters would become the most important person in Barbra's life and change her dramatically. But, although he would be the driving force on most of her subsequent projects, he was not a major factor in *For Pete's Sake.* "He *was* useful to me and the picture," Yates says, "because not only did he persuade Barbra that she would indeed look better thinner, he also helped beat the hell out of her to keep her weight down. But the relationship didn't seem to be a big deal at the time, not like it developed during *Funny Lady.* Jon was not on the set the whole time or anything like that, and no floods of tears."

Once filming began, Yates came to understand why Streisand had a reputation as "difficult": "I think that her main problem is that she is full of ideas and quite often they're right. Some people think she's difficult because she has always spoken her mind. With me, she asked questions and criticized and queried the way things had been done before. I rather liked that—I think it's terrific as long as it's constructive. And it had to be, because, after all, she was the person who was going to be on the screen. But I didn't find it overbearing in any way. I found it stimulating, in fact."

Yates also found a new trait in Barbra—she was reluctant to rehearse. "It was just at the end of the period when she liked to talk a lot," Yates recalls. "Now she had a feeling that rehearsals weren't good for her, that maybe she was going to be much fresher if she didn't rehearse."

Obviously, Barbra had been influenced by Redford's feelings on the subject. But there was an ironic twist: "Eventually she came around to rehearsing because Michael used to need rehearsal. When we filmed, Michael used to take a little longer to get there. Usually, one of Barbra's first takes was the best."

Not all of them, however. "I remember saying to her once after a take, 'That was absolutely terrible!' She collapsed laughing and said, 'No one's ever said that before. Thank God!' I think she was really grateful. I mean, that's what a director is for. He's not personally attacking someone if he tells them they're doing something terrible. A director is there to be used as a mirror . . ."

The working relationship between Barbra and Peter Yates was a good one; the *For Pete's Sake* company was happy. The director and his star continued their personal friendship after work. "My wife and I used to spend a lot of time up at her house, and it was almost as if she liked being with us because we had been married for some time. She was between marriages at that point. I feel that friendships and family ties are awfully important to her. She is a much more human and warmer person than the image that is projected of her."

As filming neared completion, there was one major scene to film: the climax, where Henry rides a stampeding bull. Barbra's reaction? "All I can remember," Yates says, "Is her saying 'Oh, God!' She was absolutely terrified. But she was very good, and she did do it. But she insisted that *I* do it once to show her—it was wickedness more than anything else."

When *For Pete's Sake* was released in June of 1974, it received surprisingly good reviews and was a box-office winner. But it is the film that many Streisand fans hold in least regard. Coming after her moving performances in *Up the Sandbox* and *The Way We Were,* this film seemed a regression. It had been said that Barbra signed for this film because she feared the public would accept her only in zany comedy or musicals—this was before the success of *The Way We Were.* Standing on its own, *For Pete's Sake* isn't a terrible film. It had funny moments, and marvelously played turns by Molly Picon as Mrs. Cherry and Estelle Parsons as Henrietta's insufferable sister-in-law. If it had starred an actress of whom we do not expect as much, it would have been a perfectly acceptable film. But as a Streisand vehicle, it fails. And it was heavily criticized because of Henrietta's willingness to do *anything* for her husband. In an age of women's liberation, this was not considered by many to be acceptable behavior.

Peter Yates today defends his film from all assaults. "People want me to say it's the one film I regret making, but it isn't. It was not a heavy social document. It was made to be frothy and light and charming and amusing, and I don't think there's anything wrong with that. I think its success at the box office proves that there's a lot of room for that kind of film.

"I don't think there was anything objectionable about her behavior. If somebody falls in love with somebody else, they're inclined to behave as their emotions tell them; they do all kinds of things they're not supposed to do."

Barbra's reaction to the film can be gauged by something she said in the *Playboy* interview. She was asked if it's a myth that when she doesn't sing in a film it isn't as successful. "Yes, it is a myth," she responded. "Because I did four films in a row that were not unsuccessful: *The Owl and the Pussycat, What's Up, Doc?, The Way We Were,* and, in its own stupid way, *For Pete's Sake.* The only one that wasn't a success was *Up the Sandbox,* which I was really proud of."

Told of Barbra's comment, Yates says, "At the time, she loved it. And she liked it even more, I'm sure, when the checks came in. She had a big piece of it. I think it's

With Michael Sarrazin

174

"Oh, God . . ."

not on the level of the other films she mentioned. But I think it's wrong to call it stupid. I think a better expression would be lightweight, but not stupid because to call something that a lot of people have enjoyed 'stupid' is to criticize the taste of those people. You would certainly think that Barbra and I could've produced something a bit more solid and a bit more worthwhile than that. But I would much rather make *For Pete's Sake* than a violent rape story about the streets of Hartford or something. At least you feel that you have given some pleasure to people."

Whatever Barbra's feelings about *For Pete's Sake,* she surely remembers it fondly as the film that brought her and Jon Peters together. After she found out that it was he who had designed the short hair she admired, she summoned him to her Bel Air home. She kept him waiting an hour, and he wasn't happy. He was becoming "angry enough to leave" when she finally greeted him. He told her he was not used to being kept waiting and that she was very rude. Barbra was taken aback by his forthrightness; usually, everyone around her walks on eggshells trying not to offend her.

She apologized, then asked Peters if he would design a wig for her. He replied that he didn't do that, it was beneath him. Again, Barbra was impressed, and obviously there was an attraction between these two. At one point, Peters told her as she was walking across the room, "You've got a great ass." Streisand loved it. "I couldn't believe it," she has said. "He was treating me like a woman, not like some famous *thing.*"

"I had expected this big woman, and in walked this little girl," Jon explained. "I was very surprised that she was little and petite and had a pretty body."

Jon was a man, like Elliott, with whom Barbra could be completely herself. "Jon is the first man who has really told me exactly what he felt as he was feeling it," she said soon after they met. "It gives me a true sense of security, since I know that he is always completely honest with me. It has allowed me to be more open with him than I've ever been before."

In 1975, after a year with Jon, Barbra gave a revealing interview to Elizabeth Kaye of *McCall's.* "In the beginning he was really crazy, a nut," she said. "He took me to a party once and said he wanted to go for a walk with me, then put me on his shoulders and wouldn't let me down. He was so vital, so verbal, really terrific and alive."

Barbra told another interviewer, "When I met Jon, I had a feeling that he was going to be important to me, but I knew the big test would be when Jason met him. Finally I invited Jon over to the house and he and Jason kind of stared at one another for a long time. Then Jason said, 'Are you a good swimmer?' and it was as if Jason just knew that Jon would be the kind of man he would like, for soon after, Jon and Jason were out in the pool. Jon was teaching Jason how to do the breast stroke. They've been friends ever since."

The attraction between these two high-voltage people was intense. "Obviously, I love Barbra," Jon has said. "She's powerful. She's gentle. She's beautiful. She's fun to be with. She's ten different people, and I love them all. On our good days, we could fly over the universe.

"Barbra Streisand is the most beautiful woman that I've ever seen in my life, and from the moment that I saw her I felt that. And I've done the hair of the most beautiful women in the world. So I think she has the classic beauty of all time, for me. I have never seen anyone who looks like Barbra so to me that's beautiful, as opposed to the conventional sense of beauty."

Of Jon, Barbra said, "He is a very strong man, and I like that. I'm probably in the worst position in the world for finding a good man; most men are so weak. Jon wasn't the least bit intimidated by me or my success. I used to say to him, 'C'mon, be a little intimidated'—but he never was."

Barbra Streisand had obviously met her match. Elliott Gould analyzed the attraction of his ex-wife to this Hollywood hairdresser, on the surface an unlikely candidate to woo and win her: "Barbra is most happy when someone else is in charge. It takes a lot of persistence to dominate her because she's a very strong woman."

Again like Elliott, Jon could match Barbra's horror stories of childhood deprivation: He saw his father die in front of him; took to the streets, was sent to reform school as an "incorrigible," ran away to Europe, married at fifteen, divorced, became a boxer to keep from starving, and finally succumbed to family pressures and entered his mother's family's longtime business, hairdressing. "I figured it was a good way to meet women."

Jon's childhood was more harrowing than Barbra's, and his rags-to-riches story within his profession rivaled hers. After working in several family beauty parlors for a couple of years, he borrowed money and went into business for himself. Within just a few years, he owned three Jon Peters Salons, one of them the top Beverly Hills shop. By the time Peters met Streisand, he was already a millionaire.

His marital status was something of a complication when he met Barbra; he had been married for seven years to Lesley Ann Warren, a young actress who had scored a success on TV's *Cinderella* but whose career had never fulfilled its promise. Her marriage to Jon Peters was shaky when Barbra entered their lives. "Just as I was leaving the house one day," Lesley Ann has said, "Barbra called to ask about one of Jon's hairstyles she had seen someone wearing at a party. But she wasn't the 'other woman' until after Jon and I split."

It is an ironic footnote that Lesley Ann Warren was Elliott Gould's costar in the short-lived *Drat! The Cat!* "I was totally fascinated with Barbra," Lesley says. "I asked Elliott how she did her makeup. I vocalized to her albums. Jon had never heard of her until I took him to the Hollywood Bowl [in 1967] to see her. Isn't life bizarre?"

Because Jon was still married to Lesley Ann when he and Barbra began dating, they tried to keep their relationship a secret. Naturally, the attempts failed, and once again Barbra found herself in the middle of a parking-lot skirmish. This time, Jon broke an ankle grappling with a photographer. Soon after, he and Barbra went public with an interview in *Women's Wear Daily*.

Barbra made it clear in this and other interviews that meeting Jon Peters had made her "the happiest I've ever been." She and Jon built a sprawling ranch house on his land in a canyon about a half mile from the beach in Malibu. The house is of rough wood with massive windows and earthy accessories: quilts, red Moorish rugs, primitive pottery. This rather masculine decor is offset by touches of Barbra: her collectibles, favorite things like a beaded bag and shawls, Art Deco statuary, objets d'art. Every corner of the house is filled with Barbra's treasures. Outside, there are twenty acres over which she and Jon have planted two thousand trees and hundreds of shrubs.

Moving into this house was a big step in Jon's efforts to make Barbra more natural, more relaxed, more in touch with the earth. "I'd never thought of living in the country," she told Jane Ardmore in *Ladies' Home Journal*. "I was allergic to fresh air. When I was a kid, I went to camp—my mother sent me away from the time I was five. I developed asthma. I even had asthma attacks the first few nights we were here. Too much greenery; I wasn't used to it. I said, 'Look, Barbra, you're *not* five years old, your mother *hasn't* sent you away from home, you're not at camp, and you can leave anytime you want.' The minute I conditioned my mind, I stopped being allergic. I love it here. You are very much in touch with the earth, with the natural things that happen. I never used to walk or ride a bike. I never breathed deeply before.

"The pressures of this business can destroy you, like they did Judy Garland," Barbra said. "You have to be very strong to avoid it. The thing that keeps me sane is living here. It's away from it all. I don't hear any traffic sounds. I don't answer the phone much on weekends. I garden or walk or ride my bike."

Barbra and Jon, 1975

"He treats me like a woman, not like some famous thing."

She also cooks. "Jon likes me in the kitchen. But that's O.K. I enjoy cooking for him. You cook something, you make it with your own hands and it becomes part of his body. It's a very organic thing."

When Barbra began gardening, she approached it typically: she learned the Latin names for every one of the flowers she was planting. She began horseback riding, joined Gilda's gym to get herself in shape, started eating health foods and tried to resist her overpowering urge for junk, wore less makeup, dressed not only casually but often in a way that could only be described as "funky."

Some of Barbra's new activities were difficult for her to get up the courage to try. "I thought there was no possible way that I could learn to snow ski. But I decided that I had to go, and I went, and it was wonderful. I was doing something that I was afraid of doing. I was conquering so many fears. I went up in that chairlift and knew I'd have to get down, and I thought, 'That's it. I'll have a heart attack. There's too much fresh air up here.' But four days later I was skiing down from the top of the mountain and I was learning so much: what it feels like to fall, that the snow is soft, that you don't get killed, that you survive. It was very exciting for me. I spent that whole year skiing."

Obviously, Jon Peters was the best thing that ever happened to Barbra. He was helping her get in touch with who she really was, not the fantasy. Their relationship was idyllic; even their fights brought Barbra pleasure: "We're able to love because we learned how to fight. We kick and scream and call each other names. Then it's out of our system. I've learned that you can hate someone and still love them, you know?"

But the press would soon impinge upon the idyll and make Barbra and Jon feel like a persecuted minority. It started slowly, with snide comments about Barbra and her "hairdresser boyfriend," and innuendoes that Peters was a Hollywood social climber who left Lesley Ann Warren for Barbra Streisand because Barbra was a bigger celebrity.

Things became more uncomfortable for the couple when it was announced that Jon, who had never produced a record, would produce Barbra's next album, *Butterfly*. The press reaction was harsh: Was Streisand, who had had such an unerring instinct in her career moves, making a mistake because she was in love? Would Jon Peters destroy her career out of ineptness in an attempt to be her Svengali? And wasn't Jon obviously using Barbra to get ahead in the world?

The reports angered both of them. Barbra sprang to Jon's defense—and her own. "Do they think I would let Jon produce a record if I wasn't absolutely sure he could do it? I believe in instinct, I believe in imagination. I believe in taste. These are the important ingredients and they're all the things he has." Jon added: "Barbra is far too much of a professional to get involved with me professionally just as a romantic gesture. And of course they're going to think I hit the jackpot by being with Barbra. And sure I'm partly out to prove to people that I'm not the hanger-on they think I am. What they forget is that I made a lot of money before I met Barbra."

"I know it's making people angry," Barbra said. "It's like when I first came out here and had three film contracts, never having had a screen test. People want you to pay your dues. But Jon will either deliver or he won't."

A few months before the album was released, press reports began appearing that Jon *hadn't* delivered. Joyce Haber's Los Angeles *Times* column carried an interview with Al Schmitt, a veteran recording engineer who told her he had been called in to fix what Peters had messed up. "Barbra has this tremendous thing of knowing exactly what's right for her," he said. "But now, it seems, that's gone out the window. She's never let anyone direct her career this way."

Schmitt went on to say that Columbia had been unhappy with seven or eight songs recorded for *Butterfly*. "This album has a flat, one-dimensional sound," he said. "It needs to be opened up. It needs climaxes. Peters is a nice guy, but he's not a record producer. Jon said to me, 'I have a business to run; I can't be here every day.' I worked for three days on *Butterfly* and left because we couldn't come to an agreement. Essentially, Peters wanted all the money, and I'd be doing all the work."

A few days later, Haber's sleep was disturbed by an early-morning phone call from Barbra—she was upset by Haber's interview with Al Schmitt. "Is Schmitt trying to imply that I've given up my career for Jon Peters?" Barbra asked. "I don't even know this Schmitt. The only thing he said that's true is 'Barbra has this thing of knowing exactly what's right for her.' With that I must agree. This is possibly the best singing I've ever done. It's the most open, the most free, the most happy. That's what Al Schmitt told Jon.

"I'm an artist," Barbra went on. "Jon and I have to deal with ourselves on two levels—as creative people and as lovers. The reason we're calling it *Butterfly* is that when we first met he said I reminded him of a butterfly. He gave me this one hundred-year-old Indian butterfly. Both of us gravitate toward butterflies."

Barbra explained to Haber that Schmitt had been fired—he hadn't left. "He's being vindictive. From a sound point of view, Columbia may have wanted more amplification. You can have one hundred mixers on one song. Schmitt did three cuts. I didn't like them. I wanted this soft, then rising."

Haber also quoted Charles Koppelman, Columbia Records Vice President. "Under no circumstances," Koppelman said, "would Columbia sanction an album with Peters and Barbra unless I was convinced it was absolutely right. I've had about ten meetings with Peters. He's an immensely talented man. Schmitt told Jon he wanted to coproduce with him. Obviously, he was upset because Jon was going to be on the gravy train. He told Peters, 'I've been in the business twenty-five years and you've been in it twenty-five minutes.' It just sometimes happens that twenty-five minutes produces genius. This album is not only one of the best, it'll be one of the biggest Barbra's ever made."

Butterfly, upon its release, was obviously a Jon Peters production. His cover design featured a cube of butter on which a fly had lighted; inside, eighteen of the thirty-seven photographs featured Jon with Barbra, several in affectionate embraces. The arrangements on *Butterfly* are simple and clean, and not—as with some earlier albums—in competition with her voice. Barbra's performances are indeed fresh and free, and she uses her voice in some exciting new ways, especially with "Grandma's Hands," the moving Bill Withers soul song on which her vocal gymnastics are very impressive.

When she sings the suggestive lyrics to "Love in the Afternoon" and "Guava Jelly," it is not difficult to imagine her smiling coyly across the room at Jon. When she sings "I Won't Last a Day Without You," it is clear that *Butterfly* is an album recorded by a woman in love.

The reviews of *Butterfly* were generally scathing; critics seemed unwilling to admit that Jon had produced a good album. Despite such negative criticism, and the ensuing general notion that the album was a flop, *Butterfly* was a commercial success; its sales were similar to Barbra's previous four albums. While it is not a milestone recording, it did strongly indicate that Barbra was becoming more and more comfortable with and adept at singing pop and rock music.

It also proved that Jon was indeed a capable man whose instincts and tastes were on a par with Barbra's. She let it be known that Jon would be producing and directing her in a remake of *A Star Is Born* which they had been preparing. Again, the criticism was particularly severe. But there was time before things would get really bad for Barbra and Jon: she first had to complete her contractual obligation to Ray Stark by making a sequel to *Funny Girl.*

Funny—But Not Much Fun

Barbra didn't want to do *Funny Lady,* Ray Stark's sequel to *Funny Girl,* chronicling Fanny Brice's later years and her marriage to showman Billy Rose. She was reluctant to play Fanny Brice again, and the music she would sing in the film—Billy Rose standards from the thirties and forties, plus new "Broadway belters" from *Cabaret* composers John Kander and Fred Ebb—seemed to her a step backward.

Jon Peters voted against it—"She can't play Ray Stark's mother-in-law all her life," he said—but Stark applied a great deal of pressure. Doing *Funny Lady* would release Streisand from her contractual commitment to Stark, which she felt was tying her down and limiting her options, especially now that she was changing so much personally and professionally. She read the script, and rationalized doing the film: "What this script is about is losing one's fantasies and illusions and getting in touch with and appreciating reality," she told *Newsweek.* "The script is about *really* learning to accept yourself. That's what I've started doing in my own personal life."

And, while Barbra was essentially playing herself in *Funny Girl,* she saw this sequel as a chance to create a real character. She told *Playboy,* "In *Funny Lady,* I was trying to *act* the character of Fanny Brice—a certain tough veneer that was hiding her vulnerability. Also, I sang Jewish songs like she did, which I didn't do in *Funny Girl.* More attention was paid to the externals, like calling people Kid, because Fanny had a hard time remembering people's names. In *Funny Girl,* I *was* the character. It was scary. I read certain conversations that have never been published and it was very peculiar, we were very much alike in a very deep area, in spirit. Her essence and my essence were very similar. That is a little spooky, you know?"

Stark, perhaps to make Barbra as happy as possible, surrounded her with familiar faces. Herb Ross was signed to direct, and Peter Matz was set as conductor-arranger. Omar Sharif again assumed the thankless Nicky Arnstein role, and James Caan was cast as Billy Rose. Caan was clearly chosen for his potential comic/romantic chemistry opposite Streisand; he bears no resemblance to the short, pudgy Rose. Robert Blake, a closer physical match, was rejected for the role, and Barbra explained why: "It comes down to who the audience wants me to kiss. Robert Blake, no. James Caan, yes. And he has to be able to talk as fast as me." One of Stark's associates defended the choice of Caan: "If an Arab can play Arnstein, a glamour boy can play Billy Rose."

Also in the cast were Barbra's old friend Roddy McDowall (he photographed the *Third Album* cover), Ben Vereen, and Carole Wells. Stark coaxed legendary cinematographer James Wong Howe out of retirement to photograph the film, and award-winning George Jenkins would design the production.

The story of *Funny Lady* more or less picks up where its predecessor left off. Fanny receives her final divorce decree from Nicky just as her latest show is closing. Faced with the encroaching Depression, even Ziegfeld is unable to finance new productions, leaving Fanny out of work and indecisive. She meets Billy Rose, a brash show-biz neophyte, whom she eyes with suspicion. But after recording a ballad he has written, she allows him to talk her into starring in a revue he is putting together.

Rose's inexperience results in disastrous out-of-town tryouts and only through Fanny's intervention is the show salvaged. Its Broadway opening is a huge success. Among the first-nighters are Nicky and his new bride, a wealthy older woman. Backstage, Fanny is crushed to learn, after confessing to Arnstein her undying love, of his remarriage. Billy realizes this is not the time to share his romantic feelings. He has fallen in love with Fanny and wanted to top the opening-night excitement with a marriage proposal.

Realizing that Nicky is forever beyond her reach, and Billy is a man she likes and with whom she is compatible, Fanny later accepts his proposal, and they both see their union as based on friendship and business interests rather than romantic fireworks. Fanny thinks about the differences between her involvements with Nicky and Billy and sings, "Isn't This Better?"

Fanny moves to Hollywood to create her Baby Snooks character for radio, but Billy must stay in Cleveland for his new Aquacade show. In California, Fanny runs into Nicky, and the old flame ignites in her. A reunion is arranged for them, and Nicky suggests they have an affair—he has left his wife and made a financial arrangement with her. When Nicky fails to ask about the welfare of their daughter, Fanny realizes he is more shallow and self-involved than ever and finally disabuses herself of her romantic notions. She flies to Cleveland to give Billy the good news, but once there she catches him in bed with the star of his Aquacade, Eleanor Holm. Billy tells Fanny, "To her, I'm Nick," and Fanny understands that Billy needs more love than she can give him. They agree to divorce.

Years later, Billy turns up at Fanny's home and urges her to star in a new show of his. They reminisce and kibbitz with each other, but Fanny refuses to say yes or no. She tells Billy she'll decide in a few days. As the movie ends, the audience gets the impression that simply being asked was enough for Fanny.

Once filming began, Barbra's enthusiasm for the project did not increase. There was unusual tension between her and Herb Ross, who felt she was not giving the film her all. "Up until *Funny Lady,*" Herb Ross said after filming was completed, "I thought Barbra's possibilities were limitless, but that film was a curious experience. She was in love at the time, and she didn't seem to want to make the picture or play the part. She simply wasn't there in terms of commitment, and one of her greatest qualities is to make a thousand percent commitment."

Barbra admits that Jon was a distraction. "He doesn't want to be around when I'm working," she said at the time. "And I don't want him to be because my concentration goes right out the window. The other day he came to rehearsal, for instance, and the musical director asked me if I wanted three bars or four in a certain spot. I didn't know and I didn't care. If Jon hadn't been there, I would've known exactly."

To a Los Angeles *Times* interviewer she said, "It's hard, when you're feeling happy, to be asked to produce tears. To do that you have to go looking around inside you for something that hurts. I'm not going to work for a while after this. I've discovered a whole life to live away from show business and this time I like it."

But Barbra wasn't distracted enough not to work hard most of the time. James Caan told a reporter, "You do not play with Streisand . . . you work your ass off. All that guff about ego clashes on the set is pure B.S. . . . press-agent stuff designed to bring people who eat gossip into the theater. We worked very well together . . . and I mean worked hard."

Neither did Streisand's distraction extend to a lack of interest in her image on film. The first few days of filming, she said to James Wong Howe, "You know my left side is the best. My right side doesn't photograph as well." Howe was able to convince her, though, that she didn't have to worry quite so much. "There were a couple of occasions," Howe said in an interview shortly before his death in 1975, "when Mr. Ross had to stage the action so that her right side was featured. I took a little more time to make sure that everything was right, and when she saw the scene, she said, 'The right side isn't bad. I guess I don't have a bad side.' I said, 'No, Barbra, you don't.' Then she said, 'Now I'll be able to concentrate more on my acting, because being photographed on the right side won't bother me.' Actually," Howe went on, "there are very few women stars who don't have a 'good' side and a 'bad' side, but a little extra care in lighting and camera angle will usually take care of the problem."

Bob Mackie and Ray Aghayan designed the clothes for *Funny Lady*—right for the period, but largely unflattering to Barbra. In an interview with Joyce Haber in the Los Angeles *Times,* Mackie gave his thoughts about Streisand, almost as stream-of-consciousness.

If the only prerequisite for someone playing Bill Rose had been to "be able to talk as fast as me," Bob Mackie might have been a prime contender for the role: "I think Barbra overbooks herself. She's always late. One day she was on time. I was 10 minutes late, and she said, 'Hi, I'm on time.' She's one of the shyest ladies and I think her shyness is often misconstrued as rudeness. She's very much like those ladies in the past glamour days—Crawford, Dietrich. You don't look twice. They're always like a foot shorter. Then they get before a camera and they grow. She was very strong when she started in *Funny Girl.* She was terrified. Study that face. That was a different kind of Hollywood to contend with. They were used to Sandra Dees. Barbra had a fabulous cameraman, Harry Stradling, Sr., who shot her incredibly well. She taught him and he taught her. A wonderful thing was happening there. The lady can feel the lights: She'll say, 'It's not hot enough here, I need another back light.'

"On *Funny Lady* we have James Wong Howe, who's 75 and fabulous. She has a beautiful chest. She honest to God does. The prettiest chest in Hollywood. Nobody's ever seen it. Why doesn't she show it? Barbra buys clothes and never wears them. She loves things. She's a collector. She's a Taurus, and they love to possess a lot."

There was a major problem for Barbra during filming. For the scene after she decides that Nicky Arnstein isn't worth her love, she takes off in a biplane to tell Billy Rose the news while singing "Let's Hear It for Me," a number written to match the excitement of "Don't Rain on My Parade" in the first film. Barbra had to fly in a thirty-seven-year-old biplane owned by director George Roy Hill. "Oh, I nearly had a heart attack," Barbra said. "I was so scared, but I knew I should do it myself. We went up and the plane just kept going. The pilot was fiddling with the radio. The first thing I thought was, 'He's kidnapping me!' Then I thought, 'The radio's dead; the guy can't land.' What happened was that they radioed him he couldn't land because it was so crowded at Santa Monica airport. Here I am risking my life in this open cockpit for a movie! And then Herb tells me we have to do it *over!*"

Once *Funny Lady* was ready for release, Ray Stark organized a premiere in Washington, D.C., to benefit the Special Olympics, a sporting event for retarded youngsters run each year by the Kennedy family. Before the opening of the film, Barbra would perform before the President, Washington dignitaries, and a live television audience.

Peter Matz recalls that the entire event was a backstage nightmare. "Barbra was very upset by the time we started rehearsals. She had agreed to do it only because it was for the Special Olympics—she had vowed never to do any more television. Then, when it was too late, she realized that it was really a Ray Stark promo for the movie, a hype.

As Fanny Brice

186

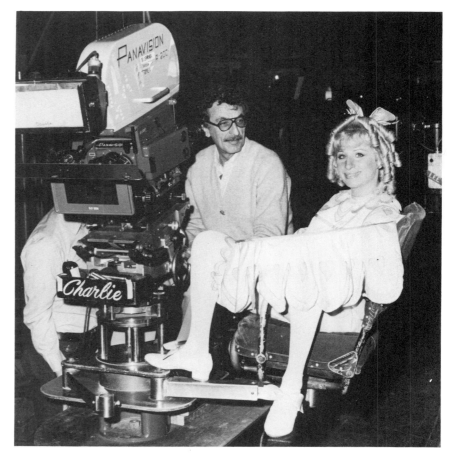

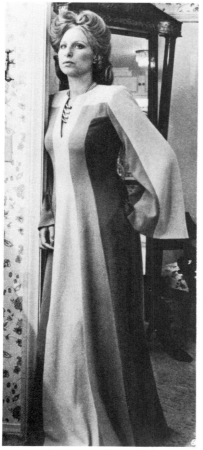

As the mature Fanny Brice

With James Caan. Reportedly, the "talcum powder bit" was improvised

At a London press conference

Nobody realized that until it was too late, after people were committed to it. Barbra felt real bad about it; she felt she had been hyped again, and she gets crazy when she feels she's been hyped. It was a bad situation. It was phony.

"And there were so many other things going wrong. The music got flown somehow to Las Vegas instead of Washington, and we couldn't rehearse on Saturday, only on Sunday, the day of the show. We had no time for much rehearsal, no time for camera blocking. Barbra and I were nervous wrecks—that's not the way to do it. She and Jimmy Caan were upset about his performing live with her on some songs—that's not what he does. He was very uncomfortable, and I don't blame him. It was bad, just bad."

Barbra was so nervous just before the show that she vomited. But despite all this craziness behind the scenes, the show was excellent. Barbra came out in a gorgeous black gown, and after a roaring ovation from a crowd she said she thought would be "stuffy," she began a flawlessly beautiful rendition of "The Way We Were"—in a very high voice. "My voice always gets high when I'm nervous," Barbra said. The nervousness didn't show, and the bit with James Caan went very smoothly. "It came off," says Peter Matz, "because every one of us is a professional. But that doesn't make the nervousness any less real just before you go on."

The evening was a smashing success. Barbra received a medal from President Ford and danced with Senator Edward Kennedy, and the audience reaction to *Funny Lady* after the live show was highly favorable.

Funny Lady, in fact, received some excellent reviews—one ran under the headline, "Barbra, you're just great!"—and it did excellent business, further cementing Streisand's position as the #1 female box office draw.

But there were dissenters, and some of them were critics who had heretofore been solidly in Streisand's camp. The most critical and damaging review came from Pauline Kael in *The New Yorker.* "When Fanny marries Billy Rose," Kael wrote, "a friend of hers asks, 'Why him?' and Fanny replies 'I fell in like with him.' The main problem I had with *Funny Lady* is that I fell out of like with Barbra Streisand."

Kael trashed the film, said Streisand looked like a "transvestite" in the clothes designed for her, and criticized almost every aspect of the movie. "You can see that the moviemakers weren't just going to make a movie—they were going to kill us. That's the thinking that has all but destroyed the American musical, and it may destroy Barbra Streisand, too. There's a vast difference between an actress trying to do something new and an actress trying to wow the public by doing what got applause before. Streisand is in beautiful voice, and her singing is terrific—too terrific. It's no longer singing, it's something else—that strident overdramatization that turns a song into a big number . . . the dialogue throughout is sharp and bitchy, and Streisand's inflections are beyond criticism—she doesn't deliver a wisecrack, she detonates it—but the cracks, too, are high-powered, designed to blitz us rather than to reveal character. This Fanny Brice isn't human. Streisand's performance is like the most spectacular, hard-edge female impersonator's imitation of Barbra Streisand. And her imitators have actually come so close that when she repeats herself she seems to be taking off from them, showing that she can outdo them. It's a performance calculated to make people yell without feeling a thing—except adoration."

The review was harsh and personal—a foretaste of what was to come with the critical reaction to *A Star Is Born*—but as a Streisand vehicle, *Funny Lady* was indeed a disappointment. Its biggest problem was the writing. "Jay Presson Allen's script was really emasculated," Peter Matz says. "The original script was strong, about a woman maturing, which is always a good theme for Barbra. It got gradually distilled and weakened."

The songs, too, were weak, with a few exceptions. "How Lucky Can You Get" is dramatically performed, but "Let's Hear It for Me" suffers from inane lyrics and a hokey production. "Isn't This Better?" the one new ballad in the picture, was melodically warm, but its lyrics stamped it as strictly a character song.

Funny Lady received several Oscar nominations, including nods to Peter Matz, Kander and Ebb for "How Lucky Can You Get?" and Mackie and Aghayan for costume design.

A small measure of controversy arose when Eleanor Holm, Billy Rose's ex-wife, called *Funny Lady* "just ridiculous." "Fanny Brice no more caught us in the kip than the man in the moon," she told a reporter. She admitted that she had been paid to allow the use of her name in the film. "They told me that the girl who was going to play me would have no lines—and she didn't. What they didn't tell me upfront were those conversations about me between Fanny and Billy. In my contract it says that nothing derogatory would be said about me. What did bother me was toward the end of the movie, when Fanny asked Billy, 'How much did that bitch,' meaning me, 'peg you for?'

"Ask anyone who knew us then. I just wanted out so I walked with no money. It took me two-and-a-half years of our fourteen years of marriage to do it. Billy was worth 15 million dollars when I left him. I eventually got a settlement of $250,000, pieced out bit by bit over ten years.

"And that whole business with her taking the plane: it never happened. I guess they put it in so Barbra could get to sing that song as she flew. Maybe Fanny did fly a plane, but I know damn well she didn't fly it from California and catch me in that kip. The whole movie is baloney, and so untrue it's laughable!"

What controversy there was about *Funny Lady* soon faded. Barbra reportedly sent Ray Stark a present after filming was completed—an antique mirror, on which she had written in lipstick, "Paid in Full." But this was, after all, a love-hate relationship, and Barbra followed that up with a plaque saying, "Even though I sometimes forget to say it, thank you, Ray. Love, Barbra."

In October 1975, Barbra released one of her most critically acclaimed albums of the seventies, *Lazy Afternoon*. The record was a result of a first-time collaboration between Streisand and Rupert Holmes, a young singer-songwriter whose first album, *Widescreen*, had been released the year before. Streisand was attracted to Holmes's meaningful lyrics and lovely melodies, and he contributed four songs to the LP, which he also produced.

Song for song, *Lazy Afternoon* was Streisand's most lyrically substantial album in years. "My Father's Song," written by Holmes expressly for Barbra, spoke of a young woman's memories of her late father and his humanistic approach to raising her ("Whatever you are, you're going to be/Whatever you are is all right with me/ You're gonna be what you want anyway/ These are the words I heard my father say.").

On the album jacket, Barbra wrote background notes for each of the songs (something she should do more often!). Of this one she said, "Soon after Rupert and I met, he played a song he had written expressly for me, about the father that all of us have wanted and needed at some time or another. Although we had only known each other for a few weeks, we were already communicating on the level of long-time friends and, both flattered and touched, I asked him why he had written this particular lyric. He explained that he thought it might reflect some of my own feelings. I told him that my father had died when I was fifteen months old, and that I considered his song a very personal gift. This cut means a great deal to me."

"By the Way," co-authored by Barbra and Rupert, is a gentle song about a woman allowing herself to love again after being left by her lover ("By the way, he began to say, 'Love takes time, I'm in a hurry'/ Anyway, that's all yesterday—let's get back to us/ Why can't we make love fall by the way?")

"I Never Had It So Good," by Paul Williams and Ron Nichols, deals with what Irvin Kershner spoke of earlier—the fact that love makes ordinary people feel special. ("I never had much money/I've never won a race/ My jokes don't end up funny/And I've had doors slammed in my face/ But I think you've charmed me/ I always hoped that someone would/ I never had a love like this before/I never had it so good.")

Stevie Wonder's "You and I" appealed to Barbra because of the simplicity of its sentiments ("Here we are, on earth together, it's you and I"). Wrote Barbra: "Sometimes it's just that basic."

"A Child Is Born," with music by Dave Grusin and lyrics by Alan and Marilyn Bergman, is a touching expression of the awe inspired by the birth of a baby. The music was written originally to underscore the abortion sequence for *Up the Sandbox,* a fact which gave rise to the Bergmans' lyrics.

"Widescreen," the album's finale, was sung by Holmes on his first album. "I was drawn to its incredible melody and theatrically truthful lyrics," Barbra wrote. "As a fourteen year old, leaving a movie theater on a stifling summer afternoon, the hot, humid reality of Brooklyn often made me long to return to the air-conditioned dream palace. At this point in my life, however, I don't want to go back into that dark place; I'd rather deal with the heat and humidity of living. Feeling this, I somewhat hesitantly asked Rupert if he could write new lyrics . . . He understood and, on the way to the session, came up with words that more honestly reflect my own thoughts about the fantasy of movies versus the reality of living: "Widescreen, dreams are more than you; how can lies be true? All we have is life, and mind, and love we find in a friend. Let the movie end."

Lazy Afternoon received excellent reviews and rose to #12 on the *Billboard* chart. "Shake Me, Wake Me," Barbra's first disco attempt, was released as a single and proved popular in dance clubs. "My Father's Song," the album's other single release, was only a fair success on the pop charts, but hit #11 on *Billboard*'s Easy Listening/Adult Contemporary list.

In February 1976, after a long delay caused by Columbia's lack of confidence in the album's commercial potential, *Classical Barbra* was released. A collection of popular lieder by such composers as Debussy, Schumann, Handel, and Fauré, the album was only a qualified success. Its sales were respectable considering the highly unusual material, but it has never been certified Gold.

Barbra's performances are lovely and sweet, but it is somewhat disappointing that she does not utilize her full range. The vocals are undemanding, and take on a sameness with repeated listenings. Larry Verdugo, writing a retrospective review of the album in *Barbra* magazine, said, "It is difficult to judge Barbra's efforts, for there is no real standard by which to measure them. One cannot put this work up against the recordings of Elizabeth Schwarzkopf or Victoria de Los Angeles, for while these three artists are temporarily sharing material, the vocal techniques and approaches are too different. Schwarzkopf and de Los Angeles, of course, sing utilizing the entire spectrum of the

Recording *Lazy Afternoon* in 1975

soprano voice. They are masters of style and technique, not to mention ornamentation. They couple these skills with their own emotional sense to produce models of interpretive finesse. Barbra projects little of this. She stays within her own familiar range and vocal projection. Her moods, while warm and appropriate in the Debussy and Cantaloube selections, are disturbingly without feeling. One waits in vain for some special, even idiosyncratic, touch—some sign that she is out to illuminate these songs. Instead we get reverence. Awe. Despite all this, the album does yield pleasure. The Streisand sound is enjoyable to hear in this unfamiliar surrounding."

Reportedly, Barbra's biggest fear in releasing this album was that it would be ridiculed by classical purists. Martin Bernheimer's review in the Los Angeles *Times* summed up the general critical reaction: "Apparently, she is one of those rare artists who cares about music in general—not just *her* music. And she has done something about it. Streisand's classical fantasies have now become public property. Mmes. Lehman, Los Angeles and Schwarzkopf need not look with much alarm to their laurels, but it isn't snigger time either. The biggest problem with *Classical Barbra* would seem to be its intended frame of reference. Is this supposed to be a collection of high-brow music hoked up for the low-brow masses? Or is it a serious attempt to meet the demands of Debussy and Schumann on their own terms? The results would seem to suggest both. And neither. If she had hoped to set the music world on fire, she may be disappointed. But if she was concerned about becoming the laughing-stock of the musical sophisticates, she needn't have worried. It is nice to know that at least one pop idol is willing to take artistic risks. A sense of adventure isn't everything these days. But it helps."

The cover of *Classical Barbra* is graced by a photograph which, if it is not the most beautiful ever taken of Streisand, is certainly in the top five. It was shot by famed photographer Francesco Scavullo, who has a rare talent for capturing Barbra's beauty. The experience of taking Streisand's picture, Scavullo told this writer in 1977, was sometimes a trying experience. "I spent a whole afternoon out at Barbra's ranch breaking the ice before I took my first picture of her," he said.

Their first session together was almost the last. "She kept directing me, telling me how to take her picture. Finally, I put the camera down and told her, 'Why don't you take pictures of yourself?' and I walked out of the room. She asked my assistant, Sean Byrnes, 'Is he mad? Did I insult him?' Sean answered, 'Yes,' and she came after me. Finally I told her, 'You have to trust me, or why bother having me shoot you?' After that, everything was fine and she adored the pictures I took of her. I love shooting Barbra. I think she's one of the great beauties today."

Scavullo would go on to take other stunning photographs of Streisand, and she is the only person to whom he has ever granted photo approval. "Barbra has photo approval with everyone. But I don't mind, because we always agree on the best shots. That *Star Is Born* logo, with Kris—we both marked it off on the contact sheet."

Barbra's next preoccupation was with the preparations for the remake of *A Star Is Born*. She wanted, she said, to "accept responsibility for my own creative vision" in films. No one could have foreseen the extraordinary reaction that vision would generate—both pro and con.

PART FOUR

ACCLAIM
AND
CONTROVERSY

1976-1981

Let Me Do Everything

A Star Is Born, the story of a disintegrating, drunken actor's love affair with an up-and-coming actress and how his self-destructive personality affects them both, has long fascinated Hollywood. It was filmed with Janet Gaynor and Fredrick March in 1937 and remade in 1953 with Judy Garland and James Mason. Nineteen thirty-one's *What Price Hollywood?,* often mentioned as the "first" *Star Is Born,* was actually a very different story with some similarities.

The idea to remake the story once more began in 1973 with Joan Didion and John Gregory Dunne, who wrote a "rockumentary" about married rock singers, one on the way up, the other on the way down. Their script was a gritty look at the rock music milieu, and after Barbra turned it down several times, there was interest in making it with a real-life couple like James Taylor and Carly Simon.

When the property was again presented to Barbra, it had been through three possible directors, six possible costars and several rewrites. By then, Barbra had met Jon, and he liked the idea; he felt it would help contemporize Barbra's image. Now that she was in love, the script's love story appealed to Barbra—perhaps she and Jon could capture some of the magic of their own love story on film. Barbra agreed to do it, if she could be the executive producer, and Jon the producer. Warner Brothers readily agreed—they were anxious for a Streisand musical.

It was at this point that the press began to take an inordinate amount of interest in the project. Joyce Haber kept her Los Angeles *Times* readers abreast almost weekly of all the behind-the-scenes moves regarding Barbra's *A Star Is Born.*

She detailed, in one column, Jon's plans to direct and co-star in the film. In another column, she announced that Jon was planning to co-author a rewrite of the script. She quoted a European executive of Warners as saying about the possibility that Jon would costar, "I never asked Jon if that was true, because I was afraid he'd say yes."

Then Haber devoted a column to the speculation that Elvis would play opposite Streisand. "I told you last fall," Haber wrote, "that Kris Kristofferson, who was first choice as costar, bowed out because La Streisand's company (and her company certainly includes her beloved Jon) insisted that Kristofferson's name be placed below, not above, the title. No one, to this date, has admitted that Kris is out."

The tone of Haber's columns—that Jon was a Svengali trying to control Streisand while inflating his massive ego—was carried over and amplified by an article in *New Times* magazine in January 1975. On the cover was an artist's rendering of Streisand totally bald, and the headline, "Barbra Streisand: a star is shorn." The seven-page article by Marie Brenner gave a minutely detailed chronological account of the genesis of *A Star Is Born,* with no attempt to conceal the contempt in which the author held both Barbra and Jon. Calling the film "Hollywood's biggest joke," Brenner quoted Jon as saying, "The whole world is waiting to see Barbra's and my story." She described Jon in his beauty salon, talking on the phone to agent Sue Mengers. "He stares at himself in the full-length mirror, oblivious to the scene around him: women in smocks having their hair washed, blown out, curled and frosted. 'OK, OK, OK.' Peters, a self-styled 'street fighter,' is, for once, listening." She later described a scene in which Jon was convinced by then *Star Is Born* director Jerry Schatzberg that he couldn't star in the film because he can't sing.

The entire piece depicted Peters as a blustering, arrogant, egomaniacal hotdog "fascinated with himself" and possessing no excess of taste and intelligence. Barbra came off in a hardly better light, as a woman who would go along with any idea Jon Peters happened to come up with.

Joyce Haber then reported that Jon had considered, then rejected, the idea of suing *New Times* and Marie Brenner for libel. Haber quoted Jon's publicist, Steve Jaffe: "Jon decided the magazine is of little importance and Brenner's not a serious or highly regarded writer, so there was no point in a lawsuit." Instead, Peters and Jaffe sent Brenner flowers and a note: "Dear Marie: We feel awfully sorry for the life you've chosen."

By early 1976, *A Star Is Born* was ready to begin filming, with First Artists presenting and Warner Brothers distributing. Two years of haggling over who would do what resulted in Barbra as executive producer, Jon as producer, Kris Kristofferson as costar and Frank Pierson as writer/director. Pierson, a highly regarded screenwriter *(Dog Day Afternoon)* agreed to tackle the umpteenth rewrite of the film on the condition that he be allowed to direct. He had directed only once before, and the film was neither a musical nor a hit. Streisand agreed to hire him as director, with the proviso—not in writing—that the effort be a "collaboration" between them. Pierson agreed, and set to work on the script.

Originally Rupert Holmes was hired as musical director, but only two songs from his score—"Queen Bee" and "Everything"—were used in the film. Paul Williams and Kenny Ascher were then asked to provide rock songs for Kris Kristofferson's character, John Norman Howard, and pop tunes for Barbra's Esther Hoffman, a singer-songwriter in the Carole King mold.

Once filming began in the spring, it was clear that the production of *A Star Is Born,* after two and a half years of frustrations, problems and personality clashes, was continuing in exactly the same way. Everyone involved was tense: Jon, because if he failed in his first effort as a producer, it would be at the expense of a $6 million film; Barbra, because she saw the film as a personal statement, the first time she had laid her own artistic vision on the line; Pierson, because he grew more and more to resent Streisand's efforts at collaboration and Jon's "intrusions," and Kristofferson, because he felt out of his league in the same picture with Barbra and wasn't sure whom to listen to: the executive producer/director, the producer, or the nominal director.

His insecurities were especially hard on Kristofferson. "I was more afraid of this than Ranger School," he said. "I thought it was going to be the one regret I'd carry with me to my grave. Barbra didn't think I'd even read the script before I came, and I studied the son of a gun. She said, 'You never knew your lines before you got there, did you?'

"I said, 'Are you out of your mind?' She asked me once before the movie, 'Are you scared to do a movie with me?' And I said, 'Of course.' She said, 'Are you willing to stretch?' and I immediately came back with, 'Are you ready to get down? I'll stretch as far as you can get down.' "

As filming progressed and problems grew, Streisand, Peters, and Pierson worked out their frustrations with heated, sometimes bitter, verbal clashes; Kristofferson worked out his by drinking tequila with beer chasers from the start of the day onward.

The powder keg that was the *Star Is Born* company finally ignited on a day Barbra later called "enormously tense and emotionally explosive." In order to film a rock concert at which John Norman Howard drives a motorcycle off the stage into the crowd, Peters arranged, with the help of promoter Bill Graham, a real rock concert at Sun Devil stadium in Tempe, Arizona, featuring acts like Peter Frampton, Graham Central Station, Montrose, the L.A. Jets, Santana—and Barbra Streisand and Kris Kristofferson filming *A Star Is Born.*

The thought was terrifying. Graham put the whole thing together in three weeks, and he, Peters, Streisand and Pierson would be responsible for keeping the crowd of

70,000 youthful rock fans under control while the inevitable filming delays kept them from being entertained.

In the midst of all of this, someone at Warner Brothers had a bright idea: Why not invite members of the press to Arizona for the weekend? Day one, Barbra, Kris and Jon can meet the press, day two the reporters can be a part of the concert happening. It would be great publicity for the film, and take care of all those interview requests at one time. In a moment of weakness or insanity or both, Barbra agreed, and Warner Brothers flew a hundred journalists, including this writer, to Arizona.

The first day, when we would be introduced to the principals and granted interviews, was broiling hot by ten in the morning. After a quickly wilting brunch, Barbra, Jon, and Kris came to the area of the stadium field where the dining tables had been set up, posed for photographers, and then "table-hopped," granting several groups of journalists separate interviews. Although some writers would later try to make it seem that they had had private conversations with the trio, there were no exclusive interviews granted.

Streisand, needless to say, was the center of attention. She certainly *seemed* tense, her dazzlingly blue eyes squinting as she strained to hear a question or thought out her response. Some of the questions were stupid—"How does it feel working with your husband?"—and most of them centered on all the rumors that had surrounded the production for almost three years. Barbra was combative. "So what if Jon was a hairdresser! I mean, people say, 'My God, she's going with a hairdresser!' Is that not supposed to happen? It's a very narrow way of thinking. A lot of producers started off selling dresses in New York. They said the same kinda thing about me. 'How can she act when she's just a singer?' No one is *just* anything. Who says I'm a singer? Who says I'm an actress? I'm a person. I happen to sing. I act. I paint pictures. I design clothes. I wear many hats."

Why had she decided to take on so much responsibility with this film? "It's a matter of maturing—not even as an artist but as a human being—when you can take responsibility for your own ideas. It's scary—it is. Power is a frightening thing. But I was always timid about that before. I'd say, 'I have this great idea, but if you don't like it, O.K.'—I never fought for it. I don't work that way anymore. Now I say, 'I have this great idea. If you have a better one, I'll take yours, but if not, we're gonna use mine.' I never had the power before because I never took it. There were movies I didn't want to make, scenes I thought should be different, but I always gave in. Not anymore."

Then Streisand looked at the assembled reporters. "How come nobody said anything about my hair? I had it *curled*. I have straight hair. All my life I wanted curly hair."

Does Jon still do your hair?, some asked.

"Only when we're making out." Then, more seriously: "Jon has done a lot to open my life. He's a very strong man. I'm basically lazy, and Jon looks after the business side of things. He's exposed me to a lot of things I wasn't aware of before, like gardening and health foods. He fights for what he believes in. He doesn't let people walk all over him." She paused, changed thoughts. "You know, being a woman today is a constant test. You have to be more assertive, more aggressive than you were brought up to be."

Someone brought her back to the movie, asking, "Why remake *A Star Is Born?* The Judy Garland version was wonderful."

"Yeah," she replied, "but our movie is different. Those were the fifties, this is the seventies—it's a whole other bag. Different kind of music, different attitudes between people. And in the other film she just loved him. Well, I don't believe it. As you experience life, you also hate the person you love." Does she identify with the character in the movie? "Oh, yeah. When we first read the script by Dunne and Didion, the male character was named John, he drove a red Ferrari and had a red jeep, which my Jon does, and he was a Gemini, which Jon is. It was kind of a mystical thing—it was destined

With Kris Kristofferson

(below right) Barbra to Pierson: "I don't know how to go around the bush. I just tell you what I feel."

"I'd like to have the perfect twin, one who'd go out as I came in."

to be. I wrote a lot of things into this movie that come from my own life. I will be revealed in this picture more than ever before."

Kristofferson joined the group, and it was obvious that there were animosities between the two stars. As Barbra expressed her admiration for Bruce Springsteen, Kristofferson piped up, "Maybe you should have hired him for this movie."

Barbra ignored the comment, but a reporter interjected, "She's said some nice things about you, Kris."

Kristofferson sulked. "She said I was an asshole!"

Barbra looked at him, then turned to a reporter. "Listen, I call him an asshole, but he's nice. I told you he was beautiful and I told you he was honest and that he'll forget, but call him an asshole and *that* he'll remember."

After Kris left, a comment was made about the rumors that he was coming to work drunk every day. Barbra skirted the issue, saying, "Kris is frightened a lot of the time, but that's part of the role, too. He has a macho femininity about him. He's what a man should be."

A few reporters talked to Jon, who was overshadowed by his movie's two stars. Most of the questions had been asked before, and he answered them patiently. What were his qualifications for becoming a movie producer? "Business is business. It was high pressure before, though not as intense as this. I didn't use Barbra to get into the business—I knew this business. People like to think I came from nowhere, but that's not true. I don't think producing a film is any great magic. It's just a matter of a lot of hard work and dedication and getting the best people you can. I feel lucky to be working with a person of Barbra's experience."

There were unique problems with this particular film, he admitted. "I was real jealous when they did a scene together in a bathtub. I made him wear underpants. It's real hard to watch your old lady on the screen making love to another guy, especially if you know they used to go out together."

The next day, the largest crowd in Arizona history jammed into Sun Devil Stadium for a rock concert. The tension was as thick as the hot air while the sun-drenched stadium writhed with 70,000 perspiring bodies. Filming was not going smoothly; Streisand, Kristofferson and Peters were having an arms-flailing argument in front of the masses, unaware that the microphones were on. There were interminable waits between rock acts; then interminable delays and retakes in filming. The crowd began to get impatient and shout, "No more filming! No more filming!"

Barbra came out to cheers from the crowd, thanked everyone for coming, and explained why it was so important for them to cheer again when Kris performed his number, and gasp in horror when his motorcycle roars off the stage. Hoping to get the mercurial crowd on her side, she told them, in their own jargon, about the film. "We're gonna do rock 'n' roll today. And we're gonna be in a *movie.* In our movie, we're *real* . . . we fight, scream, yell, we talk dirty, we smoke *grass.*" The crowd loved it; she had them. "So listen, what we're gonna do now is meet my costar, Kris Kristofferson. A great performer. So, when he comes on, I know you all love him anyway, but you have to love him even more, you know, so we won't have any problems. So, in the lingo of the movie, I say, All you motherfuckers have a *great time!*"

The crowd went crazy over Barbra's little speech and again when she returned to sing for them. "I was totally petrified about performing that day," Barbra said later. "I had to get up in front of 70,000 kids who had come to hear Peter Frampton, and I didn't know whether I'd be booed off the stage."

She wasn't. When she sang "People" and "The Way We Were" to a prerecorded accompaniment ("I didn't bring any strings with me"), it was obvious that many of those kids had come to see *her,* not just the rock groups. The applause and cheers were now deafening. Then Streisand announced that she wanted to sing a new song, from the movie. "It's called 'Woman in the Moon.' Like, who says it's a man in the moon? It could be a *woman* in the moon, right?" A wave of agreement, mostly from the females in the audience, and a warm reaction to the song. "Now, I'll sing a song for you that I wrote myself. I hope you like it. If you don't I'll be *crushed.*"

She sang "Evergreen" somewhat differently than it ended up, and it was obviously a terrific song. The crowd roared approval. "Do you *really* like it?" Streisand was being negative again. "I'm really glad you like it, because that's the first time I ever sang that song in front of people."

Finally, the last of the filming was completed, a few more acts performed for the crowd, and the day was over. It was a "nightmare," but the crew accomplished what it had set out to do—stage a real live rock concert for the benefit of a movie and obtain usable footage during it. It was a rare accomplishment, and even some of Jon's harshest critics had to give it to him—he had pulled this one off.

Barbra and Jon were pleased to leave Arizona, and not for just the obvious reasons. "When we were in Phoenix," Jon later told a British interviewer, "our two children were almost kidnapped. And that frightened the hell out of me because I have a little boy and my love for Barbra and my own desires had put me into a situation of jeopardy for him. So, the lifestyle, I would say, and what comes with it—nothing is for free and it's probably her biggest fault."

Once filming wrapped, Barbra moved a team of editors to the Malibu ranch and began preparing the final version of the film; this was the first time she had this control, and she pushed everyone around her to exhaustion, editing, dubbing, looping, and adjusting the sound levels. Larry Grobel met her at this point in preparation for his interview with her for *Playboy,* and he later described the scene: "I watched her edit and dub the last seven minutes of her movie. With her screen image in front of us 20 feet high, Barbra fiddled incessantly with an electronic control board, bringing the drums up, the guitars down, her voice out. She would stop the film and have it run backward. She would hear things no one else could—finding fault with a certain beat, a missed stress. And although the engineers wanted to wrap up and go on vacation, she remained and worked until exhaustion overtook everyone. That, I was to discover, is how she works."

When Barbra and Jon delivered the finished product, Warner Brothers executives were delighted. It was obviously going to be a big hit, and not only had this maligned duo brought the film in on time and under budget, but they had spent less money on it than the 1953 version had cost.

"It was the most horrible experience to let it go," Barbra told an interviewer. "On the last day, I wanted to take the last number and cut it and have all different kinds of strange angles and have it look like a Mike Jagger rock and roll concert. And then the big decision was whether to leave it for 7½ minutes in one place or to cut it—that was my last and most difficult decision. If I showed you the film at my house, I would show you the cut version because I have two versions. I said, 'Why can't I release it in half the theaters with the cut version and half the theaters the one-take version?' I couldn't make up my mind. But wouldn't it be great if a city had two theaters, let's say, and in one theater it played one way and in the other . . . And you'd say, 'It was interesting, wasn't it? That last number with all those cuts in it.' And the other person would say, 'What cuts? I saw it with one take. What are you talking about?' Then they'd have to go see it again. You know it would really be fun. Maybe sometime we'll do it that way."

A month before the film's scheduled release at Christmas 1976, "a black cloud," as Barbra later put it, was cast over *A Star Is Born.* Frank Pierson wrote an unprecedentedly intimate and bitter article about his experiences directing the film and published it in *New West* and *New York* magazines. Entitled "My Battles with Barbra and

Jon," the fifteen-page piece described in great detail the day-to-day problems Pierson faced trying to direct the film and deal with his producers, whom he characterized alternately as inept, meddlesome, petulant, childish, petty, frightened, frightening, and egomaniacal.

The article dealt too with highly personal matters between Barbra and Jon; Pierson recreated angry conversations and arguments between them for the edification of his readers. After one such fight, he wrote, Barbra sought his protection: "Later, as I walk to my car, Barbra darts out of the hedges, running stooped low behind cars in the dark. 'For God's sake, take me home!' she says. She shivers, huddled in a corner of the dark car. 'He gets so furious. I don't know what to do.' I offer to take her home to sleep at our house. But Jon is not home when we arrive at her place. Small and tired and scared, she walks into the gigantic house, all the lights shining."

Pierson's article spoke of Barbra's film-making ineptitude and her almost tyrannical demands on everyone around her, driving the crew to illness: "In the small hours of the morning, Paul is sent off to rework the lyrics. Barbra is a little panicky; we are running out of time. Paul won't consult others for outside help. We begin to look ourselves. Paul grows angrier and angrier. 'How can I write when I have to talk with her all the time and nothing ever gets finished because before I finish the damn song she's already asking for changes?' he shouts."

Re-creations of conversations between himself and Barbra studded Pierson's article. "She is upset with me. 'I don't feel you really want to love me. All my directors have wanted to make me beautiful. But I feel you hold something back; there's something you don't tell me. You never talk to me.' I realize she's serious. 'I love you,' I say, 'but I'm not the demonstrative type.' I talk about the need for distance, for tranquil and objective judgment of the film. She can knock directors and actors clean out of the practice of their profession with 10 percent of her energy. I have to guard against it."

At another point in his narrative, Pierson wrote, "I have never been so tired, not since World War II. I begin to realize that Barbra and Jon are frightened, and their fears are focused on me. 'If this film goes down the drain,' she says, 'it's all over for me and Jon. We'll never work again.' I point out the obvious. 'All you have to do is offer to sing, and they'll fall all over you to do a picture. Why are you trying to panic yourself this way?' 'I know,' she says, 'but what will happen to Jon?' "

Later in Pierson's piece: "The hours pass. The strain begins to tell. Jon is suddenly standing before me, yelling. I tell him to keep his voice down, because I can't hear him. I suggest he fire me. Suddenly he is confused. 'I'm sick of you,' he yells. 'I'm waiting until the production is finished. Then I'm going to punch you out!' It is a nightmare that has no end."

The publication of "My Battles with Barbra and Jon" was talked about from coast to coast, and many observers chortled over the fact that Barbra was finally being revealed as the megalomaniac they always had known she was. The woman herself was "devastated." When she read the article, she told *Playboy,* "I felt like the painting called *The Scream* by Edvard Munch, a scream with no sound. And perhaps like the Africans who felt their soul was being taken away when their picture was taken."

In a TV interview with Geraldo Rivera after the film's opening, Barbra was asked about it. "Pierson's article was so immoral, so unethical, so unprofessional, so undignified, with no integrity, totally dishonest, injurious. If anyone believes it, without examining who that person is, to try to put a black cloud over a piece of work before it's even released. That's the most important indication of who that person was.

Barbra in *Playboy:* "He broke the confidentiality of the relationship between a director and an actor, which is a very intimate, private relationship that has a great deal of honor attached to it. I was deeply hurt. He tried to make me look ridiculous and unprofessional. A lot of things are done and said in the heat of passion of the creative experience, and it's all part of the process. It happens on many films.

"The experience of making this film was a nightmare for all of us. One time I was a little sharp with him and I apologized. I said, 'I have a problem with tact, I only know how to be direct with you. I don't know how to go around the bush, I just tell you what I feel.' He said, 'That's O.K., I agree with you and then behind your back I do what I want anyway.' So we had two different styles, you see. When things got worse, I had to assume more responsibility."

At a UCLA film seminar a few days after the opening of the film, Barbra and Jon turned the tables on Pierson, indicating that it was he who did not know the fundamentals of film-making and that she had to handle a great many areas because of his incompetence. She amplified this in the *Playboy* interview. "Look, maybe he's right. Maybe he's this terrific director. Maybe it was the combination of our chemistries that didn't work. In my opinion, he didn't know how to deal with actors. When I asked him one day what he thought of the difference in playing a scene in one of two ways, he said, 'I'm neutral.' I said, 'Frank, if you ever want to be a director, you can never be neutral—lie, make it up, explore your feelings, anything—because the actor has to have some feedback, some mirror, some opinion, even if it's wrong. He didn't try to talk to the actors, give them a sense of their characters, a sense of their own importance in this film. Every extra is important, every detail!

"He put down *my* sense of detail when I made suggestions about the sets and the costumes. He seemed to look on it like, Oh, God, how meddlesome. But he had accepted his position from the start as a collaborator and even seemed to welcome my contributions, since he had never directed a musical before. He knew I was more than just a hired actress, he knew that this was an extremely personal film for me, that my responsibility as executive producer extended into all those other areas. But once we started shooting, he seemed to forget our agreement."

Pierson's article was a blow to Barbra, but the worst was yet to come—the reviews. The first notices, from Los Angeles, were disarming. Richard Cuskelly in the Los Angeles *Herald Examiner*, wrote, "Streisand is, at last, free to be herself. She gives a performance of such startling simplicity, it is as if we're discovering anew why we fell in love with her in the first place."

Daily Variety showered the film with compliments: "A superlative remake. Barbra Streisand's performance as the rising star is her finest screen work to date, while Kris Kristofferson's magnificent portrayal of her failing benefactor realizes all the promise first shown five years ago in *Cisco Pike*. Jon Peters' production is outstanding, and Frank Pierson's direction is brilliant. Selznick himself would be proud of this film."

Almost all the New York and national reviews, however, were brutal, attacking not only the film but Barbra, her hair, her clothes, Jon, and the music. Janet Maslin in *Newsweek* called the film "almost as self-destructive as its suicidal leading man," termed Kris Kristofferson "hapless," expressed surprise at "the actress's demolishing her own performance as thoroughly as she ruins his," and criticized the "simple adobe hut in the desert" which Esther and John Norman build after their marriage: "It's impossible to believe that the Streisand character could ever live in such a place, because there aren't any closets."

Rex Reed chose *A Star Is Born* as the "worst movie of 1976," and called it a "stupid, cacophonous and unnecessary rock and roll remake of the old potboiler that drowns in a lot of noise and body odor. Barbra Streisand looked and sounded ridiculous trying to be Grace Slick and Kris Kristofferson looked like the Werewolf of London stoned on cocaine and sounded like a dying buffalo. Her clothes looked designed by Lawrence of Poland, her hair looked fried in possum fat, the music was execrable, the

At a party on the set.   *(opposite)* Barbra and Jon react to the cheers of fans at the Hollywood premiere.

dialogue sounded like it had been rejected by *The Gong Show*. A total disaster, about as contemporary as a 1965 student riot."

By far the most vicious and personal attack against Barbra was launched by John Simon, the erstwhile theater critic for *New York* magazine. His review of *I Can Get It for You Wholesale* had lauded Barbra's "Chekhovian brand of heartbreaking merriment" and said that she was "gifted with a face that shuttles between those of a tremulous young borzoi and a fatigued Talmudic scholar," but in the ensuing fourteen years, Simon had changed his mind about Streisand.

"O, for the gift of Rostand's Cyrano," he wrote, "to evoke the vastness of that nose alone as it cleaves the giant screen from east to west, bisects it from north to south. It zigzags across our horizon like a bolt of fleshy lightning; it towers like a ziggurat made of meat. The hair is now something like the wig of the fop in a Restoration comedy; the speaking voice continues to sound like Rice Krispies if they could talk. And Streisand's notion of acting is to bulldoze her way from one end of a line to the other without regard for anyone or anything; you can literally feel her impatience for the other performer to stop talking so she can take over again.

"... Kris tells Barbra, 'When you hook into an incredible marlin, that's what it felt like hearing you sing.' Funny, it feels like that to me when I see her face. ... And then I realize with a gasp that this Barbra Streisand is in fact beloved above all other female stars by our moviegoing audiences; that this hypertrophic ego and bloated countenance are things people shell out money for as for no other actress; that this progressively more belligerent caterwauling can sell anything—concerts, records, movies. And I feel as if our entire society were ready to flush itself down in something even worse than a collective death wish—a collective will to live in ugliness and self-debasement."

"I read these things and I started to cry," Barbra said. "I couldn't even control myself, it was *so* devastating to me. I had heard so many good things about the film at preview showings, then they say it's a piece of trash. I didn't know who to believe. And it hurt me deeply that the reviews were so personal. They weren't reviewing the film, they were reviewing *me*. I'm criticized for my looks, my nose. It's awfully late in the game for that. Why can't I be judged for the quality of my work, and not the way I look? I was terrified that the movie would be a bomb. It would have killed me, I think. And it certainly would have put a terrible strain on my relationship with Jon."

If it is any consolation to Barbra, John Simon has been equally savage with others, notably Liza Minnelli. His tragic flaw is a total inability to appreciate on any level any actress whom he does not find physically attractive.

Many of the other reviews chastised Barbra for what the critics saw as her preoccupation with her own image on film. They accused her of lingering on herself when it was Kristofferson's reaction that was relevant, and of including scenes simply because she thought she looked good. In Britain for the film's premiere, Barbra responded to the question, "Would you put in what you consider to be an ugly shot of yourself?"

"Oh sure," she said. "Like in the death scene. I didn't want to wear any make-up. I wanted to look like a person who really got up and found out that her husband was dead. And my biggest fights when I was editing the film were because I always have a tendency to cut away from myself when I can't stand it anymore. But then it looks cut. I probably would be a better actress if I didn't see with the director's eyes. Because I become very objective and I stage scenes in my head, and then I have to go in and try to do them. Sometimes I wish I had another actress so I could be more objective."

In New York, magazines and newspapers tried to top each other in mocking Barbra and the film. "A Star Is Boring," several headlines read. *The Village Voice* editors thought a little harder and came up with a cleverer pun: "A Bore Is Starred."

"The worst reviews I've gotten were from the New York critics," Barbra said. "I heard that when one of them watched *A Star Is Born,* he talked back to the screen. I mean, the New York critics *hated* the film! I wish I could be like Shaw, who once read a bad review of one of his plays, called the critic and said, 'I have your review in front of me and soon it will be behind me.' I wish I could be above it all like he was. It's difficult to take. I cry a lot. There are times when I get so wiped out I just want to quit—get out altogether. But then I'll get a nice letter from a fan and it all seems worth it."

Barbra got a great deal of fan mail about *A Star Is Born.* The critics may have hated it, but the public loved it. It broke box-office records across the country—there were stories of people camping out in snowstorms to get into theaters—and the film quickly became Barbra's biggest hit ever, grossing between $75 and $100 million. The film's love story struck a chord with the movie-going public, and its music—railed against by most critics—helped sell eight million copies of the soundtrack album, the biggest soundtrack sale to that date. According to Jon, he and Barbra made more money on the soundtrack than on the film.

It was clear that the public was still enchanted with Barbra; *A Star Is Born,* in fact, won her millions of new, young fans, some of whom had never seen a Streisand film before. How could "the worst movie of the year" become its biggest hit next to *Rocky?* John Simon's explanation hardly suffices; the tables have to be turned. Why were the critics, who had lavished praise on Streisand for almost everything she had done before, suddenly turning on her with such ferocity? Barbra tried to explain. "People are always behind you when you're struggling," she said. "But then, when you reach the top, some of them resent you and try to tear you down again."

But that was only part of it. The critics, for whatever reason, obviously felt Streisand needed a dressing down. She was getting too big for her britches. Who was she to produce, cowrite, codirect, and edit a movie? That Sylvester Stallone did so with *Rocky,* as self-indulgent a film, and became the darling of the press, points up an inescapable fact: the criticism of Streisand was in no small way a result of male chauvinism.

Barbra and Jon had their own theories about why the reviews were so vicious. "It's hard to be an idol, hard to be a legend, because then you're something superhuman," she said. "You're *expected* to be superhuman. Somebody told me something Eva Le Gallienne said about actors—'Actors are expected to be astrophysicists and we have to be reviewed by cloners.' That's what *she* said!"

Jon added: "Hollywood is a make-believe world that fascinates a lot of different people. The elitist society of Hollywood and the press could not believe that I could make that adjustment. They were confronted with their own feelings of inadequacy. Because it frightened them, that a hairdresser could possibly succeed when in fact they kept on doing the same thing year after year. It angered them—why should *I* have the opportunity? Why should Barbra Streisand allow me to produce a movie? When the movie opened and it was good and a big hit, it made them really furious. They attacked Barbra and me personally—not even the film."

Because of her intense involvement in *A Star Is Born* and her desire to fight back against all the negative press, Barbra made herself available for the promotion of the picture to a greater extent than ever before. She attended gala premieres in Los Angeles, New York and several European cities and, with Jon, submitted to televised interviews by Geraldo Rivera, David Sheehan, and Barbara Walters.

The Walters interview was a charming half-hour segment following an interview with another famous couple, President-elect and Mrs. Carter. Walters first spoke to Jon, who disarmed her with an open admission that yes, knowing Barbra had opened doors to him. Then she introduced her viewers to Barbra outside the ranch's main house, and they discussed the acreage and Barbra's gardening interests. Once inside, Walters described the house's decor and screened a film clip from *A Star Is Born.*

She then interviewed a relaxed Barbra and Jon about their meeting, their working relationship, Barbra's criticism by the press, and whether they would soon be marrying. "I've asked her three times," Jon said, 'but she keeps turning me down." "It'll come," Barbra said. When Walters pressed them about marriage, asking how they justified their living together to their children, Jon replied, "The children look to see what you feel about each other. They don't check to see if you've got a piece of paper."

Barbra then spoke of some of the drawbacks of stardom. "People can be very cruel. People coming in back of me saying, 'Hey, her nose is not that big. Are you Barbra Streisand? You look like Barbra Streisand. Hey, hey, you look pretty good in person!' or 'You look better.' Do you know what I mean? They treat performers sometimes as if they're not *alive*, as if they're a piece of celluloid on the screen. It's a painful feeling because . . . I'm a human being, you know? And it will probably never be different because I refuse to play those games."

At the end of the interview, Walters asked them whether they saw themselves still together as old people. "Yes," said Jon. "No one else would have us," Barbra laughed.

As *A Star Is Born* continued making money (it became the biggest-grossing musical of all time to that date), it also began winning awards. At the 1977 Golden Globe ceremonies, the picture was honored five times in the "musical or comedy" category: Best Picture, Best Actress, Best Actor, Best Song ("Evergreen") and Best Music Scoring. Barbra and Jon glowed as they posed with a Golden Globe in each hand. Kristofferson, accepting his award, made a point of thanking "the lady" for all she had done.

Kristofferson later expounded on his gratitude to Barbra. "She made me look better than I've ever looked in a movie, you've got to admit that," Kris told Geraldo Rivera. "I know that this is probably the most favorable treatment that I'll ever get. I feel terrible that she's getting such criticism because she's a great filmmaker."

Barbra had nothing but praise for Kristofferson's contributions. "I had envisioned certain things between the two characters, and Kris's characterization of this person was beyond what I had dreamed. There were certain scenes in the movie that I had hoped for and when they came off, again as I said, they were beyond what I had ever dreamed them to be."

"I'm so proud of the damned thing," Kristofferson said. "Just being a part of it, you know, I feel like I got swatted in the tail with luck."

A Star Is Born changed Kristofferson's life. When he watched his performance as a rock star drinking himself to death, it hit too close to home. "I realized it was my own life I was seein' on the screen." He vowed he would never drink again. "It was like seeing myself through [his wife] Rita's eyes—when I saw the corpse at the end, I had a weird feeling of sadness, like a character in the *Twilight Zone* who sees a coffin with his name on it. I feel so goddamn lucky to have found out in time—I'd been drinking heavily for twenty years."

Once all the hubbub had died down, Barbra admitted the experience had been a draining one for her. "I'm very tired," she said. But neither she nor Jon regretted taking on the project. As he put it, "I would love to have everyone love what I do and love everything Barbra does, but I think that we cannot live our lives for that. We have to live our lives for us and do the things that we believe in. If we fail, we fail and if we win, we win. That's really where it's at for me."

Streisand Superman

Barbra spent the spring of 1977 accepting awards. In addition to her Golden Globes, she won the People's Choice Award as the public's favorite actress, and *A Star Is Born* was chosen as the year's favorite film by the readers of *Photoplay.* Barbra made a rare appearance at the "People's Choice" ceremonies, thanking people for their letters of support.

When the Academy Award nominations were announced, the film and its stars' acting were passed over, but Barbra and Paul Williams were nominated for composing "Evergreen," the film's theme song. At the Oscar ceremonies, Streisand, after a spirited introduction by Jane Fonda, sang the song to a thrilled audience. The award for Best Song was presented by Barbra's friend Neil Diamond, who said that he wanted Barbra to win so much he had told her he would announce her name no matter who won. But he didn't have to fake it; "Evergreen" was named best song. Barbra glowed as she accepted her second Oscar. "Never in my wildest dreams did I ever imagine I'd win an Oscar for writing a song," she said. "I'm very excited and very grateful."

How did Barbra, who had written just one song before, come to write an Oscar-winning melody? "I was going through a period of feeling very inadequate because so many of our songstresses (I'd guess you'd have to call them that) today write their own songs; and I thought, 'God—how talented they are to write their own songs and be able to sing them!' And then my guitar teacher—I wanted to play my own guitar in the movie—told me she wrote her own music and lyrics, and I asked her to play some stuff for me. I was so *impressed* with the fact that she wrote these songs, and it felt really terrible. I remember getting very emotional and very insecure and very upset about it because I thought, 'I only sing. I only sing these songs that other people write.' I remember going into the bathroom and I started to cry—it sounds like I cry a lot, doesn't it? I really don't cry a lot. I wish I could cry more . . . but I've been crying a lot lately.

"Anyway, Jon came into the bathroom and told me that if I put my mind to it, I could write a song, and I said to myself, 'I've got to do something like that.' So one day I was sort of bored during my guitar lesson—I want to play like Segovia and I can't—and I just started to fool around with chords. And instead of *A Star Is Born,* a song was born! It just came out of absolute impatience."

The rest of the year, Barbra relaxed, recovered, and spent months being interviewed by Larry Grobel for *Playboy.* "The interview sessions became, at times, a battle," Grobel wrote in introducing the interview. "When I touched on subjects that weren't comfortable for her, she would answer evasively or glibly and I would tell her what I thought of her answers—and get on her nerves. Because she'd always demanded a great deal of control of interviews in the past—including the TV chat with Barbara Walters, for which Streisand had unprecedented first-rush approval—and wasn't getting that sort of control in this case, things often got emotional . . . But she clearly regarded this interview as something special. It was going to be her definitive statement, she said, in which she would talk about subjects that had been rumored but neither confirmed nor denied. Because we talked for so long, some of her lengthier comments—such as those on critics who have constantly attacked her—had to be sacrificed; but what remains constitutes, I believe, the most extensive study of Barbra Streisand—in her own words—in which she's been willing to participate."

Grobel's interview is indeed an extraordinary document, an incisive look at Barbra that will remain primary source material for Streisand biographers for years to come, just as it has been for this one. It appeared in the November 1977 issue, with a sexy cover picture of Barbra displaying "the best legs since Dietrich," as Garson Kanin put it. She was the first female movie star to grace *Playboy's* cover since its first issue in 1953—that time, the subject was Marilyn Monroe. Grobel has said, "I was told the Streisand issue was one of the best-selling issues they ever had." During the photo session, Streisand took off her sneakers and socks. "Hey, guys," she laughed, "now you can say I took it off for *Playboy!*"

Grobel's interview reveals Streisand as a thoughtful, intelligent woman. Of her reputedly large ego, she said, "It's true that I have a very healthy ego; anybody who creates does. To have ego means to believe in your own strength. To not have the fear that anyone can take something away from you. And to also be open to other people's views, because they can't take your view away. So yes, my ego is big, but it's also very small in some areas. I'm very secure in one way and very insecure in another. I'm consumed with self-doubt, which, I believe, is also necessary. My ego is responsible for my doing what I do—bad or good."

Streisand described for Grobel how she would often make up elaborate lies to deny to people who recognized her that she actually was Barbra Streisand. "In my growing up process, I now admit I *am* Barbra Streisand. Once, I took my son to a gym class and this little eight-year-old girl comes up to me and says, 'You look like Barbra Streisand.' Feeling mature, I said, 'I am.' She looked at me for a long time and finally said, 'No, you're *not*.' I told her, 'Kid, you won't believe it, but for years I've been denying who I am. Now that I've decided as an adult to admit it, you come up and tell me you don't believe it!' My biggest nightmare is that I'm driving alone in my car and I get sick and have to go to the hospital. I'd say, 'Please, help me,' and the people would say, 'Hey, you look like . . .' And I'm dying while they're talking and wondering if I'm Barbra Streisand."

"When did you become a sexually agressive woman?" Grobel asked. "In just the past three years," Streisand replied. "With my relationship with Jon. When you have a relationship that really has love and trust, trust to be yourself, with your good and bad qualities, that's a very liberating thing. To be yourself. With no images. I was always playing games with men. That image game. And I never even thought that I counted. I was always trying to please them. In the song 'Lullaby for Myself,' the lyric says, 'Your aim becomes to please yourself and not to aim to please.' "

"Actually," Streisand said at one point, "I believe women are superior to men, I don't even think we're equal." "That sounds like a female chauvinist talking," Grobel responded. "*How* are women superior?"

"You would have to read *The Natural Superiority of Women,* by Ashley Montagu, in which he says the biological facts show that emotionally and constitutionally, among many other things, women are stronger than men. What is wonderful about the book is that it is designed to bring the sexes closer together. There is a constant war between men and women that is largely complicated by ignorance, and Montagu shows statistically that men have more heart attacks, ulcers, nervous breakdowns and suicides. Their façade is killing them. I have enormous compassion for men, which really came into focus with the birth of my own son. This little boy who wanted to be held and comforted

A Star Is Born sweeps the 1977 Golden Globe Awards.

At the 1977 Academy Awards, Neil Diamond presented Oscars to Barbra and Paul Williams for writing "Evergreen."

and soothed has to grow up in a world where he cannot cry because it is 'unmanly.' I think women are further along with their own liberation. We accept the fact that women can be weak yet strong, soft yet tough, shy yet aggressive. But there's much to say on the subject, much to discuss; it's an article all in itself. In the end, I think we are two slightly different animals who need the same things—mothering and fathering, love, understanding and respect."

About her continually changing image, Streisand commented, "It's so important to me to have no image. None. And if you look at my career, I always try to break my own image. My big fight has always been: Don't put me into a mold, 'cause I'm not going to go into it. Just when you think you can imitate me when my hair's long, I cut it short; when you think my hair's brown, I make it red; when they imitate me with long nails, I cut 'em off. I don't want that kind of success. I want to grow as an artist. As a human being.

"I'm at a place in my life where I'm almost realizing my dreams. The other day, I was so anxious about it I started to cry when I said the words. 'Oh my God, I'm almost getting everything.' It was a total emotional experience. Because I am so used to complaining, to being negative, that to be in a happy place is a whole new way of life for me.

"The other day, while I was driving to the doctor's, I was having an anxiety attack. I was in a rage about several things that set me off. I was feeling miserable, upset, like I was going insane. Like, maybe I *am* insane. I'm such a terrible person and maybe I really am these awful things you read about and how do I deal with that and live with myself? But in my therapy group, these people are psychologists, work in offices, on computers, from all walks of life—and we're all alike. And I think, You mean, it's not just show buisness? And then the therapist said, 'Look, you're all mad, and so am I; there's only one difference: I respect my madness.' He stripped half of my anxieties away. It was OK to be crazy, we're all crazy, and if you can respect your own madness—far out."

Seven months after the release of *A Star Is Born,* Barbra's album *Streisand Superman* was released. It continued her mastery of the pop genre, which she was beginning to dominate as never before. "Evergreen" was her first hit single since "The Way We Were" in 1973, but now she was a potent force in contemporary music. Her follow-up single, "My Heart Belongs to Me," was another big hit, and *Streisand Superman* climbed to #2 on several charts. It was unable to wrestle the #1 spot from Fleetwood Mac's *Rumours,* however. *Rumours,* which had replaced the *Star Is Born* soundtrack at #1, remained in the top spot for a historically long period of time.

The "superman" concept grew out of a sexy outfit Streisand wore in *A Star Is Born.* During a sequence in which she and Kristofferson are building their desert house, there is a fleeting scene of Barbra, wearing tiny white shorts, knee socks, and a form-fitting T-shirt with the "Superman" logo on the front. Audiences cheered this revealing look at Streisand's fabulous new figure and her raised-fist power salute—a tribute to women's liberation.

For the album, Barbra posed for photographer Steve Schapiro in the same outfit. It was this, in fact, which gave *Playboy*'s editors the idea to put Barbra on their cover—her outfit there is the same, except the *Playboy* logo has replaced "Superman."

Streisand Superman is a good album, containing wonderfully sensual interpretations of Roger Miller's "Baby Me Baby," Kim Carnes and Dave Ellingson's "Love Comes from Unexpected Places," and Billy Joel's "New York State of Mind." There are two songs not used in *A Star Is Born,* "Lullaby for Myself" and "Answer Me," the latter written by Barbra with Paul Williams and Kenny Ascher.

Barbra congratulates Roslyn after her opening at Hollywood's Studio One.

With Olivia Newton-John and Lou Rawls at the 1978 Grammy Awards.

She won for "Best Pop Vocal Performance—Female" for "Evergreen."

Another Streisand composition, with Ron Nagle and Scott Mathews, is "Don't Believe What You Read." A rocker, it's sung angrily by Barbra and was inspired by an item in *Los Angeles* magazine: "A pigeon is born: Barbra Streisand has this almost cuckoo thing about birds, so it was no surprise that when she and Jon Peters moved into their Malibu nest, her flock followed. What is surprising is that her aviary is *indoors,* and her feathered friends are allowed to fly about freely, dropping little messages all over the place. Now the word is that Barbra has become almost Howard Hughesesque about germs (the *human* variety), and sequesters visitors in one corner of the living room, allowing the birds full flight of the house."

In the song, Streisand says, "Makes me feel so foolish 'cause they called my house a cage—but there's nothin' I can do. Just puts me in a rage!"

Inside the album, she commented further on the ridiculous item: "Seems like so many magazines have no respect or regard for the truth. They print items like this without ever checking facts. There is no caring if the parties get hurt or their reputations ridiculed. One night I invited Neil Sedaka and his wife to come over and play some music and she told me later that she was afraid to come because she has read I had birds flying around on the loose . . . I find it such a waste of time to have to constantly refute these idiotic statements. Now, the truth is . . . I have a cage with two parakeets in it. Just like a typical Brooklyn girl would have. I can't even comment about the germ fetish remark, which makes me into a double *cuckoo!*"

The magazine's editors, told of Barbra's denial, said they had the item from a reliable source and stand by it. Later told of Barbra's song, one editor commented, "Good—it'll get us free publicity." But Barbra had the last laugh—she never mentioned the name of the publication that had inspired her wrath.

During the summer of 1977, Barbra's half-sister, Roslyn Kind, performed at the Backlot, a Hollywood nightclub. Once the president of the Barbra Streisand fan club, Roslyn has a pleasant voice and assured stage presence, and her show was well received. Barbra attended opening night, and joined a standing ovation for Roslyn at the show's conclusion.

Were Roslyn not Barbra's sister, she might well be able to carve out a credible show business career. But although she is a good performer, she is invariably compared to Barbra, and the comparison hurts her. Despite this, she and Barbra are very close and Roslyn divides her time between managing a bakery in Westwood, California, and doing an occasional singing stint.

Much of the controversy surrounding Barbra Streisand had abated by 1978, but the acclaim had not. *Playboy* readers voted her "Jazz Songstress of the Year," and the American Guild of Variety Artists named her, for an unprecedented third time, "Female Singing Star of the Year." She won the prestigious Anti-Defamation League designation as "Woman of the Year in the Arts," and was once again announced as the #1 female box-office attraction, a position she had held for a decade. In March, she won still another Golden Globe, this time as World Film Favorite, her fourth such win.

Barbra's four Grammy awards in the 1960s were soon accompanied by two more. "Evergreen" was named Song of the Year in a tie with "You Light Up My Life," and Barbra was voted Best Female Pop Vocal Performer, her first such award since 1964.

Looking lovely, Streisand accepted her award with grace. "Gee, I'm really surprised," she said. "I really am! It's funny—I know I won four Grammies but I didn't remember for what because it was such a long time ago, you know? So I looked in the book and . . . I mean, it's such a knock-out to me, to win one of these again. It's just really . . . I really want to thank you all."

Cries of "We love you Barbra!" came from the audience, and Streisand smiled nervously. "Thank you," she said. "I love you, too."

Later, interviewed by David Sheehan, Streisand said, "We won the Academy Award *last* year. I thought we were forgotten. It seems like a long time ago. It *was* a long time ago that I won Grammies—in 1963, '64 and '65. So, to win this now and seeing all these young kids . . . thank God I was young when I started."

"It doesn't make you feel old, does it?" Sheehan asked.

"Yeah," Barbra responded.

In May 1978, Barbra performed at a benefit concert saluting Israel's thirtieth anniversary. Rumor had it that ABC television planned to air the concert only if Streisand's appearance were guaranteed. It was, and the program was televised the following night. Streisand's appearance was saved for last, after Barry Manilow, Carol Burnett, Paul Newman, Ben Vereen, Pat Boone, and Sammy Davis, Jr., had done their turns. She took the stage wearing a lovely antique lace gown and sang "Tomorrow" from *Annie,* investing that simple song with more meaning than it had ever had before. Powerful versions of "Happy Days Are Here Again" and "People" led into a thrilling rendition of the Israeli national anthem in its native language.

Broadcast by satellite to an audience in Israel, Barbra's appearance included a phone-and-video interview with Israel's former Prime Minister, Golda Meir.

Later in May, Barbra's thirty-second album, *Songbird,* was released. It was a mellower album than *Streisand Superman,* similar in many ways to *Stoney End* in its pop romanticism. It was not a powerhouse record, a fact not lost on the *Hi-Fi Stereo Review* critic: "[It] might at first be looked on as one of her throwaway efforts, an album made only because the sales department needed a new one . . . but that, you see, is the kind of conventional entertainment-industry thinking that Streisand has always fought . . . This time out she has created at least three memorable tracks, and considering the level at which Streisand functions you really shouldn't need any more notice than that to go out and grab the album. First there's 'Tomorrow' from *Annie,* a soppy, soupy song that sounded old and worn on the night the show opened; here it's transformed (in much the same way as 'Cry Me a River' and 'Happy Days Are Here Again' were earlier) into something absolutely personal and unique—pure Streisand. Then there's Neil Diamond's really lousy 'You Don't Bring Me Flowers,' with which she merely breaks your heart, and finally, 'Honey, Can I Put On Your Clothes,' in which she throws off enough sexual steam to fog up Gloria Steinem's aviator glasses for good."

The album's single, "Songbird," was a solid hit, breaking into the Top Ten.

By 1978, Jon Peters had won grudging admiration from industry observers. He produced a film without Barbra—*The Eyes of Laura Mars,* starring Faye Dunaway and directed by Irvin Kershner—and proved that *A Star Is Born* wasn't a one-shot ride on Barbra's coattails. An indication of the newfound esteem in which he was held was an admiring article in the New York *Times* written by Janet Maslin, who had complained about the lack of closets in *A Star Is Born.* Calling Jon and Barbra "Mr. Peters" and "Miss Streisand" throughout, Maslin characterized Jon as disarmingly honest, personable, and competent. She quoted Frank Pierson, of all people, as calling Jon "open, changeable and a very bright guy with enormous energy and curiosity," and Faye Dunaway as adding, "He has great instincts, and he's totally unafraid to admit he's wrong."

Later, Maslin wrote, "The hardest thing about becoming a movie producer for Mr. Peters has been, he says, 'the loss of equilibrium. A lot of the time, I didn't know who I was—because I was, for a long time, a very successful hairdresser. I walked into

The birthday salute to Israel

221

the beauty shop and people had respect for me . . . Then, when I left that business and went into this one, all I read was that I was a pimp and a conniver and a nobody latching onto a star's wings. I would meet people, and they would look at me funny because they'd read all those things about me. It was a very painful time."

No one looked at Jon "funny" after *The Eyes of Laura Mars*. Although only a moderate commercial success, the film was stylishly produced, and Jon's production credentials were unquestioned. Barbra recorded the love theme from the film, "Prisoner," and the record was a Top Ten hit. *Billboard* said of it, " 'Prisoner' is a booming, dramatic ballad with a compelling rock undercurrent of fiery instrumentation. It also features some of Streisand's gutsiest singing to date."

Barbra's next single, released two months later, came about in a curious way. Gary Guthrie, a disk jockey in Louisville, Kentucky, noticed that Barbra's version of "You Don't Bring Me Flowers" on *Songbird* and Neil Diamond's performance of his song on his latest album were in the same key. He decided to fiddle around and produce a "duet." He played his "dream" rerecording on the air, and a flood of favorable phone calls ensued. That was quickly followed by loud complaints from record-store managers, who were unable to sell any copies of a record customers were very anxious to buy.

The story got out, and after a series of phone conversations, meetings and negotiations, Barbra and Neil (former Erasmus Hall High School classmates and still friends) recorded an actual duet. The record took just four weeks to reach #1 across the country. A record trade magazine noted "thundering phones, listeners will wait all day to hear this."

It became Streisand's biggest hit (and, of course, Diamond's), and proved a selling point for the next album, *Barbra Streisand's Greatest Hits, Volume II*. The contrast between this album and *Volume I* points up the extraordinary transformation of Barbra Streisand—fifteen years after her first album, she was a more potent force in the recording industry than ever before, and with totally contemporary material. Her first *Greatest Hits* album contained songs like "People," "Second Hand Rose," "My Coloring Book," "Sam, You Made the Pants Too Long," and "Happy Days Are Here Again." Released in 1969, when musical tastes were changing dramatically, it fared rather poorly, peaking at #32 on the *Billboard* chart. The second collection was 30 percent rock and 100 percent contemporary, and it hit #1 amid strong Christmas-season competition. Obviously, many record buyers felt that an album containing "The Way We Were," "Evergreen," "Stoney End," "Sweet Inspiration/Where You Lead," "You Don't Bring Me Flowers" and five other solid hits would make a pretty fair Christmas present.

Winner...and Still Champion

Barbra began 1979 with an album in the Top Five, a new film project underway and another string of accolades. *Seventeen* magazine announced that Barbra Streisand and Bob Hope had been voted by its readers "The man and woman teens admire most." Hope's surprising selection made news across the country. The teenagers polled also selected Streisand and John Travolta as their "Favorite Stars of 1978." *Photoplay*'s readers selected Barbra as their "Favorite Motion Picture Actress" for the second straight year. *People*'s reader poll named Streisand (with Paul Newman) as favorite movie performer, in spite of Barbra's long absence from the screen. The magazine readers' "Dreamiest" screen teams turned out to be Streisand with Redford and Streisand with Kristofferson.

As "dream teams" go, Streisand and O'Neal wasn't exactly chopped liver either. Barbra chose her former leading man and lover to costar with her in her next film, a welterweight battle-of-the-sexes boxing comedy called *The Main Event.* Although the film would be produced by Barbra and Jon through her Barwood Films and First Artists, she did not look upon it as an expression of her personal vision as an artist: in this one, she'd be more the hired actress than the obsessed creative octopus. Howard Zieff, fresh from *House Calls,* was hired to direct the film from a script by Gail Parent and Andrew Smith.

O'Neal's casting opposite Streisand created what press interest there was in *The Main Event.* After the debilitating barrage of publicity surrounding *A Star Is Born,* Barbra and Jon must have been relieved to discover that the greatest interest centered around whether Barbra and Ryan would rekindle their romance. Jon told a reporter exactly what the newsman wanted to hear when he said, "Ryan's a real professional, but if you think I'm cool about it, hell no. Would you be? Once I walked into a rehearsal and there they were kissing, and I just kept on going."

Jon deserved sympathy—this was the second time in a row Barbra was playing love scenes with a man she had previously played them with for real. Ryan stressed in several interviews that his affection for Barbra was no longer romantic but still strong. He told Rex Reed, "I've known her intimately for years. I've watched her grow up. Let's say I have a combination to the electric gate to her house on the movie star maps. We have a certain Pat and Mike teamwork. The Goyim-Jewish thing works."

And Ryan had the following exchange with Rona Barrett on a televised interview: Rona: "Do you think you really have to like someone to show that kind of warmth that the two of you have for one another on the screen?" Ryan: "Yeah, you have to love them." Rona: "Are you saying that you *love* Barbra Streisand?!" Ryan: "Yeah." Rona: "You do? What does Jon Peters think about all of this?" Ryan: "I think Jon understands it better than either Barbra or anyone else for that matter."

The Streisand/O'Neal rapport served the *Main Event* story line very well. It was a star vehicle, tailored to the public's perceptions of its two leads. Barbra played Hillary Kramer, a fast-talking Beverly Hills perfume tycooness who is informed by her lawyer and ex-husband (Paul Sands) that she has been wiped out financially by her accountant. Her only remaining asset is a contract with a retired prize fighter, Eddie "Kid Natural" Scanlon, to whom she has been paying thousands of dollars for several years as a tax dodge. She decides to convince the "Kid" to resume his career for their mutual financial benefit.

Through a series of verbal and physical skirmishes, Hillary manages the Kid's comeback to the point where he is about to win a major fight. If he does, she realizes, she will lose him—and she has fallen in love. She throws in the towel and the film ends in a clinch.

Ryan's "Kid Natural" is boyishly macho and well aware of his instantaneous effect on the opposite sex—particularly his sleazy girlfriend, played with a riotous tuberculous cough by Patti D'Arbanville. O'Neal's personal passion for boxing and his experience with the sport added a credibility and ease to his performance, his most charming since *What's Up, Doc?* "One of the reasons Ryan did this picture," Barbra said, "is because he loves boxing so much. I trusted him implicitly for the authenticity of what was happening. You gotta really hand it to Ryan. He took a terrific beating in this role."

Barbra's Hillary Kramer has a schizophrenic quality that is by turns endearing and annoying. A sophisticated, high-powered businesswoman, she turns into an incompetent, silly thing the minute she gets near a boxing ring, full of girlish goofs and Lucille Ball-like dizziness. Many critics found the inconsistency unbelievable, but each characterization on its own terms is quite enjoyable.

As with *A Star Is Born,* Barbra was intrigued by the fights people in love often have. "Men and women are always fighting," she said during a promotional trailer for the film, "so why not physicalize it? But what happens, something that starts as a little joke starts to develop into a kind of passionate exchange. We had to figure out a set-up for it, so we figured we'd make them pose for publicity pictures—the two of them in boxing gloves . . . It's a sexual dance scene, really—man and woman stalking each other."

The fighting in *Main Event,* unlike *A Star Is Born,* was confined to celluloid, although there were some moments of strain. "Sure there was tension on the set," Howard Zieff said upon the picture's release. "There always is when you're working with a star of Barbra's clout. But it was healthy tension—a give and take attitude. Barbra's been around long enough to be aware of her good and bad points. She's a pro. I knew going in that this would not be a 'director's picture'—but a Barbra Streisand vehicle. She's too big a star for it to be otherwise. When an audience goes to see a Barbra Streisand movie, they go to see Barbra Streisand. No matter what the critics say about her, her fans will come. Nothing will affect their attitude toward her. She transcends whatever is written about her—first, because she has a voice that nobody in the world has; second, because she is a special force. You realize what a big star she is when you go out for a hamburger with her. Fans mob her, like they used to mob Valentino and Garbo. She's *that* popular

"Barbra doesn't stop," Zieff added. "She is not one of those stars who say, 'I've had enough.' She has never had enough. She wants to work as hard as you want her to work. She wants to find the ultimate performance. And what I like about Barbra is that she's willing to do it six times, eight times. She's not saying, 'Well, you got it. Let's go on to the next one.' No. She wants to try it another way, which I love. A woman that strong can step on a lot of toes, but she does it right."

Zieff may have soft-pedaled his feelings about Barbra so as not to affect the critical reaction to the film, because he refused to be interviewed for this book, saying the experience had been an unpleasant one. Ryan O'Neal denies that Barbra created any problems. "Barbra was not overbearing during the shooting of the film, and she never slanted things her way. Sure, she oversees all the details of a production, but so does Kubrick.

As Hillary Kramer

224

At Golda's Gym, "firming things up"

Ryan helps Barbra display her assets

With Paul Sand and Ryan O'Neal

Jon visits the set

"I worked harder with Barbra than with Kubrick on *Barry Lyndon*," Ryan told Rex Reed. "She works 15 and 16 hours a day, checking to make sure we all do our jobs, but she does it in a feminine way. Yet that ruffles some men. I feel that people are unfair to Barbra. She's a delicately made creature, a great lady and I would never have done *The Main Event* without her."

Main Event audiences had more of a chance than ever to see just how "delicately made" Barbra is, thanks to her scanty and clinging wardrobe for the film. Streisand had gotten her figure into fighting trim and proceeded to show it off constantly: under the opening credits in exercise tights; coaching O'Neal ringside in satin shorts; jogging in skin-tight ski pants. Her "great" derriere was the focus of attention in not a few shots, to the dismay of some critics. The Detroit *Free Press* complained, "Unfortunately, what is seen all too frequently, for some puzzling reason, is Streisand's rear end. Although [it] seems reasonably decorative and is probably quite comfortable to sit on, it does little to advance the plot and may even slow it down a bit." Others were more appreciative, like the Denver *Post:* "Streisand, who is sensitive about rumors that better bodies were superimposed on her figure in previous pictures, sets out to prove what a very fine figure she really has."

Again like *A Star Is Born, Main Event* contained some Streisand "messages" about relationships between men and women. One critic noted perceptively that Streisand tends to sugar-coat her feminist views, making them more palatable by presenting them in a comedy framework. One of the scenes in which this is done most appealingly is toward the end of the film. Hillary and the Kid are discussing their future plans the morning after their first night of lovemaking. O'Neal feels exploited as a sex object and wonders if Streisand, who had initiated the sex, still respects him. He insists on marriage; she ponders her future career possibilities and refuses to commit herself.

Streisand fought to have this scene filmed despite the objections of Zieff, and in fact shot it herself after the production had closed down. Again, Barbra's instincts were correct; it is one of the best sequences in the film. Barbra explained, "What is exciting is not for one person to be stronger than the other; not for the man to be stronger than the woman; and not for the woman to be stronger than the man; but for two people to have met their match and yet they are equally as stubborn, as obstinate, as passionate, as crazy as the other."

The Main Event was released in June of 1979. Streisand gave no interviews and made no public appearances in connection with it. (Marty Erlichman has often said that a factor in Barbra's mystique is knowing when to hold back so as to avoid over-exposure.) The reviews, while lacking the venom of those for *A Star Is Born,* were decidedly mixed. *Newsweek* noted, "For both its funniest and most exasperating moments, Streisand must be held accountable . . . one gets a massive dose of 'star presence' and a character who behaves so erratically as to defy sense and patience."

The Chicago *Tribune* took another view: "*Main Event* is a good time at the movies because Streisand is obviously enjoying herself . . . her Hillary Kramer, like virtually every comic Streisand character, is a spunky young woman who uses cleverness and cutesiness to get her way. And, of course, Streisand's strange look can be played as very young or very adult."

The Miami *News* added, "Main Event is a happy movie—even, at times, a naive one. It asks a lot from its audience, but it gives a lot, too, in terms of solid laughs, endearing performances and diverting entertainment."

The Los Angeles *Times's* comments typified the negative reaction: "It is a forced, vulgar and indulgent item which, in the occasional way of star turns, is not wholly satisfactory for the star. The portrayal is strident and hyperactive and misses a lot of the vulnerability that softened the assertiveness in her earlier roles."

As Howard Zieff had predicted, none of the reviews had any effect on the film's box office. It was not in the blockbuster category of *A Star Is Born,* but it was one of the year's top grossers. In spite of the film's success, First Artists was forced to disband in 1979; its *raison d'être,* the assurance of creative control for actors through the clout of its stars, was rendered obsolete by the rapidly increasing number of individual performers who were donning producer hats on their own films. The company had also been hurt by unsuccessful attempts to branch out into music and TV.

Not surprisingly, Barbra decided to record a theme song for *The Main Event.* She had performed under-the-titles songs for *What's Up, Doc?, For Pete's Sake,* and, most effectively, *The Way We Were* and *A Star Is Born.* What *was* surprising was the type of song she chose: disco, then the hottest genre in pop music.

Paul Jabara, who had just won an Oscar for writing disco queen Donna Summer's hit "Last Dance," was hired to write the theme song for *Main Event,* along with Bruce Roberts. Working with Streisand was a dream come true for Jabara, whose idolatry of Barbra went back to *Funny Girl* on Broadway, which he admits to seeing at least a dozen times. In the early seventies, Jabara wrote an off-Broadway show, *My Name Is Rachel Lily Rosenbloom and Don't You Ever Forget It,* about an aspiring actress from Brooklyn who talks like, sings like, acts like, and idolizes Streisand. It was to have starred Bette Midler, but that fell through and the show had only a short off-Broadway run.

"On the way over to Streisand's house to talk about *Main Event* I was an absolute wreck," Jabara says. "I couldn't believe that I was actually going to be writing a song for her."

Jabara wrote *two* songs, one a ballad and one a dance number. Barbra chose the latter, asking Jabara and Roberts to add a second melody, "Fight," in order to tie the song more closely to the film.

"The first time I heard her sing the lead in, 'Extra, extra, I'm in love . . .' I said 'Oh, my God!' and started shaking," Jabara enthused during the recording sessions. "She does that to you. To have her actually sing my words and music was so devastating . . . I had to set a whole new set of goals for myself."

Despite insubstantial lyrics, "The Main Event/Fight" was excitingly sung, rose to #3 on the *Billboard* chart and represented still another breakthrough for Barbra. It established her as one of the most effective female disco singers after Donna Summer— and paved the way for another memorable duet.

"I Will Never Give Up"

Barbra's foray into disco disappointed many of her long-time admirers, to whom this new musical genre was anathema. But her success with it won her millions of new, young fans who didn't know from *Funny Girl*—they accepted Streisand as a rocker and a disco queen. It was an extraordinary development. Here was a woman who had begun her career singing Harold Arlen and Cole Porter; she came from a Broadway background and had captured the imaginations of millions in the early and mid-sixties. Now, as we entered the eighties, she was winning over those people's kids by singing—better than most—a completely different kind of music. It was a level of adaptability, and a record of successfully attempted changes, that no singer before her had ever achieved. And the greatest successes were yet to come.

Streisand's next single, her biggest disco hit, left in its wake a slew of participants claiming credit for bringing Barbra and Donna Summer together to record "Enough is Enough". Paul Jabara, who wrote the song with Bruce Roberts, has a reputation for unorthodox tactics in selling people on his music; he reportedly locked Donna Summer in a restroom in Tijuana until she agreed to record "Last Dance." In an interview with this writer for *Us* magazine, he described a similar ploy with Barbra. "I was trying to get her to include 'Enough is Enough' on her *Wet* album. But it didn't have any water in it." (Streisand was preparing a concept album in which all the songs pertained in some way to water.) Jabara wrote a somewhat gratuitous opening to the song, "It's raining/It's pouring/My love life is boring me to tears . . . " and asked Barbra if he could come over and play it for her.

"The day before," Jabara says, "I asked Donna if she wanted to come with me to Barbra's for lunch. She immediately said, 'I'd love to!' When I called Barbra, her son Jason answered. I told him to ask his mother about bringing Donna to lunch with me. He screamed, 'Donna Summer!' It turns out Jason's the biggest Donna fan in the world. So I owe it all to him.

"The minute Donna and I arrived at Barbra's, I said, 'This is the duet I've been trying to get you two to do.' They both got excited. Barbra kept asking, 'What part do I sing?' I knew if I could just get them together, they'd do it."

Charles Koppelman, the executive producer of both the single and the *Wet* album, offers a somewhat different version of these events. "Jon called me while Barbra was doing *The Main Event,* and asked what I thought of Barbra and Donna doing the title song in duet. I thought it would be too difficult to bring everything together while the movie was going on, so we put it off."

When the moment came, Koppelman says, Jabara wasn't the only one present. "Gary Klein [the record's producer] and I were there that day, but Paul likes to think no one else was around. It was as much Jon's doing as Paul's. And Gary and I had a lot to do with it coming off, too. There were a lot of problems, two different record companies and so forth. It's easy to have an idea, but a lot harder to pull it off."

Cowriter Bruce Roberts, asked about how it was "pulled off," said, "It was crazed from the start. We got them together, locked them in a room in Barbra's house in Malibu and played them the song . . . and taught it to them."

Jabara spoke of his uncertainty about whether the duet would ever take place. This was related to Koppelman, who said, "That was just his paranoia. It was always going to be in my mind, and in Jon's and Barbra's and Donna's. When you're a writer, things seem very tentative. We've worked with Barbra and we knew that once she committed herself to this project, that was it."

There was, predictably, a great deal of press attention given to this pairing. Fireworks between the "dueling divas" were breathlessly anticipated, but there apparently were few. Summer was two hours late for the recording session because of a concert the night before at the Universal Ampitheater. Barbra reportedly cracked, "I haven't waited two hours for anybody!" But, Donna reports, Barbra was "very understanding of it. She wasn't angry, she didn't act nasty, she understood—usually artists do."

Both superstars were nervous about this meeting of titans. "Barbra and Donna," Jabara says, "were both intimidated by the other, and couldn't understand why the other person should be intimidated. It was crazy." Koppelman confirms, "They *were* nervous. They had a lot of compromising to do. They would wonder, 'Is her line better than my line?'" Streisand was better at holding the long notes and, it was reported, Donna actually fell off her stool after losing her breath while Barbra sang on, unbothered.

"They were not temperamental at all," Koppelman says. "They worked real hard, a lot of hours. If they were temperamental, they never would have been able to compromise enough to make the duet come off as fairly as it does. But it did get a little tense at times."

"Whenever morale was down in the studio," Jabara says, "I would rush over and tickle Donna and tell her I wanted to make love to her. And she would turn to me and say, 'What do I need this for?' Then Barbra would come up and yell, 'I'm ill. I'm having palpitations. It's all your fault.' But when things were really bad, they'd start giggling and acting like little girls."

For Jabara, the pinnacle moment was when all the troubles were forgotten and Barbra and Donna got down to recording the song. "There was Streisand, hands flaring, and Donna, throwing her head back—and they're both belting, sparking each other. It was a songwriter's dream. Seeing them on their stools opposite each other was so mind boggling, my head nearly turned 360°, like Linda Blair's did in *The Exorcist!*"

The song, a belter in which both singers get to use their voices as never before, was the biggest hit in both their careers. The twelve-inch disco version became the first such record to be certified Platinum (over one million units sold). The other three versions, the Columbia single, Barbra's *Wet* album and Donna's *On the Radio* LP, all went Platinum as well. The song reached Number One in the United States, England, Spain and Australia.

The *Wet* album, released shortly after the "Enough Is Enough" single, sold well, largely on the strength of that song, but it represented an incongruous environment for the hit. *Wet* was a gentle collection of love songs reminiscent of Barbra's mid-sixties albums. Several of the songs were standouts: "Kiss Me in the Rain," "After the Rain" and "Niagara" by Marvin Hamlisch, Carole Bayer Sager and Bruce Roberts, a lovely ballad which calls to mind "The Way We Were." Barbra also sings a lovely "Come Rain or Come Shine" by Johnny Mercer and Harold Arlen and a surprisingly satisfying reworking of the Bobby Darin novelty hit, "Splish Splash." The album's only real clinker is "I Ain't Gonna Cry Tonight" which, while it might be easy to dance to, contains astonishingly silly lyrics.

Wet was a hit album, but it failed to match the excitement surrounding the single; the whole was less than its parts. Still, Barbra's recording career was at a fifteen-year

At the 1980 Grammies

With Neil Diamond after their memorable duet

Performing at the Bergman tribute

With the Bergmans at the concert's close

peak. At the end of 1979, *Us* magazine named Streisand and Summer as the decade's leading singers.

At the February 1980 Grammy Awards, "You Don't Bring Me Flowers" was nominated as Record of the Year, and Barbra and Neil's vocal was nominated in the "Pop Duo or Group Performance" category. The record won neither award, but it hardly mattered: Streisand and Diamond stole the show with an electrifying performance.

It was the first time Barbra had ever sung at a Grammy ceremony, and the significance of that wasn't lost on the show's director, Marty Pasetta. He had the couple come on stage, unannounced, after a commercial. As soon as the audience could tell who was emerging from the backstage shadows, a huge roar went up, and for almost a minute Barbra was unable to begin. The crowd reaction was unrestrained—they burst into applause half a dozen times during the song, cheering when Barbra hit difficult notes, when she altered the melody line, when she affectionately stroked Neil's face at the song's climax. When the performance was over, a standing, cheering ovation ensued. It was a memorable moment, dramatically presented, and although Neil had microphone problems and Barbra, obviously nervous, was not always successful in her attempts to experiment with her vocal, the overall effect was thrilling. A year later, on a special devoted to the year in TV, host Tom Brokaw presented the duet as a highlight and afterward said, "When it's that good, it will live on for a long, long time."

If what went on in front of the audience was unforgettable, so was what went on backstage, if reports are to be believed. Los Angeles *Herald Examiner* columnist Mitchell Fink wrote of the behind-the-scenes chaos Barbra's presence created: "Streisand's appearance—especially the way she ran back and forth from the backstage area to a concealed van in the parking lot—caused such a complete breakdown in the normally tight security system that accompanies this type of broadcast that 1) it overshadowed a very rare television performance by Bob Dylan; 2) it made observers forget that reigning disco queen Donna Summer was blanked in all major categories; and 3) for a time it even obscured the news that the big winners of the night were the Doobie Brothers . . . When Streisand started playing her little cat-and-mouse games with the press, all hell broke loose. Photographers climbed all over each other as they made vain attempts to obtain choice shots. Security police screamed at one another in equally vain attempts to restore order . . . and the people who really control what goes on backstage—Hollywood's biggest name press agents—threw their hands in the air, realizing that for this year, at least, they had indeed blown the whole thing."

Streisand was now at a point in her career where, because of her extraordinary status as an artist and her increasingly rare public appearances, every live performance of hers was a major event. Such was the case again when Barbra joined a group of friends of Marilyn and Alan Bergman for a concert tribute for the benefit of the American Civil Liberties Union, at the Los Angeles Music Center on June 1, 1980.

Other performers included Bea Arthur, Joel Grey, Jack Jones, Norman Lear, Melissa Manchester, and Carmen McRae, but, not surprisingly, Barbra was the highlight of the evening. The show began twenty minutes late, but when the curtain went up, the warm-up act was standing center-stage. Barbra Streisand. Wanda McDaniel reported the reaction in the *Herald Examiner:* "The roaring ovation (several minutes long), virtually made it impossible for Streisand to launch into her dreamily hummed introduction to "The Way We Were." If you can imagine Frampton at the Forum multiplied by four, that was what happened in the sedate Pavilion when Streisand stepped into the spotlight for an exceedingly rare concert appearance."

Barbra's presence, of course, was a result of her close friendship with the Bergmans. "When you're singing for people you love," Barbra told the audience, "it's easy. Alan and Marilyn give so much emotion to a world that so desperately needs it. I'd dedicate a song to them, but this whole *evening* is dedicated to them."

Following, "The Way We Were," Barbra sang an expansive version of "After the Rain," prompting a second ovation. She promised to be back, and introduced Jack Jones. Bringing Streisand out first was a master stroke by the show's director Joe Layton: it showed the audience that the evening's star was indeed there, and allowed them to sit back and enjoy the rest of the show without constantly anticipating Streisand's entrance.

The other performers sang dozens of Bergman hits, including "Pieces of Dreams" (Jack Jones), "I Believe in Love" (Melissa Manchester), and "Summer Me, Winter Me" (played up-tempo by Michel Legrand). After Legrand completed this number, Streisand reappeared to sing the more languid version of the song against Legrand's accompaniment. "Michel," she said to him, "you write the most extraordinary melodies. If you were only Jewish, they'd have an evening like this for you, too!"

Barbra then sang a warm, powerful version of "What Are You Doing the Rest of Your Life?" and the discarded version of "The Way We Were." The concert's closing moments were pandemonium. As Wanda McDaniel wrote, "The balcony contingent fairly lost their composure as Streisand went on to encore the show with the first lines of 'You Don't Bring Me Flowers' . . . it came to the point in the song for Neil Diamond's vocals and the audience—in unison—slid to the edge of their seats, anticipating the improbable [Neil Diamond was not on the bill]. When the spotlight hit a harmonizing Diamond, rising from the choice orchestra seats and making his way to the stage, the musicmania thundered through the hall, shaking the chandeliers. . . The songstress waited for the clamor to subside. Teased Streisand, 'I don't think they recognize you, Neil.' "

After the duet, the Bergmans reappeared for several bows with Barbra and Neil. By this time, the audience was on its feet, cheering and reluctant to have the evening end. Army Archerd, writing in *Variety,* summed up the show's impact: "The hall has never heard such a rave reaction from any audience in which we've been present . . . Streisand was never in better/greater voice."

Barbra's next major accomplishment (and any Streisand biography must by necessity be a litany of accomplishments) would turn out to be her greatest recording triumph. It gives one pause to realize that Streisand's biggest selling album came after nineteen years of recording and thirty-five LPs, most of which went Gold.

Producer Charles Koppelman, interviewed by *Billboard* magazine, talked about how *Guilty* came to be. Streisand's recent duets had come about under Koppelman's tutelage—Barbra had not sung with another pop star before Neil Diamond. "Obviously," Koppelman said, "a lot of it has to do with confidence, as well as the way the idea is presented and followed through. Barbra was always willing to experiment with creative ideas, but it's not the easiest thing to put these projects in motion; to put egos aside and let the creative process happen."

Koppelman liked the idea of Streisand singing with others, which he saw as making "one plus one equal three" and on a par with the marquee draw of pairing Streisand with Redford, Kristofferson, O'Neal, or Caan. Barbra began thinking about whom she would like to work with next, and after attending a 1979 Bee Gees concert at Dodger Stadium in Los Angeles, asked Barry Gibb not only to sing with her, but to produce her next album and write some songs for it. Gibb, anxious to express his creativity away from his group, readily agreed. But, in Koppelman's words, it was "not the easiest thing"

With Barry Gibb at the post-Grammy Awards party in New York, 1981

to bring these two pop superstars together. Gibb told *Billboard,* "I wasn't going to do the album at one point. I was an absolute nervous wreck before we started. Barbra is rumored to be a tough lady. I'd heard about the time 'Evergreen' was written and how Paul Williams was sent backwards and forwards to write lyrics—and I was afraid that was going to happen to me. But the wonderful thing is, it never did. Apart from the fact that Barbra's a total professional, she's a very nice lady. You can't go wrong with an artist like that."

The fact that Gibb has been a Streisand fan "for as long as I can remember" helped immeasurably in the collaboration. Gibb says his favorite songs include "People" and "The Way We Were." When Barbra asked him to produce the album as well as write for it, he was delighted. "We set out to make the great Streisand LP that she never made," Gibb explained. "It started off with them suggesting a few songs, which we listened to. We then submitted five of our own songs and Barbra liked them and asked us to write five more." The album contains only one song not written expressly for Barbra—"The Love Inside," which Gibb wrote over a year earlier.

One song, "Carried Away," was not used on the album, but Gibb says Streisand discarded none of his material and did not ask for any lyric changes. She did, however, have reservations about some of the sentiments expressed in one song, "Woman in Love." Gibb recalled, "She questioned the line, 'It's a right I defend/Over and over again.' At first she felt that it was a little bit liberationist; that it might be a little too strong for a pop song."

That was about the extent of the disagreements, though, and the line remained. As the recording sessions progressed, everyone felt very good about the potential of what they were doing. "We could tell about halfway through," Gibb said, "that we had something very different than she'd been doing and that it could be an extremely big album."

Guilty contained two duets between Streisand and Gibb, but Barbra was concerned about overdoing the duet approach, and Columbia agreed to release the solo cut "Woman in Love" as the album's first single. It was an inspired choice. Released five weeks prior to the album, the single hit #1 just as the LP was reaching the record stores.

Guilty took little time to become Streisand's best-selling album ever. It was only the second album ever to *debut* at #1 on *Variety*'s "Top Fifty LPs" chart, and it went to #1 on all the other major charts within a few weeks. It was the first time since *A Star Is Born* and "Evergreen" that Barbra had enjoyed concurrent #1 status on both the album and the singles charts.

The teaming of Streisand and Gibb and the album's huge success made *Guilty* extremely newsworthy. *Us* magazine devoted a cover to it, and reams of newspaper copy followed. The reviews, for the most part, were ecstatic. Even *Rolling Stone*'s Stephen Holden, who had (with few exceptions) been hostile to Streisand's forays into pop and rock, found the album thrilling. His review gave insightful reasons for his enthusiasm: "One reason that the Streisand-Gibb team proves to be the most sensational artist-producer duo since Michael Jackson and Quincy Jones created *Off the Wall* is that both principals are basically traditional pop sentimentalists who complement each other in convenient ways. Barbra Streisand's steel-belted soprano gives more dramatic authority to Barry Gibb's chromatic mini-arias than practically any other voice could. And because Gibb's compositions are bel canto baubles whose lyrics consist mainly of comic blather concerning love, Streisand is spared worrying about what the songs mean. Indeed, Gibb's sweet nothings are so slight that they allow Streisand to *be* a love goddess without ever having to think about playing for keeps. Though she was once a great interpretive singer, Barbra Streisand now possesses a larger-than-life image that completely overwhelms her material. These days, whatever she sings becomes an extension of her superstardom; an expression of the triumph of her will rather than a text to be revealed.

" . . . Gibb has handed Barbra Streisand some of the prettiest compositions he's written. Song for song, *Guilty* is stronger than any of the Bee Gees' or Andy Gibb's LPs. The title track fuses a Doobie Brothers-type rhythmic hook onto a tune that somehow seems Russian with a tropical lilt. 'Woman in Love' expands a melody very similar to Andy Gibb's 'After Dark' into an aural balloon that wafts Streisand's singing right through the stratosphere. And the Pucciniesque sweetness of 'Run Wild' and 'What Kind of Fool' easily matches that of their prototype, 'How Deep Is Your Love.' "

Holden concluded his review with these observations: "While *Guilty* is a romantic entertainment with no ambitions beyond making billions of hearts flutter and earning millions of dollars, it's also as beautifully crafted a piece of ear candy as I've heard in years. (It) may not be particularly nutritious, but it sure is tasty."

Most of the world agreed. *Guilty* went to #1 in twelve countries, and Columbia projects that it will sell 20 million copies worldwide. Both follow-up singles to "Woman in Love"—the duets "Guilty" and "What Kind of Fool"—entered the Top Ten. The album remained in the Top Twenty on several charts for more than ten months.

, When the announcement came of the 1980 Grammy Award nominations, Barbra and *Guilty* received five nods: Album of the Year, Song of the Year and Record of the Year ("Woman in Love"), Best Female Pop Vocal Performance, and Best Pop Vocal Performance, Duo or Group ("Guilty"). It was the first time Streisand had won an Album of the Year nomination since *Color Me Barbra* in 1966, and she had not won the award since her first album in 1963.

At the Grammy Awards, *Guilty* was the odds-on favorite, and Barbra and Barry's announced participation in the ceremonies added to New York's excitement at having the event at its Radio City Music Hall for the first time in years (It is usually held in Hollywood). After the thrill of the Streisand-Diamond performance the year before, there was much anticipation of another surprise from Barbra (neither she nor Gibb was listed as a scheduled performer).

The evening was, however, only a qualified success as far as Streisand watchers were concerned. She won but one Grammy, in the Pop Duo category, and that award was not presented on the air. *Guilty* was beaten out of all its awards by newcomer Christopher Cross, and Bette Midler was named Best Pop Female Vocalist for "The Rose." Barbra and Barry didn't perform, but they did present—and even at that, it was a highlight of the show.

Their entrance was greeted with a standing ovation, the only one not for a performance, and the TV cameras caught Diana Ross in the audience as she exclaimed "Wow!" while watching Streisand walk out. Barbra's banter with Barry highlighted the "dowager empress/street urchin" dichotomy of Streisand's personality. After hushing the shouts of "We love you, Barbra!" from the audience, she stood close to Gibb and, in a voice low and sexy, said "Barry. . . do you feel guilty?" Gibb responded, "No—why should I feel that way?"

Streisand then reverted to her Brooklyn-Jewish intonations and quipped, "I don't know—I feel like I'm cheating on Neil Diamond!" As the audience laughed and applauded, Barbra reverted to her sophisticated self and read off the "Pop Male Vocal Performance" nominees with élan.

What many saw as Streisand's "snub" by the Grammies made news, with headline writers enjoying puns on her competitor's name—"Streisand Double-Cross'd at Grammies." But Barbra, who has been treated very well by the recording academy, was a gracious loser. New York *Daily News* writers Phil Roura and Tom Poster described her appearance at the post-ceremony party under the headline "Barbra wasn't a bit cross": "Some of the guys and gals at CBS Records sure are worrywarts. Take Grammy Night, for instance. As the show wound down, the advance team for the *very private* CBS party at the Four Seasons was moaning over whether Barbra Streisand would show. She hadn't won the coveted Best Female Vocalist award.

"Was Babs in a frenzy? Would she show? And if she did, would she make life miserable for everyone? Horsefeathers! Barbra *did indeed* come—gracious and surprisingly unaffected by Grammy's snub. Continually through her dinner, she greeted guests with grace and charm and never once stopped smiling—even when love Jon Peters asked her to pose for pictures with one celeb after another. She left at 1:40 A.M."

If Streisand fans were disappointed that what many consider her best album in years wasn't recognized by the Grammies, there was immediate hope for the following year: rumors abounded that Streisand was teaming up—à la Barry Gibb—with Stevie Wonder. The news was very exciting. The combination of these two musical geniuses would surely be a stunning album, and Barbra's recordings of Wonder songs in the past—"You and I" and "All in Love Is Fair"—are wonderful.

Surely part of Streisand's musical legend is her unending willingness to experiment, to stretch herself, to adapt to new musical styles. Who knows what Barbra's musical future holds in store for her, and for us? Whatever it is, judging from the past twenty years, it will be at least interesting—and often thrilling.

Cheryl

Barbra's follow-up film to *The Main Event* was supposed to be *Yentl,* based on an Isaac Bashevis Singer short story. Streisand had been developing the property for years, and was planning to direct it.

It was therefore quite a surprise when the announcement was made that Barbra had been signed to replace Lisa Eichhorn *(Yanks)* in *All Night Long,* already filming in Hollywood. The details of Barbra's assumption of the role were even more surprising: it was essentially a supporting part, and Barbra would be taking second billing to the film's star, Gene Hackman. If all of these precedents seemed humbling, Barbra's salary was not. While Lisa Eichhorn was being paid $250,000, Streisand's fee was $4 million plus 15 percent of the film's profits. This enormous pay—especially for a part which would take Barbra twenty-four days to film—created a predictable controversy. The criticism was blunted, however, by the obvious fact that male screen stars had been receiving comparable fees for years—most notably Steve McQueen, whose box office record was far inferior to Barbra's, and Marlon Brando, who had received millions for his brief appearances in *Superman* and *Apocalypse Now.*

Streisand's signing for the role—a suburban housewife with a healthy sexual appetite—came about because the film's director, Jean-Claude Tramont, is married to Barbra's agent, Sue Mengers. Barbra had expressed interest in the role earlier, and when problems arose with Lisa Eichhorn, Mengers asked Barbra to step in. Reportedly, Streisand did so as a favor to Mengers, but Tramont denied this. "My wife and I have been together for eleven years," he told Los Angeles *Herald Examiner* writer Chris Chase. "If she had the ability to force Barbra to do a picture with me, I wish she had used it sooner."

Still, reports persisted that the later parting of the ways between Streisand and Mengers was a result of Sue's insistence on receiving 10 percent of Barbra's salary despite the fact that her taking the role at all was a favor.

Barbra wanted to play the part, Tramont insists, because she was intrigued by the goofy, sexy, soft-voiced Cheryl Gibbons, who represented a total departure from any character she had ever played before. "The part was *too* much of a departure for Lisa," Tramont said. "It's no reflection on her acting ability. Barbra brought a quality of naïveté that worked wonderfully for Cheryl's part."

The *All Night Long* story concerned George Dupler, a career man with Ultra Save drugs who throws a chair out a corporate office window after being passed over for a promotion, and is demoted to managing a remote drugstore—at night. At a time when he is questioning all the values in his life, he discovers that his son (Randy Quaid) is having an affair with distant cousin Cheryl, married to a macho lug of a fireman (Kevin Dobson).

Dupler forbids his son to continue the affair, and Cheryl drops by the drugstore to explain herself. After meeting Dupler, she makes a play for him and, despite George's resistance, they are soon having an affair too. When George's son furiously confronts him with the information, George leaves home, taking a ratty boardinghouse room.

Cheryl's unconventionality and her dreams (she aspires to be a country and western singer-songwriter) lead George to reject all the cherished notions he had lived with for years. He quits Ultra Save, rents a loft and invents a mirror that does not reverse images—"It shows people as they really are." He asks Cheryl to leave her husband and join him in this new bohemian lifestyle of his, but she is afraid—her rebellions against stuffy society were okay when they weren't taken seriously, but now . . . He finally does convince her to come completely into his life; he reconciles with his son and begins a new chapter in his existence.

Filming took place in various locations around Los Angeles, and was interrupted for months by the actors' strike. Streisand, apparently, was a pussycat—friendly, cooperative, and pliable. Hackman, on the other hand, was described as temperamental and disgruntled through much of the filming. It may have been the result of the fact that after Barbra's signing for the picture, it began to be described in the press as a "Barbra Streisand movie." Not only was Gene the star, but the film had been written—by W. D. Richter—with Hackman in mind. Whatever the reasons, Tramont admitted to Michael Sragow of *Rolling Stone* that Hackman had caused some problems. "It was always a joy, if sometimes difficult, working with Gene Hackman. He's a genius, the greatest living screen actor. Hackman is full of anger—that's what gives his acting vibrancy—but here he's able to play against that anger."

Before the film's release, Lisa Eichhorn was quoted in several publications about her feelings when she was replaced by Barbra. "It was upsetting, but at least my replacement was *Barbra Streisand.* I mean, if I had been replaced by a peer, I would have been devastated." She related two separate stories about running into Barbra, once at a restaurant. "She was just getting ready to leave, so I felt I wouldn't be intruding. I said, 'Excuse me, I just wanted to tell you how much I've always admired your work.' She didn't want to know. She looked up at me with a please-go-away look and nodded thanks, rather ungraciously. So I turned and left. She'd no idea who I was, of course, not that it would have made any difference . . . I suppose it must be tiresome having people come up like that, but it isn't hard to be gracious. I think the only reason I did it was because I saw her in *Funny Girl* when I was at school and that was what determined me to be an actress."

Despite such negative press, Barbra's fans hoped that her acceptance of a secondary role in a small picture would temporarily blunt the overly harsh criticism her last few films had elicited. The advance word was that it was a gentle comedy in the European mold, and that Barbra was playing a flirtatious blonde with pretensions of being a country singer-songwriter. How much vitriol could *that* inspire?

Quite a bit, as it turned out. The first solid hint of trouble was the Universal Pictures advertising campaign. The ad was a depiction of Streisand sliding down a fire pole, her skirt blowing up around her thighs à la Marilyn Monroe in *The Seven Year Itch.* Below, preparing to catch her, were Hackman and costars Kevin Dobson and Randy Quaid. Hackman, at least, was portrayed on a slightly larger scale than the other two. The copy read, "She has a way with men. And she's getting away with it . . . *All Night Long.*"

Talk about misleading advertising! Anyone seeing that ad would reasonably expect another screwball comedy centered completely around Barbra Streisand, and wonder why Hackman received top billing. Barbra had no say in the campaign, and it must have been an embarassment to her. Rona Barrett chastised Universal on her "Today" segment and intimated that the ad campaign would actually hurt the film.

It did. As with *Up the Sandbox,* viewers were expecting something other than what they got, and word-of-mouth on the film was bad. The initial box-office receipts were low, and they did not improve. Even more of an indictment of Universal's advertising department than the original ad is the fact that, when many reviewers praised the movie and urged their readers to go without expecting a typical Streisand film, the

With Gene Hackman

quotes were not run in the ensuing ads. In the Los Angeles *Times,* the *All Night Long* ads were run quite small and contained absolutely no quotes. Obviously, Universal decided early on to abandon the film to the scrap heap.

It was a tremendous disservice to the movie, its stars, and its director. Because while the film garnered some unexpectedly vicious reviews (most directed at Streisand) it received others that were positively effusive with praise: "*All Night Long* is one of the finest American comedies in years," the Los Angeles *Herald Examiner* critic wrote.

Michael Sragow said in *Rolling Stone,* "*All Night Long* is that rarity this season: a consistently witty and intelligent entertainment. Even rarer, it's a middle-class comedy blessed with grace, wisdom and integrity . . . (it) has a visual luster and tenderness all its own, partly because of the two stars' low-key sexiness. Coming off years of desultory work, Streisand and Hackman soar like Phoenixes. If Hackman weren't a star already, this performance would make him one. He uses all his proven gifts of sensitivity, humor and simmering violence, as well as a romantic dreaminess he's never had the opportunity to demonstrate. As George Dupler, Hackman turns a man in midlife crisis into a conquering hero. Keeping his balance as an actor while Dupler's existence turns topsy-turvy, he makes this schmo *manful.*

"Cheryl," Sragow continued, "is always on the lookout for a fling, but as embodied by Streisand, she's more than Dupler's floozy. She's his muse, the one who hurtles him past the plastic roadblocks of suburban mores and back to his true feelings. The delicacy Streisand brings to the role may momentarily confuse fans who've come to love her brassband stridency, yet it's her best performance since 1973's *The Way We Were.* Even at the start, when Cheryl appears to be an overpampered seductress, Streisand imbues her with a breathy, soft avidity that recalls Marilyn Monroe.

"Cheryl Gibbons is one of the most appealing female characters to reach the screen in recent years; impetuous but not loony, aggressive without being a ball-buster. When she runs away from her baby-macho fireman-husband, she seems nakedly vulnerable. Taking up with Dupler, she doesn't declare a feminist manifesto. She simply realizes that she must change her life."

Some critics—like Pauline Kael, Rex Reed, and Sheila Benson of the Los Angeles *Times*—had reservations, but saluted the film's "wry, stolid" humor and its "distinctive, new comic sensibility." Others, however, gave the film—and Barbra—some of the most savage notices since *A Star Is Born.*

Los Angeles magazine, the editors of which absolutely detest Streisand (they offered us the tidbit about Barbra's free-flying birds), was especially vicious. Their critic Merrill Shindler theorized that the script had been written by a monkey: "One need be only recently descended from the trees to see that *All Night Long* is a film utterly devoid of: (a) a coherent script; (b) the most rudimentary forms of character development; (c) anything that can be even facetiously referred to as acting; (d) a directorial style no more advanced than the type used to film baby's first tooth; (e) even the remotest sense of comedy . . . While Hackman occasionally seems to be trying to act, Streisand makes no pretense of acting at all. I thought I'd never see a worse portrayal of an allegedly living, breathing human being than Streisand gave in *The Main Event,* but the lustful little turnip she plays in *All Night Long* puts some of the creatures in *Freaks* to shame."

Shindler's review is symptomatic of an increasing trend in film criticism: the attempt to entertain one's readers with witty bitchiness rather than to constructively criticize a piece of work in which many people have invested their hearts and souls. Such poor excuses for criticism should raise doubts about the reviewers' ability to write about a film with true insight and intelligence.

Oddly enough, Rex Reed—who made his initial reputation through just such witty bitchiness—gave *All Night Long* an insightful, if mixed, review. He wrote in the New York *Daily News,* "It's not easy being Barbra Streisand. There must be days when she feels like the executor of a dead millionaire's last will and testament—so many contestants demanding a piece of the pie, and no way to ever please them all . . . *All Night Long* is not really a Streisand picture at all. She plays a secondary role in it, and that won't make her fans happy. They want glitz and glamour and excitement from her, and in the past she's given them their money's worth. On the other hand, there's a small but noisy band of critics who keep demanding more than variations on the Fanny Brice theme. They've suggested, goaded, reminded her in print that she should drop the antics and the Mondrian eyelids and the astronomic budgets, stop controlling her films, and just turn in a creditable acting job in something (preferably downbeat) that stretches her muscles and challenges her range as a dramatic actress.

"*All Night Long* is that kind of picture—a wry, stolid, often depressing kind of American *Cousin, Cousine,* about the truthful dreams of a band of thoroughly unremarkable middle class drones . . . it is quite jolting to see Barbra Streisand joining the crowd. The highbrow critics who write reams of endless prose in periodicals with circulations no bigger than a high school glee club will be overjoyed by this departure. Streisand fans—most of whom come from the working-class world she's portraying here—will see nothing new and find even less to shout about.

"Tramont not only sees and records American foibles with a unique eye, but gets indelible performances from American actors, too. Hackman has never been better. Clumsy and unromantic, there's a longing in his eyes that proves how touching oafs can be . . . And Streisand must be credited for playing her blousy housewife role so passively. She does what's right for the role (and the film) by remaining securely in character. At no time does she resort to stealing the show, and there are no traces of her usual Brooklyn hash-slinger-turned-Ziegfeld-girl routine."

Jean-Claude Tramont is philosophic about the commercial failure of his first feature film. "The timing may be wrong for this film," he told Michael Sragow. "These days, American anger is tinged with bitterness. At our sneak previews, the audience I thought would react the strongest to George Dupler's revolt—men over twenty-five—seemed to resent the movie! I can understand their guilt if they felt that *they* haven't amounted to anything. Guilt has always been a part of the American success syndrome. After all, every young American male is brought up to believe he *could* be President. But I think there's a new sense of resignation now."

Clearly, *All Night Long* suffered the same fate as *Up the Sandbox,* and for many of the same reasons. Like Irvin Kershner, Tramont blames television for making audiences insensitive to subtleties. "(Television) has shortened our attention spans," he said. "Life is reduced to bald statistics. That kind of reflex may affect how people react to my film. Some people who've seen it say that Cheryl's husband is not unsympathetic enough. Now, I don't want *any* villians in this film, but I thought it was pretty clear that Bobby was not very understanding of his wife. To get that across to a mass audience, I may have to show him committing unnatural acts with his dog."

Anticipation

Since 1977, Barbra had been actively preparing to make her official directing debut. By 1981, the project—*Yentl*—was coming together despite a series of setbacks and problems that would have permanently discouraged a less tenacious filmmaker than Barbra Streisand.

The script of *Yentl* is based on a short story by Nobel Prize-winning author Isaac Bashevis Singer. It concerns a young nineteenth-century Eastern European Jewish girl who disguises herself as a boy in order to study the Talmud, as her father desired of her. While at school, she falls in love with a classmate, creating tremendous complications.

Streisand bought the rights to the story in 1968. In 1975, an off-Broadway production starring Tovah Feldshuh achieved a moderate success.

Despite Barbra's reputation as a "bankable" star, she had a great deal of difficulty getting financial backing for *Yentl*. Orion Pictures, who had originally agreed to produce the film and provide between $12 and $15 million for it, withdrew its offer in 1980. Industry reports indicated that the film's ethnic theme, its large budget, the necessity of overseas filming and the fact the Barbra is a novice director led Orion to back out.

At this writing, however, Yentl is scheduled to begin filming in September 1981, with United Artists putting up the money. Streisand has had to make a great many concessions to get this project off the ground. She has agreed to star, despite the fact that she is much older than the character in the original story (reports are that the script now has Yentl as a somewhat older woman). She has turned the film into a musical, with between twelve and fourteen songs written for it by Michel Legrand and Marilyn and Alan Bergman. Jon Peters, who was originally to produce, will not; Stanley O'Toole and former Peters partner Rusty Lemorand will. Stanley O'Toole's main areas of expertise are controlling costs and overseeing the exigencies of foreign filming.

Originally, Streisand had wanted to film the movie in Poland, and she spent some time there in the fall of 1980 scouting locations. While she was there, the Polish workers' unrest began, and the threats of Soviet intervention in the problem ruled out that country as a possible location. At this writing, Czechoslovakia will provide the locales for the movie.

The venture is indeed risky, and Barbra deserves admiration for again "putting my artistic vision on the line." Making films as well as starring in them appears to be the way Barbra's career is headed. In 1977 she said, "It's a very personal thing to make a film. All we have is what is in our hearts, what is in our souls, what is in our heads. It's a total form of expression, although you're totally dependent on all the other people. You can't do it alone.

"It's just having a dream. You can accomplish your dream if you have it. And that's what the most rewarding part is, putting it all together to give somebody a feeling in their gut—something that relates to their own lives that they can feel. That they can either laugh at or cry at or get moved or understand. That's what interests me . . . bringing entertainment."

Barbra has often stated that it is her work that is important to her, not the accouterments it brings. "I don't like the 'star' part, I really don't. I like the work—the challenge of filmmaking. There's a lot of false "love me" feelings in Hollywood. "Love me.

A 1981 portrait

246

I love *you,* audience. I want to *please* you." When it's that overt, that easy to give, it also has less value—to me. I find it's a difficult process, a painful one, very intimate—and difficult to share. But I have found that the way I please an audience is to please myself. The more concentrated I am in terms of my work, the more specific I can be, the more truthful the emotion is . . . to me. If it's truthful to me, it transmits itself into that room, whether it seats 50 people or 25,000 or 75,000. Because there's nothing like the truth."

What keeps Barbra Streisand—a woman who has won every major award in her field, made millions of dollars, and had established herself as a legend by the age of twenty-four—continually working, continually struggling to make pictures her way and continually having to read terribly unkind things about herself? The knowledge that her work brings joy to millions of people.

"The audience knows the truth," she said. "That's why those are the people I care about pleasing. I guess it would be nice for the critics to like your work. But the audience knows—that's why when I read terrible things, I still try to keep hold of the letters I receive. People saying that they felt bad for a period of time and they would play my records and feel better—that I helped them in their lives, you know? "That makes me feel good. It gives me a sense of fulfillment, a feeling that I'm contributing something."

PHOTO CREDITS

AUTHOR'S NOTE

This book was produced on an accelerated schedule, and I would not have been able to meet my deadline were it not for the considerable contributions of my collaborator, Chris Nickens.

Many of the photographs are from his private collection; he researched and wrote the first drafts of several sections of the book; his extraordinary knowledge of Barbra's career and Hollywood history more than supplemented my own; and his eye as an artist was of inestimable help in choosing the photographs.

Chris Nickens is the editor of *Barbra* magazine, a quarterly devoted to Streisand's career. Its resources, through Chris and his colleagues Bob Scott and Karen Swenson, made this book much better than it would have been otherwise. Anyone interested in more information about this publication may write *Barbra* magazine, 7985 Santa Monica Boulevard, Suite 109, Hollywood, California 90046.

My heartfelt thanks to these people and all the others whose willingness to help is something for which I will always be grateful.

James Spada
Hollywood, California
April 1981

ABOUT THE AUTHOR

JAMES SPADA'S interviews with actors, authors and notables of the art world—such as Robert Redford, Julie Harris, James Michener, Studs Terkel, Gore Vidal, Stephen King and Norton Simon—have appeared in many publications, including *Us, Los Angeles* Magazine and the London *Daily Mirror*. He is also a book reviewer for the Los Angeles *Times* and writes a monthly book column for *Republic Scene*.

He is the author of *BARBRA: The First Decade—The Films and Career of Barbra Streisand, THE FILMS OF ROBERT REDFORD* (an authorized biography), and *THE SPADA REPORT*. He was Editor-in-Chief of *In The Know* Magazine and Editor/Publisher of *EMK—The Edward M. Kennedy Quarterly*.

Born and raised in Staten Island, New York, Mr. Spada now lives in Los Angeles, where he runs his own magazine publishing company. He is currently at work on his next book, a pictorial biography of Marilyn Monroe.